Unleash the Power of force.com

How to Thrive in the New Digital Economy

Jonathan Sapir

Steve Wood, Francois Koutchouk and Andy Mulholland

Foreword by Peter Coffee

There is wishful thinking that if we can just "get through this," things will go back to normal. Those days aren't coming back. That is the nature of technology, for both good and bad – it destroys old ways of operating that aren't as powerful anymore. – Bruce Rogers, Chief Brand Officer of Forbes, June 2011

Digitization is creating a second economy that's vast, automatic and invisible – thereby bringing the biggest change since the industrial revolution. – W. Brian Arthur, 'The Second Economy", *McKinsey Quarterly*, October 2011

The health, competitive power, and even survival of an enterprise largely depends on its ability to understand and harness the power of knowledge workers who are enabled to take responsibility for providing automatic solutions to meet many of their business needs. – "SOA Meets Situational Applications: Examples and Lessons Learned", *IBM System Journal*, July 2008

Citizen developers are here to stay and will fundamentally change the future of IT work. How you embrace them will determine the future of IT within your organization and define the role IT plays in the creation of new innovative business practices. – Mike Rollings, "Citizen Development: Reinventing the Shadows of IT", *Gartner, Inc.*, February 2012

Table of Contents

Executive Summary

A new Gartner report[1] says that **by 2014, citizen developers will build at least 25% of new business applications**. A citizen developer is defined as an end user who creates business applications for consumption by others using corporate-IT-sanctioned development and runtime environments.

This has profound implications for the future of IT in your organization.

For citizen developers to succeed, they will need a new set of tools, as well as a new approach to application development and delivery. There will also be a critical new role to be played by IT in supporting citizen developers and bringing them out of the shadows.

Unleash the Power of force.com addresses this new wave of IT – what it is, what it means, and how your organization can take advantage of it. This book describes:

- the burgeoning digital economy and how it is driving the need for citizen developers;

- the foundation and building blocks for a consistent enabling platform to support citizen developers;

- an implementation plan for a smooth transition to citizen application development; and

- a comprehensive description of force.com as a ready-to-go, complete citizen developer enabling platform.

This book will give you a comprehensive understanding of the enormous challenges that IT faces today, and what can be done about them by leveraging the power of force.com.

---

[1] Mike Rollings, "Citizen Development: Reinventing the Shadows of IT",

Foreword by Peter Coffee

Peter Coffee is VP and Head of Platform Research at salesforce.com.

Eight years ago, I wrote an *eWEEK* column about a breakfast conversation with salesforce.com Chairman and CEO Marc Benioff: we discussed the notion (still novel at the time) of a Platform as a Service. This would enable the construction of custom applications, executed in a massively scalable environment, provisioned to users in the same manner as salesforce.com's thriving lineup of CRM and related business tools. At that time, Marc and I agreed that both enterprise and ISV developers would need some powerful incentives to give up traditional ideas equating possession with control.

Three years later, I joined salesforce.com because I believed it offered the best vantage point from which to tell developers that those incentives were now in place: that a cloud-based platform could offer developers faster time to market and superior applications that could be more quickly discovered and more easily adopted by more customers in more places.

Oddly, those crucial advantages of a true cloud PaaS are still largely unrecognized, with only the benefits of elastic capacity and some incremental cost reduction sucking most of the oxygen out of the room in conversations about cloud platform opportunity. As I pass my five-year milestone with salesforce.com, I'm glad to help Jonathan Sapir and his contributors in advancing the conversation to a higher level.

I'm privileged to have this chance to share a vision of what's to come for application development in a global, accessible cloud – and for the enterprises that seize the opportunity.

Getting the Cloud through the Door

Since 2007, I've met with CIOs, system integrators, and ISV developers in India, Indonesia, Australia, Singapore, China, Korea, Brazil, Colombia, Mexico, Canada, England, the Netherlands, France, Spain, Germany and Italy – plus more U.S. cities than it would be useful to list.

Those conversations have touched on every task domain from retail financial services, to high-performance scientific computing, to entertainment venue management and motion picture production. Many of those conversations have taken place during the most turbulent economic times that most of us will ever experience: that's been an important part of the context for considering the cloud, and the times to come will continue to call for the benefits that only the cloud can deliver.

I've spent evenings talking about programming practices for stateless, massively parallel systems over pizza with startup developers in Montreal; I've briefed the CIOs of some of the world's largest financial institutions, on three continents, on issues of data governance and cross-border compliance. Even so, despite this universal interest in the cloud, I'm still asked "Who's going to use this?" I have no hesitation in saying that "Whoever's not using the cloud today, it's just a matter of time before the business case becomes utterly compelling – and the objections start to seem quaint."

Please don't think that I'm casually dismissing the remaining concerns about the cloud. What I do notice, though, in comparing the conversations I have today with those that I had three years ago, is a 180° change in direction: from CIOs asking me, "Can you meet my needs?" to CIOs (and, increasingly, CEOs) asking me: "Can you help me tell the story to my regulators? My board of directors? My customers?"

It's less and less a conversation in which I'm selling the cloud; more and more, a consultative session helping an eager customer find a way to buy it.

Fortunately, an enterprise or independent developer who wants to deliver the benefits of the cloud can invoke a growing list of credible authorities and high-profile examples to rebut the most common objections:

- Is a public cloud secure? Ask the U.S. National Institute of Standards and Technology, which offers a six-point list of aspects of IT operation in which cloud adoption will usually *improve* security compared to legacy models.

- Is a public cloud reliable? Ask the agencies providing disaster relief in Haiti or Japan, following those countries' devastating incidents of recent years, when cloud services became a powerful aid for crucial coordination of those efforts.

- Is a public cloud cost-effective, compared to what many people persist in calling "bought and paid for" on-premise IT? Ask the IT managers who have seen daunting growth in the volume and complexity of patching and maintenance efforts for their on-premise software stacks. Increasingly, the indirect IT costs of people (and energy!) are being recognized as major burdens for on-premise operations.

- Is a Platform as a Service readily mastered by development teams with other established expertise? Ask the four different research firms that have studied developers using salesforce.com's force.com platform, with striking agreement that development time shrinks fivefold while overall cost of development and testing is halved.

Winning the Future: PaaS is Prologue

It's pointless, though, to play point/counterpoint with cloud objectors if their objections are really just excuses. If someone really does not want to change an organization's approach to application development, every rebuttal of every objection will be met by yet another espoused concern. The cloud is not adopted until the people on the front line see a positive benefit in doing that – at which point, their role changes from objector to partner in overcoming the genuine but readily addressable issues.

What makes this moment important, therefore, is the growing recognition that clouds are not a convenience or a cost-reduction strategy for IT: rather, clouds are the strategic playing field on which companies will either move forward with vigor, or cower into irrelevance. This transformation is conveniently captured in the concept of The Social Enterprise, and companies that fail to engage this opportunity are writing an undated suicide note. They've decided to die: the only question is when.

13

Here are some key reasons why The Social Enterprise is both enabled, and compelled, by the growing capability and maturity of cloud-based platforms:

- Old IT was the archiver of data that flowed as a by-product of business operations. Tomorrow's IT must be the prospector for, and refiner of, the data that emerges outside the walls: in supply chains, in conversations on social networks, in telemetry from an expanding and enriching "Internet of Things." When the data originates outside the walls, it's no longer nearly so obvious that it should be stored or analyzed inside the walls.

- When data arises in growing volume, with growing volatility, and in a growing variety of formats and contexts, it becomes infeasible to deal with that data by making capital investments in systems whose capacity will usually be excessive (therefore too expensive) – but will often be too limited (and therefore uncompetitive). The finite capacity of any "private cloud" will fail to cope with peak workloads, but its sheer mass and complexity will generate crippling IT costs.

- When people expect to have access to data from multiple devices and in multiple contexts, from a multi-screen "war room" to a pocket-sized touch-screen, the cloud becomes the essential means of providing shared truth in a scalable way. The moment a person starts using both a tablet and a PC/laptop to create work product, the cloud becomes the preferred means of assuring that all work is available from any device – without clumsy and error-prone replication schemes.

These are the most compelling reasons why building applications in the cloud, of the cloud, and for the cloud must be the mainstream model for creating new business function and delivering a distinctive customer experience. To live up to this potential, development platforms must not seek to minimize change, but to maximize opportunity. It's convenient in the short term, but ultimately inefficient, to strap wings and jet engines on an ocean liner and call it a 747: sadly, this is the approach that's taken by too many purveyors of cloudwashed development tools, which are then sold to deliberately deceived developer teams. New environments demand new vehicles to explore them.

Timing is Everything

We're starting the second decade of "cloud," and it's time to stop treating it as a novelty. How do you recognize the end of that novelty stage? A nascent technology will often bear a label of "-less" – but real breakthroughs demonstrate addition, rather than subtraction. That doesn't just happen.

For example, a "horseless carriage" doesn't smoothly evolve into a Formula 1 racer – or, for that matter, into an 18-wheeler freight truck. Either of those latter conceptions requires a rethinking of what new technology makes it possible to build and to do. Likewise, a label like "filmless camera" or "wireless phone" may express the initial novelty, but such labels also tend to conceal transforming opportunities like multispectral imaging and smartphone applications.

In a similar way, it's time to recognize that platforms in the cloud are much, much more than "serverless computing." PaaS is the future: Jonathan and his contributors invite their reader to start today.

I urge you to accept that invitation.

Peter Coffee
VP and Head of Platform Research, salesforce.com inc.

Preface

After 30+ years in the IT industry, I've experienced all the waves of business computing, starting with punch cards on an IBM 360 mainframe, through PCs and client server, the advent of the Internet, and now the cloud. It has been a fascinating journey.

With the benefit of hindsight, I've witnessed the same pattern play out with each new wave. Like the best surfers, the companies that were able to catch a breaking wave early were able to ride it to riches. Those that waited too long languished – and often went under.

The cloud is going to be even more transformative than the waves that came before it. Until now, information technology in business has been primarily about efficiency, from automating supply chains through managing customer relationships. These applications are now well understood and commoditized, and can no longer afford an organization a competitive edge, as they did before.

What we are seeing with the cloud is something completely different. Instead of simply improving efficiencies and driving down costs, the cloud will completely transform how business is conducted, how people work, and what services they provide.

While the earlier waves were one-dimensional, aimed primarily at providing a faster way to get things done, the cloud has many dimensions, including social networking and mobile computing. And all of this takes place in the midst of increasingly rapid globalization that can only be fully harnessed through the innovative use of information technology, which is advancing at a phenomenal pace.

It's hard enough for IT veterans to fully comprehend the significance of all these changes. Business users without deep backgrounds in computer technology don't stand a chance. As a result, there is a great deal of confusion, misunderstanding, and simple ignorance regarding this new wave of technology, what its impact will be, and what can be done to ride it most effectively.

This book provides business users with a broad understanding of the new wave so that they can make the best decisions for their organizations. It also describes how force.com, implemented properly, can be like an exceptional ready-to-go surfboard with which you can confidently ride the new wave. You don't have to spend a lot of unnecessary time and effort engineering, designing, shaping, waxing, and sanding your own surfboard – since it can be delivered ready-made, with everything you need already in place.

These are exciting times, but also treacherous times. A few years from now, we'll look back and be able to see which companies succeeded and which ones failed. For achieving success, I am betting on those companies that understand the power of the cloud, and are forward-thinking and open enough to unleash force.com across their organization!

Jonathan Sapir
Founder and CEO, SilverTree Systems, Inc.

Note: For current updates and timely discussions on subjects like force.com, PaaS in general, citizen developers, as well as new ideas and cutting-edge tools, please visit unleashforce.com, the web site linked to this volume. I hope and trust that this book will give you a solid understanding of what is possible today, and a context in which to make sense of future possibilities.

Introduction

Something deep is going on with information technology, something that goes well beyond the use of computers, social media, and commerce on the Internet. – W. Brian Arthur, "The Second Economy," *McKinsey Quarterly*, October 2011

Unfortunately, the business doesn't care about IT. The business will only care about what it can do to generate more business, and generate more revenue. – Daryl Plummer, managing VP and chief of research, *Gartner Predicts 2012,* December 2011

In his recent article on "the second economy," W. Brian Arthur describes how a decade before the Civil War, the United States' economy was relatively small, not much bigger than Italy's. Just forty years later, it was the largest economy in the world.

What happened in that short period of time? A vast crisscrossing railroad network that linked the entire country was built, giving access to the East's industrial goods, making possible economies of scale, and stimulating the steel and manufacturing industries. The railroads created a whole ecosystem of commerce, making it much easier for companies all over the country to start doing business with each other, bringing goods from far flung places to their local customers. This was the cloud of its time. The economy was never the same.

Arthur points out that deep changes like this are not unusual. Every so often – every sixty years or so – a body of technology comes along that transforms the economy, creating a different world for business.

Gartner calls this new driving force the "CSMI Nexus"[2] – comprising cloud, social, mobile and information. According to Gartner, the CSMI Nexus forms "a phenomenon that is changing the world as we know it, and certainly changing the IT landscape. Cloud is the means of delivery. Social is the behavioral style, the interaction style. Mobile is the access mechanism. Information is the analytical foundation on which you figure out what decisions to make."

This perfect storm of technologies is (as Arthur says) "causing a revolution no less important and dramatic than that of the railroads." They are revolutionizing business and society. This nexus defines the next age of computing.

Most organizations are completely unequipped to handle this seismic shift in information technology. Already faced with application backlogs that are measured in years (not just weeks or months), the thought of having to implement a whole new raft of solutions is a truly daunting prospect.

---

[2]Daryl C. Plummer and Peter Middleton, "Predicts 2012: Four Forces Combine to Transform the IT Landscape," Gartner Research, December 9, 2011, http://www.gartner.com/DisplayDocument?id=1871420

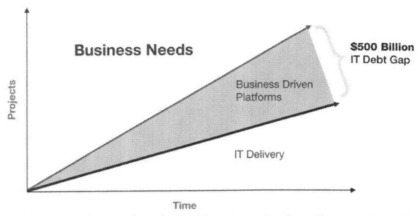

Figure 1: Gartner predicted that global IT debt totaled approximately $500 billion in 2010, with the potential to rise to $1 trillion by 2015.[3]

To make matters worse, the "official" application backlog usually only contains projects that are big enough to make the list. Behind the official list are all the applications that can't even get on the list because they don't meet the minimum bar. Unfortunately, many of these applications are needed in areas of the organization that are on the forefront of competitive differentiation – where they support and retain customers and partners, minimize risk, and maximize profit.

---

[3] Gartner defines IT debt as the cost of clearing the backlog of maintenance that would be required to bring the corporate applications portfolio to a fully supported current release state. "Gartner Estimates Global 'IT Debt' to Be $500 Billion This Year, with Potential to Grow to $1 Trillion by 2015," September 23, 2010, http://www.gartner.com/it/page.jsp?id=1439513, http://www.gartner.com/it/page.jsp?id=1439513

Agility creates a competitive advantage

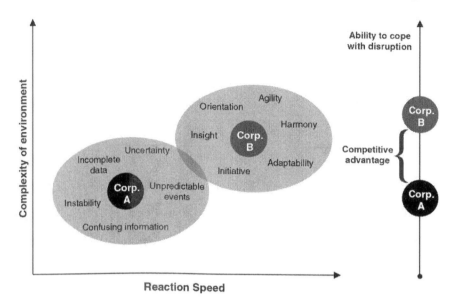

Figure 2: The ability to cope with disruption in an increasingly complex world opens up a significant competitive advantage. Source: "Business Mashups or Mashup Business?" Peter Evans-Greenwood, Capgemini.

But with the emergence of what Arthur calls "the second economy," this backlog problem is about to worsen much further:

- The need for IT responsiveness grows daily as product life cycles are shortened to months instead of years, and as the predictability of mass markets is replaced with the uncertainty of a global real-time economy and rapidly evolving consumer preferences. Organizations increasingly need to **detect events as they occur**, instead of hours, weeks, or even months later.

- Every new business venture, product, or marketing campaign needs agile IT support to **prevent the business end-users from being overwhelmed** by the flood of details and demands that go along with doing new things. And every company needs to be doing new things all the time just to survive.[4]

- Businesses have no choice but to build new applications or enhance existing ones to **leverage new (and ever-changing) technologies** such as mobile and social networking.

- As more and more work is being done outside the organization, specialized solutions need to be built to **accommodate the unique needs of a wide variety of outside partners**.

- With different kinds of customers looking for slightly different mixes of products and services, the **opportunities to make money by being responsive to custom needs** are exploding. Supporting systems need to be built to manage the increasing complexity of offerings.

- **Value-added services** are often information-based and need to be customized to meet the specific needs of each customer. What is valuable to one customer in one situation is not valuable to another in a different situation. Generic solutions don't work.

- The huge opportunities opening up in developing countries (such as India, China, and across Africa) require **a radically different mobile-driven approach to service and product delivery.**

All of these applications require a focus on time-to-value and a never-ending process of being nimble, experimental, dynamic, and continuously iterating. This is in complete contrast to traditional IT, which is "project focused: do it and forget it."

With IT struggling to address these needs in a cost-effective and timely manner, workers rely more and more on makeshift solutions, including large, complex spreadsheets, homegrown databases, and ad hoc custom software development, all beyond the oversight, control, and expertise of

---

[4] Michael H. Hugos, *Business Agility: Sustainable Profitability in a Relentlessly Competitive World,* Hoboken, NJ: Wiley, 2009

IT. These solutions are often inadequate, siloed, unsecured, and inaccurate. The problem is further exacerbated by the need to include new technology like mobile and social into almost every solution.

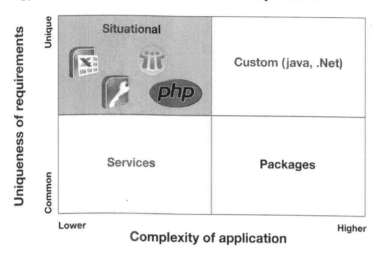

Figure 3: IT focuses on supporting packages and writing complex custom applications while users tend to be left on their own to address their situational needs with tools like Access and Excel.

Incremental improvements to these tools are not going to have anywhere near a large enough impact. What is needed is a quantum leap forward in building these applications.

Enter force.com.

force.com is a comprehensive, unified platform for building and deploying business applications. **force.com is one of those rare technologies that have the potential to truly transform your organization**. It empowers users who are closest to the problems being solved and the opportunities being exploited. force.com facilitates tremendous business agility, allowing businesses to react much faster to changes and opportunities in the marketplace.

force.com can help make organizations more innovative and competitive by enabling individuals and teams to take responsibility for building their own solutions. This is a growing need, as recognized in the following predictions from Gartner:

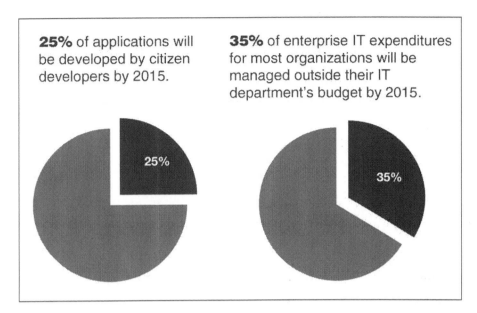

25% of applications will be developed by citizen developers by 2015.

35% of enterprise IT expenditures for most organizations will be managed outside their IT department's budget by 2015.

Figure 4: Source - Gartner press release, July 14, 2011, http://www.gartner.com/it/page.jsp?id=1744514

The trend is clear. A significant and growing number of applications are going to be written by end users, with or without the help of IT. As described in the *Gartner Predicts 2012* report, "Next generation digital enterprises are being driven by a new wave of business managers and individual employees who no longer need technology to be contextualized for them by an IT department."

The time is ripe: with tech-savvy Millennials flooding the workplace, many employees are more than willing to take a more active role in applying information technology to their work.

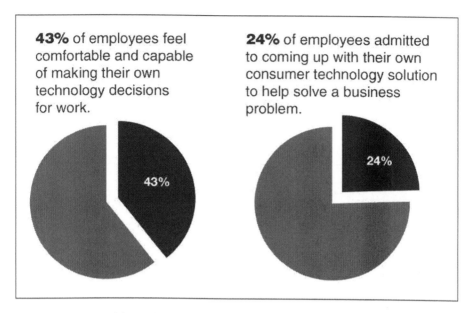

43% of employees feel comfortable and capable of making their own technology decisions for work.

24% of employees admitted to coming up with their own consumer technology solution to help solve a business problem.

Figure 5: Source - Aleks Vujanic. Accenture, "Rising Use of Consumer Technology in the Workplace Forcing IT Departments to Respond, Accenture Research Finds." December 12, 2011. http://www.businesswire.com/news/home/20111212005158/en/Rising-Consumer-Technology-Workplace-Forcing-Departments-Respond.

force.com opens up possibilities that were never within reach before. The capability to easily access and combine data and business logic residing at different places in the cloud will lead to innovation in ways never conceived of before. The ability to develop and deploy these solutions more quickly, globally, and less expensively will give nimble organizations a significant advantage over their competitors, whether they are large or small.

To unleash the full power of force.com, it is not enough to simply subscribe to it and add a system here and there; that alone will not turn a business into a more resilient, intelligent, fast, and flexible organization capable of thriving in the new digital economy. force.com provides the *potential* for such transformation. *What is also needed is a holistic implementation that includes a change in mindset, methodology and support.* This will help you meet today's business challenges quickly and cost-effectively, and give everyone in your organization the opportunity to become more efficient, effective, agile, and innovative.

This book lays out a blueprint for how to get there. Executed correctly, the holistic implementation of force.com can have an enormous impact on an enterprise, and represent billions of dollars in potential productivity gains, higher customer satisfaction, new business opportunities, faster time to market, and innovation.

Fully embracing force.com offers organizations a powerful and effective way to ride the next wave of computing, and thereby thrive in the new digital economy.

3. **An analysis of why today's development options won't suffice.** This brings to the surface the problems that need to be overcome, and an understanding of why today's development options are not a viable answer.

4. **A review of the conditions that make the power of force.com possible**. The changes that make a platform like force.com possible – such as cloud computing – are fully described.

5. **The foundation of force.com.** A comprehensive overview of key concepts, such as multi-tenancy and metadata, is provided.

6. **The building blocks of force.com** - social, mobile, workflow, and database - what they provide and what can be achieved with them.

7. **How to implement force.com in your organization**. Simply using force.com to build an application here and there will provide only a small fraction of the advantages offers. This section describes how to implement force.com to get the maximum benefit.

8. **The role of IT in supporting force.com** describes what services should be provided by IT to make the force.com as successful as possible.

9. **Migration considerations** describes the different strategies that can be used to migrate existing applications to force.com.

10. **Best practices.** This section provides a list of best practices that should be followed when implementing and using force.com.

11. **How to get started.** This section describes the basic steps you should take to start riding the force.com wave!

You can choose to be someone who makes it happen, someone who lets it happen, or someone who wonders "What happened?" I hope that with the help of this book you will be in the first category!

The Power of force.com in a Nutshell

We can't predict the future, but we can learn to react a lot faster than our adversaries. – Jack Welch, ex-CEO, GE

To understand how force.com can address the needs of the new digital economy, it's important to get a complete picture of what force.com has to offer. One of the reasons I began to write this book was to address the difficulty of **explaining the overall power of force.com**. Because the platform delivers so much functionality in so many different areas, the parable of the blind men and the elephant is a good analogy.

Much like the blind men who had such different conceptions of the elephant depending on where they stood, some users see force.com as a CRM system, while others see it as a social enterprise platform, a mobile enablement platform, a database in the cloud, or a workflow manager. Having narrow views of what the platform can do makes it difficult to appreciate that the whole is much greater than the sum of its parts – much like the elephant!

An Example

To give you a sense of the power of force.com, here is an example of an application built with force.com:

> **The application is for safety officers on oil rigs**. The basic requirement is to allow the safety officer to record information about any incident through a wizard that asks questions pertaining to the type of incident that occurred. The application allows the user to take photos and videos and automatically attach them to the report. Depending on the type of incident, the appropriate people are automatically notified, actions are taken, a matching workflow is kicked off, the appropriate government forms are automatically filled out, follow-up tasks are created, and so on. Depending on injuries sustained as a result of the incident, first aid instructions are made available and take into account the personal health records of the individuals being treated. The different roles involved can update only their part of the recorded incident.

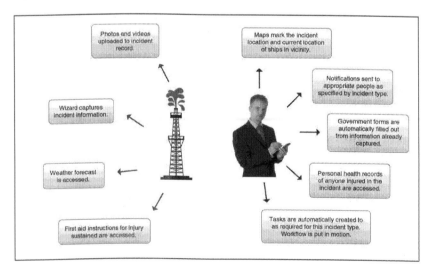

The application has to scale to accommodate a significant increase in usage and users in the case of, for example, a major oil spill. Performance must be consistently fast, and the system should provide 99.99% uptime. Many reports and dashboards are pre-defined, and the need for ad hoc reporting must be provided for. Users need to be able to look for similar incidents to see how they were dealt with, who was involved, and how to get hold of them. Mobile devices also need to be able to function without an Internet connection. There needs to be a prearranged place to store documents related to the incident. Finally, the application needs to be proactive in being able to warn of impending weather events, other incidents in the vicinity, etc.

Building and deploying this application using traditional methods would be a significant undertaking. **Using force.com, building and deploying this type of application is relatively simple**, despite the extent of the requirements, because force.com takes care of many of the requirements "out-of-the-box."

There are no decisions to be made regarding what technology to use, there is no hardware to procure, and there is no software to install. force.com provides:

- Unlimited computing power

- Guaranteed uptime and performance

- Automatic scaling and performance tuning

- Automatic backup and disaster recovery

- A ready-to-go database

- Roles and profiles for security and permission management

- A point-and-click wizard builder for smart forms

- Calendar, task, and follow-up functionality

- A point-and-click, easily modifiable workflow engine

- A point-and-click report writer and dashboard builder

- A social networking environment to facilitate real-time collaboration, recording, filtering, and rapid exception handling

- A document repository

- Easy access to external web services

- The ability to effectively capture data using mobile devices, including offline

Developers can immediately start building the business logic required without having to think about all the functionality detailed above.

There is no need for a lengthy design phase, because **much of the business logic can be built and changed, without code, by a business analyst**. The analyst can create the database, define validation rules, build the roles and profiles, develop the wizards, implement the workflows, write the reports, and build the dashboards – all without IT. The platform also allows the analyst (or user) to modify or enhance many parts of the application without programmer intervention.

As a result, **this application can be up and running and deployed to thousands of users in a matter of a few weeks**. Compare this streamlined process to what would have to be done to get this application written, deployed, and maintained using conventional methods. The application architecture would need to be designed by the technical architect; the database would have to be designed and implemented by the database administrator; detailed functional specifications would necessitate a designer writing for programmers; a technical writer would be required to ensure everything is well documented, since there is so much that needs to be tracked; and a project manager would have to coordinate the work of all personnel and all functions occurring within the process. Common functionality for things like security and permissions, workflow, support for mobile devices, and much more, needs to be built into the application, as do less common but increasingly required functionality, such as support for multiple languages and multiple currencies.

And writing the application is just one part of the equation. Then, add in the need to figure out what technology to use and how to integrate it, procure and implement the hardware and software, find and bring together the right team, plan scalability, ensure constant performance, implement backup and disaster recovery procedures – as a start. Then there is the need to make sure that the specifications are tight, because changing them later won't be easy.

Now, multiply this by all the applications your organization needs to build, and you may begin to get a sense of how transformative the power of force.com can be.

With force.com, the application architecture is pre-determined by the platform; the database is already in place and can be configured using simple point-and-click; security, workflow, etc. are all built into the platform and automatically made available to the application; much of the business logic and workflow is built through configuration instead of coding, eliminating most of the need for detailed specifications; a technical writer is no longer required because there is so much less to be documented (and in any event the system changes all the time); in many projects, the significant reduction in the size of the team needed may even eliminate the need for a full-time project manager; there is no need to worry about, or even think about, scalability, performance, backup, or disaster recovery.

When it comes to deploying the application, things are also much simpler than with the traditional approach. With no hardware to procure or software to be installed, the application can be up and running in literally a matter of minutes.

The power of the "platform"

A digital nervous system is the corporate, digital equivalent of the human nervous system, providing a well-integrated flow of information to the right part of the organization at the right time. A digital nervous system consist of the digital processes that enable a company to perceive and react to its environment, to sense competitor challenges and customer needs, and to organize timely responses. Bill Gates, *Business @ the Speed of Thought*

force.com is designed to work as one comprehensive, totally integrated unit, Like a digital nervous system, *with force.com the whole is much more powerful than the sum of its parts.* In other words, the power of force.com is the platform, not the individual tools it provides.

Highlights of force.com

Financial Power

1. **No capital costs**. force.com eliminates the necessity to procure and maintain hardware and software needed to run applications.

2. **Pay as you go.** You only pay for what you use. Applications can start off with a small number of users, and then grow or shrink as needed.

3. **One license, many applications.** Users can subscribe once to the platform, and run as many applications as they want. The monthly user fee does not change.

4. **Reduced ongoing overhead.** Support and maintenance costs are much lower because staff and resources are not tied up keeping basic infrastructure in place and running. Upgrades are transparent and require no effort.

5. **Budget predictability.** Regardless of the number of applications created on force.com, the number of users is the only effective change in cost, allowing for a scalable budget that adapts to organizational and business changes.

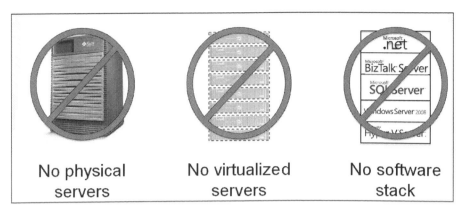

| No physical servers | No virtualized servers | No software stack |

Figure 6: With force.com, there is no hardware or software to think about – ever.

Management Power

6. **Centralized administration.** Because the software is in the cloud, it can be managed and maintained centrally – from anywhere. All users and applications can be managed from one place.

7. **Improved IT control.** force.com includes built-in tools to ensure that internal rules and policies are met. This includes access logs, built-in security, and data segmentation, isolating users from specific data and applications.

8. **Automatic audit trail.** Because all development is done within the platform, information is always available about changes made to applications.

9. **Single system of record.** force.com provides multiple applications with a single database (and thereby a single source of truth) for the entire organization to work from.

10. **Maximized time-to-value**. Because of the low startup expenses, force.com offers rapid prototyping and deployment. Applications can go live the second they are finished.

11. **Continuous upgrades**. force.com continuously delivers the latest advances in technology (e.g., social networking and mobile)

automatically. All new functionality is immediately available to any application already deployed. Previously built custom development is unaffected by system upgrades.

12. **Minimal administration and support.** Data security, backup, disaster recovery, performance, and availability are not of concern for applications built on force.com.

Development Power

13. **Build with clicks, not code**. A significant (and growing) amount of application development can be accomplished without writing any code.

14. **Totally integrated**. force.com eliminates the need to spend time and money integrating application building blocks like workflow, social, mobile, and analytics. Everything works together as a single, totally integrated platform. This means that there is a single login for all functionality, and permissions are defined once and enforced throughout.

15. **Shorter time to go live.** The force.com infrastructure is up and running, with all the services necessary for your application to go live already in place. There is no need to even think about baseline functions like security and scalability. Getting the system in the hands of the users as quickly as possible ensures faster feedback, and by accelerating the process you can avoid piling on sunk costs for efforts that may either fail or require significant adjustments.

16. **Pre-tested platform**. Salesforce.com has already built and tested the production environment, including database, database connectivity, application server, security protocols, and other application infrastructure items such as load balancing, so developers will have to make fewer technology strategy decisions and spend less time on testing before moving to production.

17. **Scale without effort**. force.com's infrastructure already supports thousands of other customers (and millions of other users), so it will sustain whatever requirements you have.

18. **Mobile-enabled**. force.com applications are automatically enabled to work on all major mobile platforms.

19. **Social-enabled**. force.com allows every user and application to participate in the social enterprise. The social enterprise enhances collaboration, facilitates innovation, and reduces the time to resolve problems.

20. **Data sharing.** Data can easily be shared across multiple applications, thereby duplicate data and eliminating redundant data stores.

21. **Single sign-on.** Users log in once and gain access to all the applications they have permission to use.

22. **Shared connectors.** The same legacy system or other cloud service connectors built for one application can be fully leveraged in other applications on the platform.

23. **Shared extensions.** Any extensions to the platform that are built for one application can be reused and extended by other applications.

24. **Reduced interrelated application complexity.** force.com provides a way to reduce complexity by being able to trigger actions across multiple applications.

Business User Power

25. **Build (and deploy) your own solutions**. Users can build solutions using a point-and-click capability, and deploy applications immediately, without waiting for IT.

26. **Save time and effort**. The platform provides comprehensive functionality, thereby eliminating the need for the user to have to deal with basic things like hardware and software, security, backup, and sharing when building solutions.

27. **Access to enterprise data**. Users have clean, core enterprise data (e.g., master files) immediately available to them to build solutions.

28. **Collaboration.** Users have the immediate ability to collaborate in a highly effective manner with other users across the enterprise and beyond.

29. **Personalized for individual users**. Solutions can be easily personalized to the specific needs of each individual user.

30. **One tool for many uses**. All users can become familiar with a single tool they can use for many purposes. This also makes it easier for IT to support, and for users to take advantage of functionality and data created by others.

31. **Fail quickly**. Because there are no planning and setup steps involved, starting a new application is almost as easy as starting a new spreadsheet. This allows users to try things out quickly and, if necessary, abandon them without having made significant investments if they don't work out.

force.com Positioning

force.com is capable of running entire businesses in the cloud. For example, Vetrazzo, a company that manufactures recycled glass surfaces such as countertops and tabletops, uses force.com for CRM, manufacturing, inventory, production planning, customer service, shipping, warranty management, equipment maintenance, plant reporting, quality assurance, channel training, purchasing, and more.

These types of applications would traditionally be written by IT in .Net, Java, and PHP. They can now also be developed on the force.com platform by IT.

Situational Applications

force.com is also capable of building *situational applications*. Situational applications are, as the name implies, solutions to very specific needs, which can include everything from a short-lived database collection serving one person, to a complete solution that includes distributed data entry, workflow, and reporting serving many people.

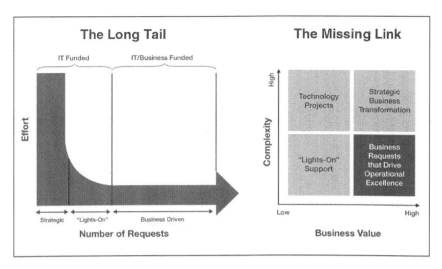

Figure 7: Situational applications are high in business value but are relatively of lower complexity and require less effort than strategic or "lights-on" applications.[5]

Situational applications are characterized as follows:

1. They are usually found at the edge of the organization, where people interact with each other, with customers, partners, contractors and suppliers.

---

[5] Sam Pakrashi, Director, Cognizant, "Rapid Response: Rebranding IT by Creating Transformational Business Value," January, 2009

43

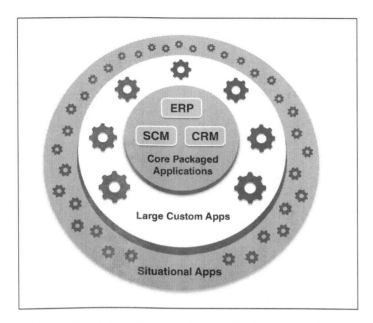

Figure 8: Solid core, flexible boundary: situational applications are found at the edge of the organization, where the opportunity for innovation, value-creation and external interaction takes place.

2. Situational applications are often required to respond quickly to unanticipated events. They therefore need to be much more flexible and agile than traditional applications.

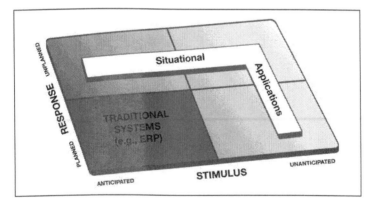

Figure 9: Unlike traditional applications, situational applications are built to address unanticipated and unplanned events.

3. The needs addressed by situational applications tend to be unique to the organization, and their complexity is usually lower than applications found at the core of the organization.

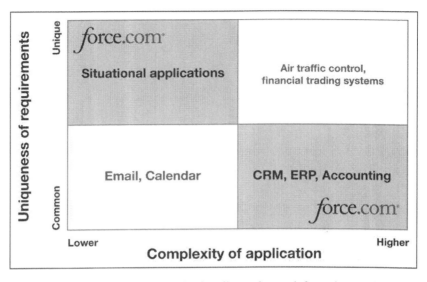

Figure 10: In this book, we are focused primarily on the top left quadrant – this is where organizations can be highly responsive, differentiating, and can garner competitive advantages.

Until now, these types of applications have been written using tools like Lotus Notes, MS Access, and the ubiquitous MS Excel, by business analysts, users, and ad hoc consultants.

These types of tools are woefully inadequate in a world where solutions need to be mobile- and social-enabled, and responsiveness to changing demands needs to be immediate for all users, including those outside the organization.

force.com is well-positioned to meet the situational application needs for organizations both large and small.

Exceptions

There are, of course, some types of applications that are not well-suited to force.com. They include:

- applications with massive storage requirements, like cell phone records or Gmail;

- streaming audio and video;

- raw computing power, such as scientific simulations and video games.

force.com applications requiring this type of functionality can take advantage of the ease with which cloud computing facilitates integration with other, complementary clouds, such as:

- Amazon for massive storage;

- Google for elastic consumer web-scale applications;

- Facebook for integration with the public social graph; and

- Heroku for customer-facing web sites.

In a Nutshell

force.com provides an entire host of powerful ready-to-go capabilities in one place. As we will see in the next chapter, this is exactly what is needed to meet the needs of the new digital economy.

The New Digital Economy

"For more than a decade, powerful new digital approaches to business, and life in general, have come on the scene, yet we are now entering an even more rapid and dramatic period of change. The phenomenon of digitization is reaching an inflection point. Three powerful forces are driving the shift: consumer demand, the push for new technologies, and the prospect of even greater economic benefits. Every company in every industry will be dramatically affected... Unlike the technology revolutions of the 1990s and 2000s, this time around the basis of competition will be set by the companies that embrace and deploy digitization in the right places at the right time... The judgments that companies make now will largely determine their relative competitive position for the foreseeable future." – Roman Friedrich, Alex Koster, Matthew Le Merle, and Michael Peterson, "The Next Wave of Digitization. Setting Your Direction, Building Your Capabilities," Booz & Company, 2011

The digital economy is triggering a third wave of capitalism that will transform business and government, and lead to extraordinary wealth creation. – John Sviokla, PwC Strategy and Innovation Advisory Group[6]

The new nexus of cloud computing, mobile technology, and the social enterprise is spawning a new *digital economy*, where things that were previously physical have now been *digitized*: translated into digital services, processes, and delivery mechanisms.

---

[6] *The New Digital Economy: How It Will Transform Business*, a research paper produced by Oxford Economics in collaboration with AT&T, Cisco, Citi, PwC & SAP, June 2011. http://www.pwc.com/gx/en/technology/publications/ transform-business-in-new-digital-economy.jhtml

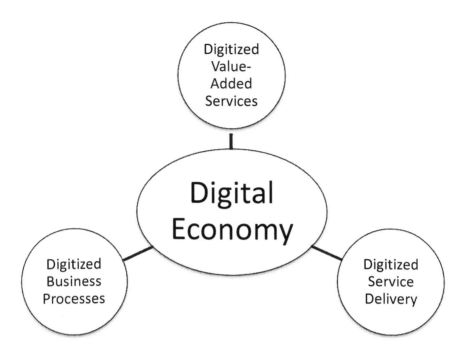

There are three primary components of the new digital economy:

1. **Digitized Processes.** More and more business processes are being executed electronically without any human intervention.

2. **Digitized Value-Added Services.** Offering differentiating digitized services is becoming the key to profitability and growth as products and services become commoditized.

3. **Digitized Service Delivery.** Transforming the delivery of physical data and content to digital is moving well beyond books and music. Conducting business through mobile devices is going to be an enormously disruptive change in the way business is performed.

Digitized Processes

This second economy that is silently forming—vast, interconnected, and extraordinarily productive—is creating for us a new economic world. How we will fare in this world, how we will adapt to it, how we will profit from it and share its benefits, is very much up to us. – W. Brian Arthur, "The Second Economy"

In Arthur's McKinsey article, he describes how business processes that once took place between human beings are now being executed electronically, in a domain that is strictly digital. He points out that, while on the surface this shift doesn't appear to be particularly consequential, it is "causing a revolution no less important and dramatic than that of the railroads. It is quietly creating a second economy, a digital one."

The digitization of business processes is occurring across a broad swath of business applications, ranging from complex, stable processes, to simple business processes involving automatic routing of information and application execution.

One of the best examples of business process digitization is the airline check-in process. Until fairly recently, when you went into an airport you'd stand in line at a counter and eventually present a paper ticket to a human being. That person would register you on a computer, notify the flight you'd arrived, and check your luggage. All this was done by humans. Today, you walk into an airport and go directly to a machine. You insert your credit card, and in a few seconds, you get back a boarding pass, receipt, and luggage tag. Behind this is a complex business process, conducted entirely between machines. Once your name is recognized, a computer checks your flight status with the airlines, your name with the TSA, your seat choice, your frequent-flyer status, your access to lounges, and ongoing connecting flights.

On the other extreme, a comparatively simple cross-functional workflow: A fast food chain needs to roll out a new point of sale system to

6,000 stores. This involves a significant number of players, all of whom need to be coordinated – vendors, contractors, stores, trainers, installers, and more. There is data to be collected and multiple decisions to be made across the workflow. The schedule needs to account for blackout dates, vendor capabilities, locations, readiness, etc. And the schedule changes frequently, resulting in a flurry of notifications and discussions. There are interfaces to other systems, orders that need to be placed and tracked, exceptions spawning additional workflows, and checklists that need to be completed at key junctures.

The time required to manage this project is significant, and the number of things that can go wrong is high. But digitized, it becomes much less daunting. Data and checklists can be captured and validated at the source through a mobile device. Notifications, reminders, and approval requests are all automated and delivered through the social network. Discussions can take place in context through the social network. Many decisions can be made automatically by the system through user-defined rules, including the automatic adjustment of the schedule, which results in a cascade of digital interactions among systems in multiple organizations.

In these examples, processes are being digitized, creating a constant conversation among multiple servers and multiple semi-intelligent nodes that are updating things, querying things, checking things off, readjusting things, and eventually connecting back with processes and humans in the physical economy.

Digitized Services

> *In an endless pursuit of innovation, companies of thousands of employees and sole proprietors alike, strive to distinguish themselves, and avoid commoditization so they can demand a premium for their goods and services.*
> – Peter Fingar, *Extreme Competition*

Jeremy Rifkin, author of *The Empathic Civilization*, writes that the Internet, mobile computing, and digital media are giving rise to what he calls the third industrial revolution, and business models that are "cybernetic, not linear."[7] Instead of the linear, start-and-stop assembly line model of the twentieth century's second industrial revolution, business is now about access to services instead of ownership of products. Business is no longer about transactions that record one-time purchases, but instead about "an ongoing commercial relationship between parties over time."[8]

So instead of purchasing music CDs, a customer buys a membership in organizations that provides them with access to huge libraries of music, which they can retrieve for their own personal use. Instead of buying a car, many people are turning to membership in companies like Zipcar and iGo that provide them with the use of a car when they need one.

Michael Hugos is an award-winning CIO who writes a blog for *CIO* magazine called "Doing Business in Real Time," and has written books that include *Business Agility: Sustainable Prosperity in a Relentlessly Competitive World* and *Business in the Cloud: What Every Business Needs to Know about Cloud Computing.* He observes that successful companies are increasingly focused on wrapping their commodity products in blankets of value-added services that are tailored to meet evolving needs and desires of specific customer segments.

This will result in a surge of requests for applications from IT. The problem for IT is that the focus of these applications is quite different from assembly line thinking, where the focus is on *efficiency*. Now, IT will need to change its focus to facilitating *responsiveness*.

---

[7] The cybernetic model is described as a system where an action by the system causes some change in its environment and that change is fed to the system via information (feedback) that causes the system to adapt to these new conditions: the system's changes affect its behavior. This "circular causal" relationship is *cybernetic*.

[8] Jeremy Rifkin, *The Empathic Civilization: The Race to Global Consciousness in a World in Crisis,* NY: Tarcher, 2009

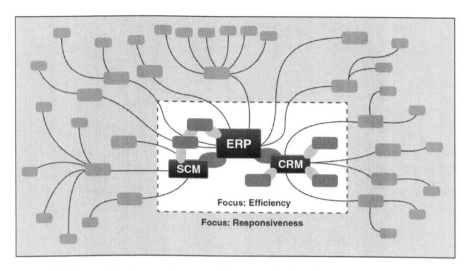

Figure 11: The applications at the core of the organization focus on efficiency. On the edge, they focus of responsiveness and effectiveness.

Hugos explains the tremendous need for a company to be more responsive if they are to succeed in a world that is relentlessly squeezing profit margins more and more. While companies must of course achieve and maintain a "good-enough" degree of efficiency, they cannot use efficiency alone to generate profits. In this high-change global economy, responsiveness trumps efficiency.

Says Hugos, in *Business Agility*:

> ***Opportunities to make money by being responsive have exploded.*** *There are far more ways to use responsiveness to attract customers than there are ways to use efficiency and low prices. This is because there are so many different kinds of customers, and each is looking for slightly different mixes of products and services. Constantly changing environments and customer needs enable responsive companies to offer continuously evolving mixes of new products and services.*

This requires us to change our thinking about what information technology contributes to an organization. We need to start asking questions like: what value-added services we can we provide customers, and how we can use IT to deliver those services?

The Value-Added Component of Products

In any deep transformation, industries do not so much adopt the new body of technology as encounter it, and as they do so they create new ways to profit from its possibilities. – W. Brian Arthur, "The Second Economy"

Hugos points out that all products have two components: the product or service itself; and the information about the product and the value-added services surrounding it. The information component is what enables a customer to find and evaluate your product, to understand how to use it, and to get the results and benefits they want from it.

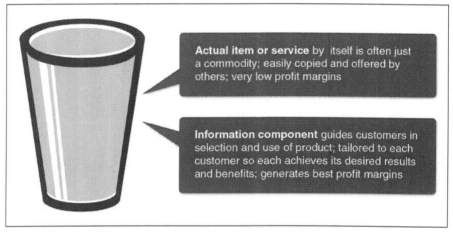

Actual item or service by itself is often just a commodity; easily copied and offered by others; very low profit margins

Information component guides customers in selection and use of product; tailored to each customer so each achieves its desired results and benefits; generates best profit margins

Hugos continues:

*This second component is where above-market prices and profits are to be found. Through the creative use of the information component, you can wrap any commodity product with a mix of value-added services that make it more useful and for which customers will pay a bit extra. Information technology lowers the cost and expands capacity to deliver the information component. **This is*** *where skillful use of IT enables a company to earn higher profits.*

Example 1: The Value-Added Paper Cup

In his book, Hugos provides the perfect real-life example of how this can work, using "The Value-Added Paper Cup."

When Hugos was the chief information officer of a national distributor of food-service disposables and janitorial supplies (like paper cups), his challenge was to make the products more valuable and earn a higher profit. He and his team devised a menu of about fifty different value-added services that salespeople could then mix and match to meet specific customer needs.

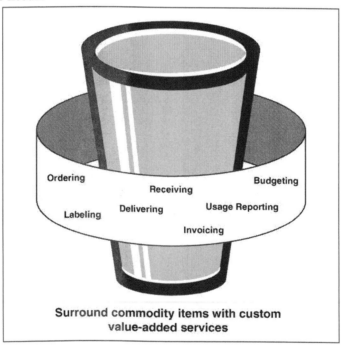

Ordering
Receiving
Budgeting
Labeling
Delivering
Usage Reporting
Invoicing

Surround commodity items with custom value-added services

The services included allowing customers to: place and track their orders online; create labels customized to the customers' needs that would allow the cups to be quickly received, stored, and retrieved; send invoices in whatever format each customer wanted; insert customer general ledger codes into every invoice line item so those costs could be automatically disbursed to their general ledger systems; and an online dashboard so the distributor could get real-time insight into usage patterns and purchasing trends.

Every company has its equivalent of that paper cup.

Example 2: Monetizing intellectual capital

Vinnie Mirchandani, author of *The New Polymath: Profiles in Compound-Technology Innovations* and *The New Technology Elite: How Great Companies Optimize Both Technology Consumption and Production*, describes how leading edge firms that have moved to the cloud are beginning to shift their business models from billable hours to intellectual capital monetization.

> *Because the cloud is always on and always connected, both the accountant and their client always share the same financial information in real-time. This allows accountants to become proactive advisors – they are no longer looking at a QuickBooks file at the end of the month or a shoebox of receipts at the end of the year. The client and the accountant are connected 24x7, bringing tremendous benefits to both – the firm generates higher value billings and the client receives more timely and impactful guidance...This is what the cloud revolution is all about – transforming business processes in ways that have never been possible before.*[9]

Example 3: Saving lives through digitization

I like this particular example because it powerfully illustrates how a small digitized value-added service can make an enormous difference to a commodity product.

---

[9] Vinnie Mirchandani, "The 'Cloud Pioneers': Dan Druker," *Deal Architect,* http://dealarchitect.typepad.com/deal_architect/2009/04/the-cloud-pioneer-series-dan-druker.html

Counterfeit drugs can make up a quarter of all pharmaceuticals sold in poor countries. They are a lucrative and lethal business, against which most consumers are powerless: if your anti-malaria pills are made of any old white powder, you may not survive.[10]

To address this, a pharmaceutical company started a mobile service in Ghana and Nigeria that allows people buying medicine to scratch a panel attached to the packaging, revealing a code they can text to a computer system, which looks it up in a database. Seconds later a reply comes back saying whether the drug is genuine or not.

When the digitized service IS the product

Companies like Zipcar and iGo provide cars, but they are not in the auto business. They are in the *mobility service provider* business. And the service they provide is primarily digital.

If Zipcar wants to gain a competitive advantage over iGo, buying and providing different cars is not going to do it. Providing a mobile service that allows the customer to locate the nearest Zipcar using geo-location – *that* is a

---

[10] "Mobile services in poor countries: Not just talk," *The Economist*, Jan. 27, 2011.

service that provides a real competitive advantage.

With Zipcar, rather than buy or lease an entire car, customers buy just the amount of car they actually need, like a day's worth, or perhaps just an hour. The car is there when they need it, and probably in use by someone else when they don't.

For this to work, Zipcar has to make sharing more affordable and more convenient than car owning. This can only be done by wrapping its mobility product with digitized services.

As a result, Zipcar provides a wide array of digitized services, including the ability to easily reserve a specific vehicle for a specific day and time from any device; a two-way text function to help members quickly and easily extend or modify an existing reservation; and a GPS link that instantly displays a list of available Zipcars near a member at any moment.

Here, the digitized service is the product. The physical product, the car, plays a very small role in the entire value proposition.

When the digitized service eliminates the physical service altogether

Sometimes, providing digitized value-added services will kill the actual physical product or service.

Take associations, for example. Associations are established to allow people in the same industry to network, provide certifications, and increase their members' knowledge.

Over the last decade, associations have used the Internet to help deliver and add value to their services. But with the advent of services like LinkedIn and Facebook, the Internet has made the actual services provided by associations increasingly irrelevant. So instead of the association providing value-added digitized services, the digitized services are themselves replacing the association; "physical" associations will for the most part cease to exist.

Digitized Delivery

Going digital will put you on the leading edge of a shock wave of change that will shatter the old way of doing business. - Bill Gates, *Business @ the Speed of Thought*

Digitized delivery of everything from content to banking and payments is enabling mobile devices to be the primary medium through which business is conducted.

Here are some examples:

- Digitizing a car's traditional paper-based owner's manual and delivering it as a mobile app allows a company to go well beyond just making the manual's information more convenient, and cutting printing and shipping costs. The mobile app allows owners to receive reminders for routine maintenance, schedule maintenance, and receive special discount offers or information about new cars. This app increases the "stickiness" and engagement levels between the customer and the dealer/automaker throughout the ownership lifecycle, far surpassing the value of the original physical artifact.

- Airlines have embraced the idea of a "paperless flight deck." Instead of lugging around 40-pound flight manuals (and manually updating binders with new pages every week), each pilot has an iPad that provides flight plans, navigation, and other data, providing real-time automatic updates. Instead of keys or codes, a real estate company uses an app to control access to the homes it's showing via a smart phone. This provides a centrally-managed ability to limit entry to specific agents at specific times. Similarly, Zipcar uses digitized delivery service via a smart phone to open car doors and enable its cars' engines to be started, eliminating the need for physical keys.

- An external plug-and-play device that allows a smart phone to be used as an ultrasound scanner stores video/images and delivers them digitally anywhere in the world for diagnosis. This type of digitized delivery service has particular relevance in the developing world.

- "Mobile wallet" apps on smart phones are capable of being loaded with money – no paper or coins needed. Mobile wallets can bring

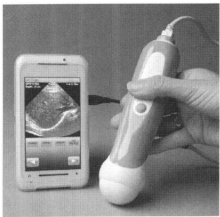

people in emerging markets such as India and Africa, who have no access to banks, into the wider financial world, helping to drive economic and social development.

- Digital delivery of coupons allows businesses to offer location/time-based pricing. Not only are paper coupons eliminated (and all the costs that go with them), but the business can present a much better targeted offer.

In all these examples, physical delivery mechanisms have been digitized, resulting in significant reductions in cost and significant increases in value-added functionality.

Conclusion

We're at a turning point with digitization, from which dramatic change will come about. Conventional wisdom has it that the Chinese symbol for "crisis" is a combination of symbols representing *chaos* and *opportunity*. How well an organization will fare will depend on how forward-thinking the people at the top are. CEOs can choose either to quickly capitalize on the opportunity being offered to help them stand out in the marketplace; or they can be onlookers, watching and waiting while the digital revolution takes place. In the latter case, they will be among the group who end up asking, "What happened?" while they are outflanked and outplayed by their digitized competitors.[11]

---

[11] Roman Friedrich, Matthew Le Merle, Michael Peterson, and Alex Koster, "The Next Wave of Digitization: Setting Your Direction, Building Your Capabilities," Booz & Co., 2011

A Radical Change in Business Use of Information Technology

In the cloud, on the web, there's no distance to slow us down, no custom infrastructure we have to build, no paperwork to get lost. We can make connections, harness resources and start interacting without ever having to wait for physical stuff to happen first. – Phil Wainewright, "From Fixed to Frictionless Enterprise," ZDNet, Oct, 2011

In the new digital economy, there are no organizational boundaries. Systems can't stop at the edge of the enterprise, and applications can't be monolithic, one-size-fits-all, or time-consuming to change. The new digital economy requires a completely different way for business to harness technology. Welcome to IT 2.0.

The shift includes the following:

IT 1.0	IT 2.0
Solution development & delivery	Solution enablement
Focus on efficiency	Focus on effectiveness
Build solutions for the core	Facilitate solutions for the edge
Focus on back-office	Focus on front-office
Big I.T.	Small I.T. services
Local orientation	Global, transnational orientation
Stable environment	Dynamic environment
In-house	Outsource
Mass production	Mass customization
Afterthought	Pre-thought

The changing role of IT

Today, we're seeing a shift from process to pattern, a shift from rule to principle, a shift from hierarchical to networked, a shift from centralized to edge-based. – JP Rangaswami.[12]

The railway companies of the last century declined because they believed they were in the railway business, rather than the transportation business. Similarly, the importance of corporate IT departments will decline if they think they are in the business of building and running enterprise software when in fact *they need to be in the business of empowering employees to be as effective and productive as possible.*

From delivery to enablement

The primary role of business computing has changed from automating transactions to facilitating interactions. – Sohaib Abbasi[13]

Today, the computing power and the networking services are becoming more and more like dial tone. Now we need to focus on what business users need to get out of technology.[14] – Yuri Aguiar, CIO, Ogilvy Worldwide

The IT department has traditionally been the focal point of automation in the organization because the primary means of production (programmers, etc.) and the sole means of delivery (the data center) were located within it. This is no longer true.

---

[12] JP Rangaswami, "Musing gently about improvisation, permission and forgiveness," Confused of Calcutta blog, January 29, 2012

[13] Informatica, "Press Release: Informatica Chairman And CEO Sohaib Abbasi Shares Vision On Future Of Big Data." August 09, 2011 http://www.informatica.com/us/company/news-and-events-calendar/press-releases/08092011-pacific-crest-keynote.aspx.

[14] Hugos 2010, 127

As a result, instead of IT spending 85% of its budget on everything *but* truly transformational technologies, it will now be able to use much of that budget to focus almost entirely on enabling the organization to thrive, by using information technology to quickly take advantage of the windows of opportunities that are opening up at a faster and faster pace.

From efficiency to effectiveness

The value proposition of information technology in the enterprise is shifting beyond operational efficiency to organizational effectiveness. Until recently, organizations focused on operational efficiency by automating transaction processing with department applications like ERP and CRM.

But this kind of efficiency is past its peak, because "there's very little left to store and automate that isn't already."[15] To increase business performance, you have to look beyond systems of record because the low-hanging fruit has all been picked. That's one reason knowledge work, which now makes up 40% of developed nations' businesses, is on the rise: there is plenty of room for expansion and innovation. Working on strategic processes of a higher order better utilizes the most important workers, and businesses gain the most by leveraging collaborative networks.

---

[15] Dion Hinchcliffe, "Moving Beyond Systems of Record to Systems of Engagement," Dachis Group, June 8, 2011. http://www.dachisgroup.com/ 2011/06/moving-beyond-systems-of-record-to-systems-of-engagement/

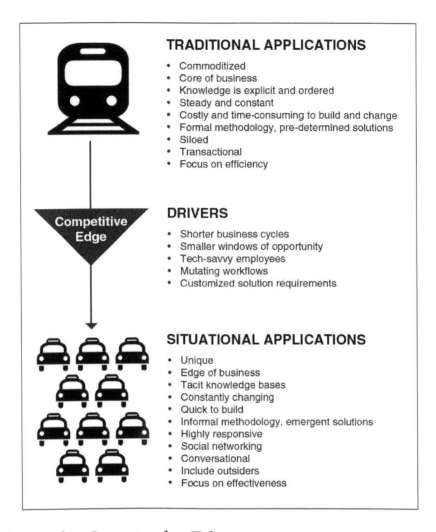

TRADITIONAL APPLICATIONS

- Commoditized
- Core of business
- Knowledge is explicit and ordered
- Steady and constant
- Costly and time-consuming to build and change
- Formal methodology, pre-determined solutions
- Siloed
- Transactional
- Focus on efficiency

DRIVERS

- Shorter business cycles
- Smaller windows of opportunity
- Tech-savvy employees
- Mutating workflows
- Customized solution requirements

SITUATIONAL APPLICATIONS

- Unique
- Edge of business
- Tacit knowledge bases
- Constantly changing
- Quick to build
- Informal methodology, emergent solutions
- Highly responsive
- Social networking
- Conversational
- Include outsiders
- Focus on effectiveness

From the Core to the Edge

The way people work is different at the edges of the enterprise than it is at the center. The edge of the enterprise is where work gets done – people interacting with each other, with customers, partners, contractors and suppliers. These "edge" operations often require creative problem-solving on a daily basis. This is where the focus of IT needs to be now.

John Hagel III and John Seely Brown, explain the move to the edge like this:

When business challenges arise unexpectedly, workers, especially those on the edges of the enterprise, need flexibility and sophisticated, responsive tools. Enter cloud computing, which allows individuals countless choices for a flexible and agile response. Sometimes it will require several false starts and untested combinations of ingredients, all of which would be impossible for a central IT department. Moreover, while edge workers lack the time to wait, they seldom have input to IT priorities, even if the department were sufficiently nimble and open to experiment. Cloud remedies don't need scheduling, approval, or prototype trials so users can apply and test solutions immediately. Since they don't require big up-front investments of money or development time, there's no downside to the user's experimenting or improvising.

So, if experimentation is made so much easier to do, there is likely to be much more of it by employees on the edges of the enterprise. Overcoming challenges reinforces positive feedback, and thereby increases motivation to perform beyond the norm.[16]

This is in sharp contrast to the way problems are usually handled today, where they are seen as obstacles to be avoided or dealt with in a "quick and dirty" manner, instead of using problems as opportunities for lasting solutions and increased worker satisfaction.

In this way, people on the edge can now "drive innovation from their vantage point and in that way impact the enterprise more quickly and persuasively. In the past, experiments took place on the edge, but the results had to be tentatively presented to the core and one hoped for the best. In reality, most of these initiatives died horrible deaths as antibodies in the core rapidly overwhelmed the brave edge participants who ventured into the core. That relationship can be very different

---

[16] John Hagel III and John Seely Brown, "The Power of the Social Cloud," Harvard Business Review Blog Network, October 15, 2010, http://blogs.hbr.org/bigshift/2010/10/the-power-of-the-social-cloud.html

today. Now, the innovations don't even have to be taken back to the core. Instead, the novel working solutions draw core workers to the edge to join in the frontier experience."[17]

Edge-based companies are also characterized by their ability to self-organize, widely distribute decision-making and quickly adapt to market changes. Dr. Sviokla of PwC likens these organizations to "special force" units, where "everyone has situational awareness, skills to take action, shared values, and decision rights to empower the edge to take action."[18]

In this environment, one of the roles of IT is to make users aware of potential problem areas, like regulatory concerns, financial and tax matters, management and security issues, and help users deal with them effectively.

From back office structure to front office unstructure

The back office environment is "structured," and has been the focus in the last twenty years with Enterprise Resource Planning (ERP). The goal of the back office is to fully automate and optimize structured processes.

The front office, on the other hand, is an unstructured operational area built around people trying to make insightful decisions around whatever facts are available. In the chaotic event-driven world of the front office, social networks are the glue that facilitates the finding of alignments between events, people, and data to "organize" collaborative responses to market opportunities. Since the market opportunities are unlikely to align exactly with the way that the enterprise would like to do business, "the enterprise has to quickly find answers to all the questions and be 'agile' in

---

[17] John Hagel III and John Seely Brown, "Cloud Computing's Stormy Future," Harvard Business Review Blog Network, September 14, 2010, http://blogs.hbr.org/bigshift/2010/ 09/cloud-computings-stormy-future.html.

[18] *The New Digital Economy: How It Will Transform Business*, 2011.

its ability to match the requirements of the market and its customers in the online globally competitive environment."[19]

From big IT to small services

Enterprise level deployment of monolithic applications is giving way to the assembly of small granular services. Instead of big-bang everything-and everyone-at-once implementations, the need is to create large numbers of small services that can be rapidly orchestrated into chosen processes, and equally quickly changed again. This allows solutions to be small, experimental, innovative, and locally relevant.

This also changes the length of time a solution will stay in service. For example, a six-month traditional application development solution may be around for many years with ongoing maintenance requiring full documentation, whereas a week-long service development and deployment may have a life of only a few months and then be scrapped rather than maintained. [20]

From dependence to independence

A new Accenture survey of 4,000 employees from across the globe finds a large proportion (43%) feel comfortable and capable of making their own technology decisions for work. There is also an increasing trend for employee-driven technological innovation, as 24% of employees admitted to coming up with their own consumer technology solution to help solve a business problem.[21]

---

[19] Andy Mulholland, "2012: the year of unstructured technologies and market change," CTO Blog, January 16, 2012

[20] Andy Mulholland, "Ten Game-Changing Technology Shifts for 2012," CTO Blog, January 3, 2012

[21] Aleks Vujanic, "Rising Use of Consumer Technology in the Workplace Forcing IT Departments to Respond, Accenture Research Finds," Accenture, December 12, 2011. http://www.businesswire.com/news/home/ 20111212005158/ en/Rising-Consumer-Technology-Workplace-Forcing-Departments-Respond

It is not surprising, therefore, that line-of-business tech budgets may soon top IT department budgets. Gartner analysts are predicting that by the year 2015, 35% of enterprise IT expenditures for most organizations will be managed outside the IT department's budget. "Next generation digital enterprises are being driven by a new wave of business managers and individual employees who no longer need technology to be contextualized for them by an IT department," the report states. "These people are demanding control over the IT expenditure required to evolve the organization within the confines of their roles and responsibilities. CIOs will see some of their current budget simply reallocated to other areas of the business. In other cases, IT projects will be redefined as business projects with line-of-business managers in control."[22]

From local to global

> *Victor Fung, the chairman of Li & Fung, one of Hong Kong's oldest textile manufacturers, remarked to me last year that for many years his company operated on the rule: "You sourced in Asia, and you sold in America and Europe." Now, said Fung, the rule is: "Source everywhere, manufacture everywhere, sell everywhere." The whole notion of an "export" is really disappearing. —* Tom Friedman, "Made in the World," *New York Times,* January 28, 2012

In the global market, more and more enterprises are moving into "new" or "emergent" markets for their products or services, and establishing local operations in these countries to support them. It is impractical to set up an IT support structure in these new markets, including the need to adjust for local rules and regulations, currency and language. Your organization cannot be trapped by the limitations of your information systems.

---

[22] "Gartner Reveals Top Predictions for IT Organizations and Users for 2012 and Beyond," Gartner Newsroom Press Releases, December 1, 2011, http://www.gartner.com/it/page.jsp?id=1862714

In this new environment, it becomes imperative to take an approach to building systems in a way that leverages centralized functionality with local flexibility.

From stable environments to dynamic environments

We are moving from a relatively stable business environment to one characterized by rapid rates of change with ever more disruptions generating increasing uncertainty and unpredictability. Turning this instability from a threat to an opportunity will require a significant adjustment not only in how systems are built, but also a complete change in mindset.

From in-house to outsource

Until now, it made sense to contain resources and processes within the enterprise because it incurred too much friction and cost to go outside for them. "Today, the opposite is true. It takes too much time and expense to acquire or build stuff in-house if it's already available on-demand from the cloud. The most successful, efficient organizations are those that can easily connect to and harness those cloud resources. … In the cloud, on the Web, there's no distance to slow us down, no custom infrastructure we have to build, no paperwork to get lost. We can make connections, harness resources and start interacting without ever having to wait for physical stuff to happen first. This on-demand access to information and resources has already transformed long-established industries such as bookselling, classified advertising and music publishing. And that's just a foretaste of what's yet to come."[23]

---

[23] Phil Wainewright, "From fixed to frictionless enterprise," ZDNet, October 27, 2011

From mass production to mass customization

At the turn of the twentieth century new flows of information through channels such as the telegraph and telephone supported mass production. Today the availability of abundant data enables companies to cater to small niche markets anywhere in the world. To do this effectively requires a new set of tools to manage, mine and present this data, followed by highly applications to help manage each unique situation.

From Afterthought to Pre-thought

"Increasingly, business differentiation and success involves or requires responsive IT capabilities."[24] In the digital economy, by definition IT must be part of every offering, and in many cases is the core. Embedding IT into products, offering value-added IT-based services and building revenue-generating purely digital products requires that IT be involved at the front end of the development process.

---

[24] "We better have a Plan B for the 'Something about Services Era'", Bruce J. Rogow, Cognizanti, Volume 4 Issue 2 2011

Taking an Outside-In Approach to IT, by Andy Mulholland

Andy Mulholland is the Global Chief Technology Officer at Capgemini.

Enterprise IT can be definable as "inside-out" since it starts from the back office, and is focused on activities "inside" the enterprise. There are only a few activities requiring access "outside," such as use of the Internet/web, and even for these, control is managed from the "inside." The important insight provides guidance regarding many current concerns such as security, new business requirements using external information, servicing customers with new business models, and increasing employee demand to use their own devices and use new services such as Amazon Web Services, or Salesforce.com.

Most problems now stem from trying to deliver this new outside world of business use from the inside. This shows a failure to recognize that the enabling technology is radically different. The Inside-Out model of traditional IT manifests in monolithic enterprise applications using client-server to support a close-coupled, state-full, or data-centric, deterministic environment. On the other hand, Outside-In is based on Internet/web architecture characterized as loose-coupled, state-less, and non-deterministic. Each and every important technology characteristic is exactly reversed, as is the purpose for which the business user or manager wants to use it! For example: The operating authority of a major airport is facing demands to improve operational management of its increasingly congested airport. On one hand is the need to improve real-time efficiency in the face of the increasing number of unplanned events like late-arriving aircraft and lost baggage. On the other hand, passengers and airlines expect that information flows will be provided both in a more timely way and in different people-oriented formats, or feeds. Large numbers of tablets or smart phones are deployed to front line staff to achieve these goals and improve operating efficiency, which means dealing with many unplanned events, from locating missing passengers to lost luggage, delineating steps to replenishing food and drink, or handling last minute gate changes.

This is just like the major shift in the early '90s when using PC network technology changed every aspect of the mini-computer requirement, delivery, and deployment model to the model we understand today as Enterprise IT.

The existing traditional inside-out IT systems of various components of an airport ecosystem – airport operator, airlines, baggage handler, food services, etc., – each separately show their planned activity to their own staff via their secure and closed enterprise IT. In each enterprise the data comes from the central ERP systems to the edge of the enterprise in the form of structured non-real-time information to show what should happen; and if it does happen, then the whole ecosystem will be synchronized and "resource planning" will have succeeded.

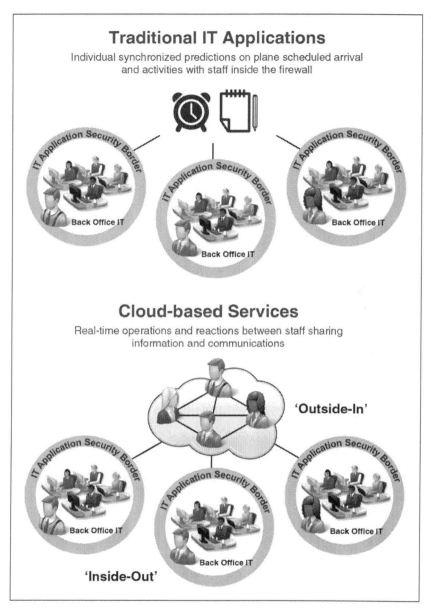

The operational improvement challenge is that in the "real" world a series of unforeseen events occurs that, to be resolved, requires the staff of the companies involved to interact together in a unique way to suit each event. The better any business can do this, the higher their customer satisfaction, and most likely the lower their costs as they optimize their responses. This is highly people-centric, using real-time data ending in a "work-around" solution or process to suit the circumstances. Most importantly, it doesn't require any of the people to be present in each other's existing enterprise IT systems (the current barrier to addressing this kind of transformation). When the event is resolved, however, there might there be a need to pass the concluding data into the existing IT systems of each company so that records can be updated. This is the "Outside-In" view: the activity occurs "outside" the enterprise and only limited access is required to pass "in" to the secure IT environment.

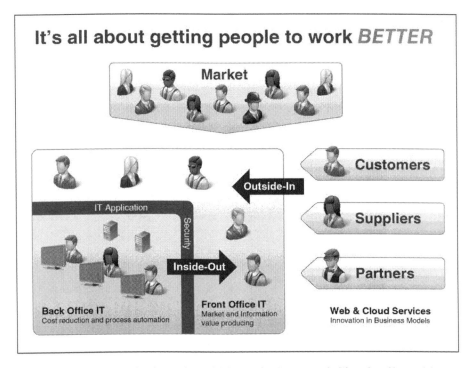

The new technologies of Mobility, Big Data and Clouds allow this to be achieved without infringing on the enterprise security model, only if they are applied in a very different way. The current good practice is to create and manage a comprehensive and cohesive IT environment within a secure boundary. For the tight coupled, state-full data-centric, client-servers applications this is entirely correct. But in the airport example above, there is a formidable challenge in permitting unknown operational staff and networks, working in unstructured ways, to enter this controlled and structured world in a secure manner.

The challenge exists around rapid and frequent introductions of new types of apps and services that allow interaction through social and collaborative tools, pooling of huge amounts of data, and the new app-based processes to be deployed around this new generation of "front office" business requirements. In adopting an "Outside In" approach, the relevant users and devices are moved outside the existing secure enterprise IT environment. In the case of the airport operations, they will co-exist on one or more clouds that permit the loose-coupled, stateless consumption of "services" on-demand that is the core of this new environment.

"Outside-In" is a completely different way of thinking about the requirement, delivery, and deployment model. But this is only to be expected, given that this is an entirely new generation of technologies used in a completely different way by business. This is just like the major shift in the early '90s when using PC network technology changed every aspect of the mini-computer requirement, delivery, and deployment model to the model we understand today as Enterprise IT.

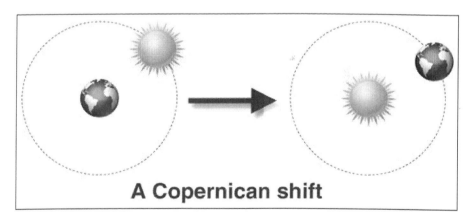

A Copernican shift

Figure 12: Stop thinking that "*We build a collection of applications that support our business.*" Start thinking that "*We build our business using technology platforms.*"

Conclusion

These seismic shifts, all happening at the same time, collectively reflect a major change in information technology in the enterprise. It therefore makes sense to refer to all these changes under the rubric of *Information Technology 2.0.*

Application Characteristics in the New Digital Economy

> *The cognitive model is to treat the computer not as a box, but a door. It's something you need to get through to get to the value on the other side. People don't want a door with 32 different kinds of handles.*[25] – Clay Shirky, *Here Comes Everybody: The Power of Organizing Without Organizations*

Applications in the new digital economy are going to be delivered primarily on mobile devices, and mobile apps will be the way people increasingly socialize, collaborate, communicate, transact business, obtain information, and perform activities.

In fact, we are very likely to drop the word "mobile" quite soon and just refer to anything with a browser as a "device" and a mobile app as just an "app." (Likewise, "cloud computing" will eventually just become "computing" – "cloud" will be a given.)

So mobile apps are a good place to look to see what the applications of the future will be like.

Situational applications

To be effective, mobile apps need to be very targeted and often single-function, such as checking flight arrivals, looking for contacts, tracking shipments, ordering spare parts, approving requests, or checking account balances. The objective is to provide simple features and functions with pre-populated data that make it as easy as possible for users to complete specific tasks.

---

[25] Clay Shirky, *Here Comes Everybody: The Power of Organizing Without Organizations*, NY: Penguin, 2008

Building behemoth applications (except for static applications like accounting) is therefore a thing of the past. And simply taking an existing application and translating it into a hundred mobile screens with complex navigation schemes is not going to work. Small, intuitive, on-demand, role-based apps and services that allow users to use only what applies to their particular situation (hence the term *situational application*) will transform the way business is conducted.

For example, service technicians might perform dozens of tasks in their daily jobs, but they could probably identify just six or seven of these tasks that are crucial for performing on the road – like confirming an order is complete, or ordering a spare part for a repair job. They don't need an entire "field technician application" involving complex navigation schemes and requiring hours of training. They just need highly purposeful, single-function applications that are aligned with their role and intuitive to use, to ensure quick adoption.[26]

Situational processes

The same applies to business processes. The first step is to deconstruct business processes so that different nodes in the process can be executed by the best possible team or service, wherever they happen to be (including outside the organization). This too requires small, targeted, single-function apps to be built so that individual apps and services can be strung together to meet the needs of each specific. This provides much more flexibility and facilitates much better responsiveness.

Bear in mind, however, that building and deploying these small apps is much easier if a common platform is used, where they can share the database, authentication, permissions, workflows, etc.

---

[26] Mahesh Lunani, "Enterprise Mobile Apps: How Role-Based Apps Will Drive Productivity and Transformation in Manufacturing Companies," Cognizant 20-20 Insights, July 2011

The Activity Stream as Work Context

The most valuable, economical way to work with situational applications will be right in the social networking activity stream. It doesn't make sense to use the applications and *then* take the resulting work product to the social network, where we "collaborate and work together throughout the day building up crucial narrative and context..."[27] What makes sense for the applications of the future is that they'll be completely integrated with the work that goes on within the social networks, thereby multiplying effectiveness and efficiency.

---

[27] Dion Hinchcliffe, "Why The Next App You Use Might Be In A Social Network," ebizq.com, August 2, 2011, http://www.ebizq.net/blogs/enterprise/2011/08/ why_the_next_app_you_use_might_be_in_a_social_network.php

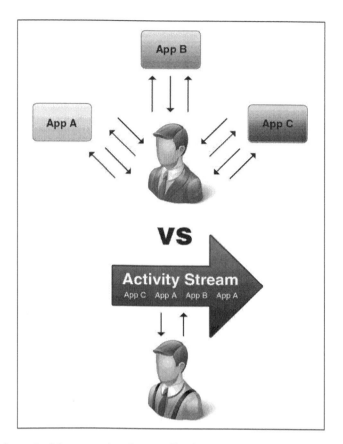

Figure 13: Instead of the user going from application to application to complete their tasks, the tasks appear in the user's activity stream as needed. For example, a manager needs to approve an expense report: instead of going to the expense reporting application, the request will simply show up in their activity stream, along with any associated notes, attachments, and a direct link to the record being acted upon.

For example, when a user needs to respond to an item in the activity stream through an application, they should not need to toggle away to the application in question – it should be accessible in the activity stream. Another example would be to allow users to upload a document to the activity stream and associate it with a particular activity. Users should also be able to take action on an approval process from directly within their activity feed. The activity stream provides context, including comments and documents, to help users make informed decisions.

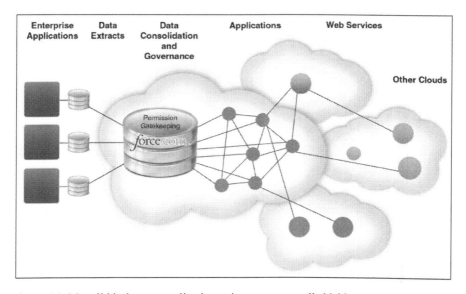

Figure 14: Monolithic legacy applications give way to small, highly-targeted, situational apps working off a single, non-redundant database, exchanging data and services with each other and other apps in the cloud. Legacy applications feed the database, and the database controls the quality and source of data, maintaining permissions for all app users.

Building these solutions requires a very different approach:

Application Characteristics		
	Traditional Applications	**Situational Applications**
Applications	A single, complex, multi-function, self-contained "package" of functionality with complex navigation schemes used by multiple business roles.	Multiple simple, intuitive, single-function apps synchronized with employee business roles. These apps can be orchestrated in a workflow as needed to accomplish business processes.
Development	Developers build large applications based on specifications given to them by users.	Users build small applications with the help of developers as needed.
Growth	An application stays in the same form over a period of years.	An application is considered a seed that will grow and evolve continuously.
Contributions	From time to time IT will incorporate new ideas into the application so it doesn't become out of touch with the real world.	The application is enriched through the contributions of knowledgeable people, and important and relevant additions are constantly being incorporated.
Stakeholders	Line of Business executives, Corporate IT.	Individual users or self-organizing small teams.
Targeted users	Generic.	Specific.
Governance	Centralized and formal.	Grassroots and community-based.
Evolution	Top-down controlled, centrally driven, dependent on available funding.	Organic, based on user feedback and participation.
Time-to-value	Many months or years.	Days or weeks.
Development phases	Well defined, following agreed-to schedule (although with frequent schedule overruns).	No defined phases, milestones, or schedules – focusing on a good-enough solution to address an immediate need.
Functional requirements	IT needs to "freeze" requirements to move to development; change is discouraged.	Changes as business requirements change; encourages unintended uses.

Application Characteristics

	Traditional Applications	Situational Applications
Nonfunctional requirements	Resources allocated to availability, security, scalability and maintainability often result in robust but costly solutions.	Little or no direct focus on scalability, maintainability, availability, etc., due to nature of platform, significantly reducing cost.
Testing	By IT with some user involvement in a formal testing phase.	By analysts and users, in a "test-as-you-develop" mode.
Funding	Often coincides with annual IT planning; requires approved budgets.	No formal budget; developed and run under the radar of corporate IT.
Stability	Fixed, highly stable.	Moving target and in a state of perpetual beta.
Ownership	Highly controlled environment.	Local team control; ownership mentality.
Adoption	Generalized.	Form-fit tools for very particular needs.
Communication	Larger group means more chance of miscommunication.	Smaller group reduces time spent on communication; less chance of miscommunication.
Problem solving	Solving general problems well requires very careful forethought and planning.	Much easier to solve a specific problem.
In-depth requirements gathering	Because the cost of developing traditional software is so high, and changes downstream are so rare and costly to implement, there is a huge incentive to anticipate any conceivable situation.	Users develop exactly what they need, which is tremendously freeing for everyone involved.
Cost	Cost is significant, so often shared by multiple sponsors.	Sponsors can spend far less and get exactly what they need.

The Inadequacies of Today's Development Options

Let's look at how the two divergent paths of software development – traditional and ad hoc – fare in the new digital economy.

Traditional Application Development

Information systems today are typically built in much the same fashion as railroads were built in the early 1900s. Building a railroad system required multiple stages of planning, agreed-upon destinations, predetermined stops at train stations, limited switching choices, moving businesses closer to train stations, and rigid schedules to maximize rail efficiency. The very nature of the railroad system leaves little room for flexibility and adaptability, which are critically important for railroads – and certain types of business applications such as accounting and manufacturing – because the risk of failure can be severe.

Figure 15: Certain types of applications need to be very carefully managed and controlled, because the consequence of failure can be severe. This is rarely the case with situational applications.

An approach with fixed plans, fixed rails, stations, and pre-determined schedules doesn't work when events can't be easily anticipated and responses need to be delivered on the fly.

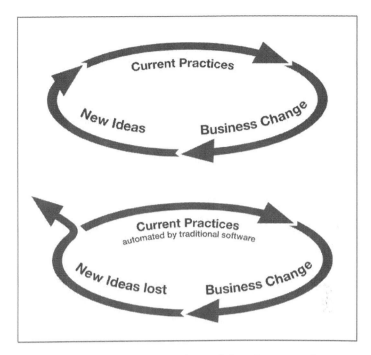

Figure 16: In the digital economy, companies can't launch new products or services or redesign internal operations without costly new application systems to support them. It is just too expensive and too much trouble to do things in new ways, so old products are perpetuated and old ways continue.

In the digital economy, the needs are quite different:

- The digital economy is dynamic and unpredictable. Success lies in the ability of workers to coordinate many information feeds, harness personal connections, and process interactions. The ability to navigate this maze effectively and quickly is based on knowledge that is frequently not written down or readily available to others.

- Workers in the digital economy must be able to build solutions that allow them to approach their activities in ways that are most comfortable. A "one-size-fits-all" approach is not appropriate.

- The digital economy is always in flux. Workers need to be able to adapt immediately as things change, without having to wait for IT.

87

- There is often no common structure and flow to work in the digital economy, making it extremely difficult IT to really understand what type of solutions workers need.

- Given the dynamic nature of the digital economy, there is a constant need for creativity and variation. Attempts to "streamline" or automate work by IT in this environment are usually doomed to failure.

- The digital economy is full of exceptions. In traditional IT-built systems like accounting, because exceptions are extremely rare, they can be handled manually with relative ease, making use of totally automated systems. Systems in the digital economy are much messier. Workers need to be able to experiment and change things. Exceptions are a way of life and too numerous to be planned for in advance.

In the digital economy, there is usually no straight line of logic or process that leads to a perfect solution in these circumstances. Instead, there is a great deal of tinkering until you get something that works – for now. Users need to be able to experiment and iterate rapidly in ways that cost little to introduce a new application, and also generate quick feedback. This makes the cost of failure minimal and the upside potentially enormous.

This is not the type of environment in which traditional IT can flourish.

Figure 17: The distance between the user and IT is just too great.

Ad Hoc Application Development

For decades, many IT organizations have been dealing with developers outside of the IT department as if they were insurgents - their weapons were Excel and Access. – Mike Rollings, *"Citizen Development: Reinventing the Shadows of IT"*, *Gartner, Inc.*, February, 2012

When applications are considered too time-consuming to write, too costly to implement, and too brittle to customize and maintain once deployed, workers cobble together a hodge-podge of inadequate solutions using tools like Excel, Access, and Lotus Notes.

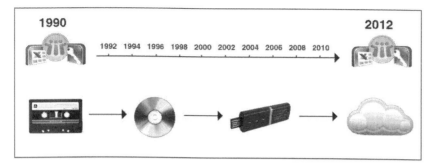

Figure 18: The great strides in technology we have seen in other areas are completely missing from ad hoc development tools.

These solutions are the right idea in the sense that they exhibit the characteristics of applications in the new digital economy: they are small, simple, role-based apps that provide only what applies to a user's particular situation.

But they share a slew of inadequacies for today's environment:

- Isolation

- Duplication of data

- Lack of security

- Lack of scalability

- Lack of oversight

- Need for hardware and software

- Inability to be included in workflow

- Inability to leverage new technology

- Inability to integrate with other applications

In addition to the inadequacies they hold in common, each of these solutions is lacking in its own particular way.

Spreadsheets

The ease with which spreadsheets can be used to build simple applications is both a blessing and a curse. A spreadsheet allows you to build a quick and dirty solution, but it often then grows into something well beyond its original purpose. Since the growth usually creeps up over time, its limitations endure, and it is rarely migrated to a more suitable environment.

This is unfortunate, because there are many serious problems with using spreadsheets as database applications. These problems are instructive when it comes to providing the right tool for building applications in the digital economy.

Security and stability. Since spreadsheets can easily be copied and shared, they are open to tampering, which leads to undetectable (and sometimes costly) errors.

Scalability. Spreadsheets are not designed to handle large amounts of data, or to accommodate a significant number of users.

Aggregation. It is difficult to aggregate data from multiple spreadsheets, especially when this needs to occur frequently, and when the spreadsheets to be aggregated are maintained by multiple users.

Data validation. Creating and enforcing validation rules are often difficult to do in spreadsheets, making data errors more likely.

Transparency. Calculations and other business rules, as well as the type of user interaction taking place, are often not transparent to the rest of the organization.

Permissions. Spreadsheets do not easily (if at all) provide the ability for each user or group of users to have different data permissions down to the field level.

Interoperability and dependency. A single spreadsheet used in isolation is easy to manage. But when a spreadsheet is used as a system, it's necessary to introduce dependency checks, because certain actions dictate the validity of further actions. For example, consolidating the results of all departments is invalid if some of those departments have not yet completed their budgeting input. A dependent process requires knowledge of the factors on which it depends. For example, the ability to indicate status is not easily managed.

Wasted resource. One of the largest drawbacks of spreadsheet dependency is the accumulated amount of time staffers devote to creating spreadsheets, and maintaining and formatting them.

Complexity. Inter-workbook links create hidden dependencies and make data consistency difficult to assess.

Carelessness. It takes some effort (often a lot of effort) to develop and maintain sound and effective spreadsheet practices. The spreadsheet's very ease of use encourages sloppy habits and lack of foresight.

Integrity. There is no audit trail. Preventing tampering without expending significant effort is often difficult. Data validation is often weak.

Quality. Novice programming can result in complex data structures and poorly developed logic.

Integration. Spreadsheets are not designed or intended to integrate with other systems.

Version control. Version control and change control are difficult to implement.

Consistency. Spreadsheets are unable to support consistent methodologies and consistent consolidation of data.

Single source of truth. Data quality, validity, and consistency problems make it difficult for the users of the application to know where the "single source of truth" resides. This is exacerbated by the diffusion of data among many disparate, siloed data repositories.

The paradox of the spreadsheet is that despite these shortcomings, users overwhelmingly embrace them and do not want to give them up.

Yet despite their obvious appeal, spreadsheets are clearly inadequate to meet the demands of solutions for the digital economy.

Microsoft Access

Microsoft Access is often used by individual information workers and small teams to track, manage, prioritize, and act upon business information. Workers can quickly build effective applications without requiring the skills of a professional developer. The information tracked may be ad hoc and temporary, for a single limited project, or it may be used by a team on an ongoing basis.

However, Access does have serious shortcomings:

Data access. Users download sensitive data to an unsecured local computer for use in an Access database.

Physical access. A desktop computer containing sensitive data or programs may be physically accessed by other users.

Network share access. Users can browse other users' desktops, and automatically gain access to unauthorized assets.

Backups. The data is not part of an enterprise backup or disaster recovery plan.

Sourcing. The data comes from sources that could be unreliable or inaccurate.

Currency. The data is not current. There is no defined policy for data expiration.

Isolated pockets of data. Data is isolated in silos, making it difficult or impossible to run reports across data in multiple applications, for example.

Use of web services. Web services cannot be taken advantage of to extend applications.

Inclusion in workflow. Users cannot benefit from being part of inter- and intra-application workflows.

Sharing across the globe. Users cannot easily make applications securely available to others around the globe. The absence of powerful user administration and permissions management makes it difficult to facilitate workflows across multiple organizations.

Mobile devices. Inability to access applications from any device is becoming more and more critical, as mobile device capability is extended and its usage becomes more prevalent.

Many organizations don't realize how much they are limiting their capabilities by continuing to use MS Access as their database for departmental applications. These limitations will become more pronounced and more significant as the organization cannot take advantage of new technologies and address more complex problems in the digital economy.

Lotus Notes

Lotus suffers from all the disadvantages of not being in the cloud: the need for hardware, software, upgrades, maintenance, backups, disaster recovery, scalability, performance, web service integration, and so on.

Other problems include a slower rate of innovation due to inherent barriers in Notes technology, the cost of migrating to new versions of Notes, and the evolution of Notes from a situational tool to an ERP-like platform, rendering it less and less accessible to its core constituents, the business developers.

Marc Benioff on Lotus Notes

You look at products like Lotus Notes and it's a product that was conceived before Mark Zuckerberg, the Founder of Facebook, was. The reality is that it's not a humorous joke. It was a great product at the time, but IBM has done a terrible job in terms of keeping it fresh.

Customers have been running this technology for two and three decades. They are hiring people out of school and they are coming into these "Productivity Applications" and are saying, "I don't know how to use this, this is not how I work. Where is my iPad? Where is my iPhone? Where is my BlackBerry? Where is my graphical user interfaces?" [Companies] are like, "well, this is graphical user interface" and "this is Windows." It's just junk and that's what Lotus Notes is honestly...

... Just look at the terrible job IBM has done with their software strategy. They've had to move to an acquisition strategy because they let these kinds of core franchises erode. They turned them into cash cows and now they are getting trampled by these next generation products. I think [Microsoft] SharePoint is very much the same thing. It's kind of the grandmother's attic. These customers throw everything into it and then they can't find it and they don't know what's up there, and they don't know how to get it out. - Marc Benioff[28]

---

[28] Marc Benioff, BusinessCloud9, November, 2010

A Digital Business Platform

It bears repeating:

> *In the new digital economy, we should expect that anything that can be digitized, will be digitized.*

As a result, we are witnessing an exploding demand for small, targeted applications, which need to be delivered rapidly, and changed often in order to respond to immediate customer requirements.

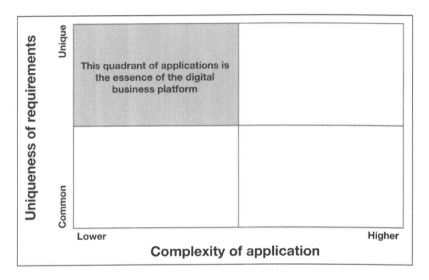

Figure 19: The applications needed fit into the top left quadrant - they satisfy unique requirements, are needed quickly and change often, but their complexity is relatively low. They don't typically require the power of Java or .Net.

In this environment, there is no time to build applications the old-fashioned way. There is no time to look for the data needed by a new application – it must be readily available, *and* it's got to be clean and it must be current. There is no time to spend on a procurement process for either hardware or software, or extra time to spend on scalability, backups, and security. Any time spent trying to pull together and coordinate whole teams of experts can result in lost opportunities. There isn't the time to write a whole lot of code.

Everything you require to get started on building a solution needs to be in place and ready-to-go. That's the purpose of a *digital business platform (DBP)*[29].

A DBP is a seedbed in which to grow solutions to everyday business challenges and opportunities – as quickly as you need them.

Figure 20: A seedbed is a good analogy for a digital business platform. A seedbed is prepared beforehand – it is leveled for drainage, and the soil is aerated, enriched and fertilized. The seed just needs to be planted, and it can draw what it needs to grow from the seedbed.

In the DBP environment, solutions are like plants: they are constantly developing; they need to be propagated, grafted, or pruned; and in some cases they need to be rooted and relegated to the compost heap. With plants, there's a constant assumption of maintenance – you're always working with them so that they'll thrive, or even just stay alive. They are

---

[29] A DBP can be thought of as *a consistent enabling platform for an enterprise front office*. (Andy Mulholland, Capgemini Global Chief Technology Officer,)

organic, malleable, and need your frequent attention in order to flourish. Just like the solutions that are necessary to meet the requirements of the new digital economy.

The charts outline what a robust DBP needs to enable the organization to succeed:

The Prerequisites for a DBP

Prerequisite	Filled by
No additional time spent on hardware/software procurement, installation and maintenance	Cloud computing
The ability of end users to take more responsibility for building their own solutions	Increasing numbers of Millennials in the workplace
The availability of off-the-shelf services that can easily be mashed together	Open API
The ability to build software quickly using clicks versus code	Greatly improved point-and-click tools
A mindset and methodology better suited to building these types of apps	A paradigm shift in thinking about how to build applications

The Foundation of a DBP

Foundation	Needs met
Infrastructure	Servers, storage, database, network must be in place, as well as redundancy, system security, scalability, availability, monitoring, authentication, backup, etc.
Metadata	Using metadata to store the applications allows the platform to change over time without impacting them.
Application framework	A framework reduces the amount of time that needs to be spent designing application architecture, and provides features that are implemented in every new application, like security, user identity, logging, profiling, integration, etc.
Security	All aspects of security need to be taken care, including servers database and application security.

The Building Blocks of a DBP

Building Block	Needs met
Central master database	Having one master store of information provides immediate availability of clean and current data.
Social networking	Communication and collaboration are critical for fast feedback, collaboration and exception handling.
Ad hoc workflow	Ability to create workflows and change them on the fly is essential.
Mobile	Mobile is the key delivery mechanism and applications need to be immediately deployable.

Each of these requirements will be explored in depth in the following chapters.

Prerequisites

The approach used to build information systems over the last forty years hasn't changed all that much. Sure, there are differences, like new programming languages and agile programming methodologies, but the overall process of building, deploying, and maintaining systems has remained substantially the same: full of frustration, tedium, and repetition, and time-consuming for all concerned.

Attempts we've made over the years to move a quantum leap forward in system-building productivity have been countered by increasing complexity and novel elements, such as graphical user interface (GUI), the web, mobile, and social networking. In addition, in our attempts to make things "better" we have added more pieces to the process – technical architects, database administrators, user-interface specialists, graphic designers, and so on. As in a perfect storm, a number of forces have coincided, making that leap forward possible:

1. Unlimited computing power is now a click away.

2. IT-savvy workers capable of building their own solutions are flooding the workplace.

3. A standard method for utilizing pre-built web services from any provider makes possible a building block approach to application development.

4. The ability to build software without coding exists.

5. A shift in thinking about how organizations work and how solutions should be built is becoming more widely accepted.

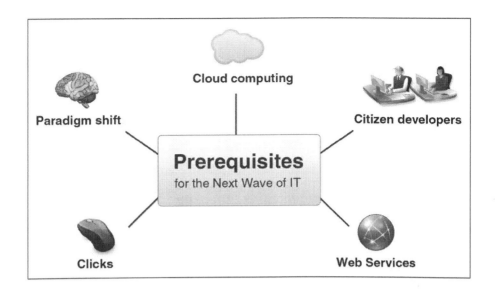

Cloud Computing Changes Everything

We're at the dawn of a new era in business. Just as the last century's electric utilities spurred the development of thousands of new consumer appliances and services, so the new computing utilities will shake up many markets and open myriad opportunities for innovation. We see this transformation playing out not just in IT departments and the IT industry but across information-intensive industries like media and entertainment. Harnessing the power of the electric grid was the great enterprise of the twentieth century. Harnessing the power of the cloud is shaping up to be the great enterprise of the twenty-first century. – Nicholas Carr, "The Clouds Roll In" (in the Afterword to his book, *The Big Switch*)

The slow-moving dinosaur firms will have trouble keeping up with more nimble adopters and fast-followers. Not adopting cloud computing ... will make it even harder to compete in the modern business environment. In the end,

103

those too slow to adopt the benefits while managing the risk are likely going to face serious and growing economic and business disadvantage. – Dion Hinchcliffe

Cloud computing has forever changed the landscape of the IT world because it provides straightforward access to enterprise-grade computing resources that are affordable and instantly available. Accessing as much of the resource as you need, when you need it, and never having to deal with the complexities of managing all the underlying mechanisms that provide the resources, makes life suddenly a lot simpler and easier.

But saving money on IT infrastructure is just the start. The advent of cloud computing presents an unprecedented opportunity for organizations to revolutionize the way in which they build information systems, and in so doing, transform their business.

According to Gartner: By 2012, 20% of businesses will have no ownership of IT assets.

The freedom and accessibility of the cloud will lead to innovation in ways never previously conceived of. The ability to develop and deploy solutions faster, globally, and less expensively will give the more deft organizations a significant advantage over their competitors, both large and small.

Benefits of Cloud Computing

Cloud computing makes it possible to create new "business operations platforms" that will allow companies to change their business models and collaborate in powerful new ways with their customer, suppliers and trading partners – stuff that simply could not be done before. – Peter Fingar, *Dot.Cloud: The 21st Century Business Platform*

Cloud computing offers an enormous amount of benefit to the enterprise, enabling an organization to return its focus to what's most important, and the ability to streamline costs while doing so:

Focus. The attention required to maintain and fund computing capacity is a distraction that dilutes the efficiency of an organization and its focus on core business objectives. Data centers are not the core competency of organizations not specifically in that business, and **no competitive advantage results from having the very best data center in the world.** Cloud computing is attractive because it allows businesses to focus on what matters most: their customers, their business processes, and the employees who nurture them.

Cost. Cloud computing reduces dependence on internal infrastructure and its associated capital expense. **Cloud computing yields significant cost savings** in the real estate required for the data center, as well as power and cooling costs. Onboarding, provisioning, and maintaining everything needed to run a corporate data center makes about as much sense as operating a power plant instead of plugging into the power grid.

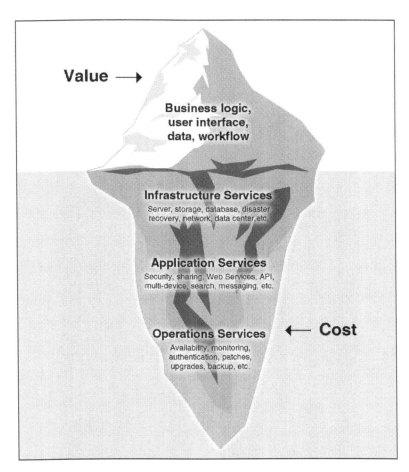

Figure 21: An application is the tip of the iceberg. All the underlying costs required to support the application are essentially "below the surface." Cloud computing eliminates those costs, leaving just the value.

1. **Quality**: Cloud service providers offer great economies of scale and specialization that few (if any) other organizations can match. Rigorous processes and procedures maximize uptime and optimize performance, best-in-breed software monitors and manages the infrastructure, and the most skilled practitioners oversee the management tools.

2. **Scalability**. Cloud computing ensures that an organization is able to meet the needs for the exponential growth in data volume resulting from the proliferation of devices, compliance, online commerce and

increased replication to secondary or backup sites, etc. It also supports massive scalability to meet periods of demand while avoiding extended periods of underutilized IT capacity. With the click of a mouse, services can be quickly expanded or contracted, without requiring overhauls to the core data center.

No forward-looking company starting up today will ever own IT assets.

---

3. **Security**. The cloud incorporates next-generation security and cloud service management technologies, as well as simplified security management and enforcement. This combination guarantees enterprise customer's security and compliance equivalent to or better than what they can expect in traditional computing environments.

4. **Performance**. Cloud computing provides the ability to quickly and confidently reap the business benefits knowing that performance will be predictable and downtime and recovery will be taken care of automatically.

The Shanghai Rule

There are of course cases where the cloud is not the right solution. But these are few and far between. Peter Coffee, Vice President and Head of Platform Research for Salesforce.com, applies what he calls the "Shanghai Rule," based on observations of activity at the Shanghai Stock Exchange.

The Shanghai Rule is where conducting stock trades faster than the competition is important. It is where small performance advantages can bring significant competitive advantage. So being 10msec faster than the competition in executing significant processes is important. That is when there can be a need for on-premise, often specialized systems. Everything else can go in the Cloud.[30]

The Rise of the Citizen Developer

Citizen developers will be building at least a quarter of new business applications by 2014. – Gartner, Inc.

As more barriers disappear and more Web services are directly available, citizen developers will be active participants in the creation of business solutions. Solutions will be cocreated without the creator being confined to departmental lines or constrained by departmental ideas of ownership. Cocreation will be synonymous with how business gets done. – Mike Rollings, "Citizen Development: Reinventing the Shadows of IT", *Gartner, Inc.*, February, 2012

To be most effective, situational applications must be built when they are needed. Sustained competitive advantage will increasingly depend on

---

[30] Martin Banks, "Coffee time in the Cloud," BusinessCloud9, January 2012

enabling self-sufficient employees to create their own software solutions for their business needs.

This was hardly feasible in the past, but an influx of Millennials into the workplace means that a great many new workers have at least a rudimentary understanding of how information systems function.

Gartner defines citizen developers as "end users who create business applications for consumption by others using corporate-IT-sanctioned development and runtime environments."

Why Citizen Developers?

> *Normal people can and will innovate of their own initiatives if enabling conditions are present.*[31] – A. Van de Ven, *The Innovation Journey*

> *Given an appropriate set of tools and services, technically savvy business users can build situational applications by themselves.* - Mike Rollings, "Citizen Development: Reinventing the Shadows of IT", *Gartner, Inc.*, February, 2012

In traditional application development, a significant transfer of knowledge between the user and the developer must take place. When a project is large enough and requires complex software development, there is no other choice. But in situational applications, there is simply not enough time for this transfer of knowledge. In fact, the idea that a developer can soak up the complex knowledge that these users, these "knowledge workers," have spent years accumulating is rather unlikely. Therefore, it only makes sense for the workers to do it themselves as much as possible, which also permits them to respond to change much faster than a whole team could.

---

[31] Andrew H. Van de Ven, *The Innovation Journey*, NY: Oxford, 1999.

Self-service development

> *The citizen developer sits on the front lines of experimentation and business innovation. The innovation sought is not solely big-bang innovation, but all types of innovation that happen within the flow of business execution.* – Mike Rollings, "Citizen Development: Reinventing the Shadows of IT", *Gartner, Inc.*, February, 2012

The speed and efficiency demanded of a resilient and responsive organization can occur only when employees find different ways to make continuous small adjustments that increase profits and decrease costs every day, every week, every month.

The only way to do this is to give employees the tools and support they need to serve themselves. "Self-service" does not mean turning business people into programmers. It means giving the right set of tools and support to the people closest to the problems, so they can build powerful software solutions on their own. The goal is to enable workers to quickly put together "good enough" software solutions to solve specific problems, significantly reducing or even eliminating the time and coordination needed from IT. It becomes possible to address areas that were previously unaffordable or of low priority for the IT department.

> *Just because a user can do a database query, create a spreadsheet, or build a simple database application doesn't mean the user is capable of becoming a competent programmer. But given the right tools, users won't have to become programmers in order to achieve significant results building their own solutions.*

In this way, force.com will encourage waves of more modest business innovations – creative new combinations of resources in some areas and novel approaches in others – that in aggregate will transform the way your company organizes and works.

Lowering the barrier to building solutions will make more people programmers – but not in the traditional sense. You could say there are now fewer typists and switchboard operators than there were in the '80s. Technically, that's true, but it misses the bigger picture. Nowadays, we're all "typists" and "switchboard operators" to some degree – but our new tools and what they make available have opened up tremendous new possibilities. The same is true of software development.

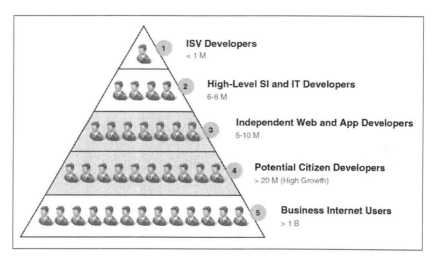

Figure 22: The potential number of Citizen Developers will eventually dwarf professional developers. Source: Evans Data, PewInternet.

For the IT skeptics

There is always great skepticism, especially on the part of IT, about whether end users are capable of developing their own applications.

Consider this:

Back in 1984 when desktop publishing programs like PageMaker and ReadySetGo appeared on the market, many advertising agencies employed high priced full-time typesetters and keyliners. Very much threatened by the new technology, these folks scoffed at the programs' lack of precision in kerning (the process of reducing the spacing between certain pairs of letters to improve their appearance), the high cost of the computers, and the

limited availability of type output machines that would accept Adobe Postscript files.

Companies that understood this attitude (such as Adobe and Aldus) were smart enough to not concentrate their software marketing efforts on the people whose jobs these products might threaten. Instead, they targeted art directors, CFOs, CEOs, and marketing and creative directors. Apple donated thousands of computers to graphic design schools to educate the next wave of designers. Many keyliners and typesetters lost their jobs as desktop publishing started to be used by innovators, then early adopters, and then the early majority. The smartest of the workforce took classes in the new technology and quickly landed the field's new high-paying jobs.

Of course there is still a need for production professionals in the publishing industry. But think of how much can be done now by non-professionals. The entire publishing industry as we knew it has been completely transformed. Today, anyone can publish anything anywhere on their own – without the need for a traditional bricks-and-mortar publisher.

Similarly, the ability to send a message over the telegraph once required an intermediary with significant skills. Now even great-grandmas can build web sites, create videos, and post blogs.

force.com provides the basis that allows its business users the freedom to become self-reliant to a significant degree. Unfortunately, most companies are trapped in IT-centric development processes, and the thought of giving business users the ability to do things themselves seems like a big leap. But in the same way that outsourcing a spreadsheet to IT is recognized as absurd today, in the future it will be seen as strange to outsource other typical business applications.

The lesson is not that experts aren't needed. Rather, it's that technology shortens the learning curve, enabling non-experts to complete the same tasks with less training and experience.

Millennials in the workplace

An important scientific innovation rarely makes its way by gradually winning over and converting its opponents.... What does happen is that its opponents gradually die out and the growing generation is familiarized with the idea from the beginning. – Max Planck, *The Philosophy of Physics,* 1936

Today's kids are much better at sense-making, improvising, and figuring things out... than most mid and senior managers. We've got to start thinking about the content and tools that will let them do it. – John Seely Brown

While end-user application development has been around for a long time, we are entering into a whole new phase of citizen developers. This is the result of the entry of Millennials (roughly, people born anywhere from the late '70s to the mid '90s) into the workplace.

When computers were first introduced into the workplace, they were viewed as mysterious and intimidating. Users learned the functionality by rote, and never strayed from what they were taught.

For the most part, the way we build information systems today still assumes a workforce that is computer-illiterate. Users must be provided with everything they need and are given little opportunity to create their own solutions (other than standalone desktop applications for private use).

Now, however, we're seeing a much more computer-literate worker – and even the older workforce is becoming more IT savvy and capable of more than we've given them credit for.

The Millennials flooding the workforce have different expectations, skills, and values. After all, they are the first generation to grow up with IT as an integral part of their environment.

> *Attracting sufficient numbers of Net Generation (Millennial) workers should be a top priority, since their talents will be critical to how companies adapt to future change... [T]he winners will be companies that embrace the Net Geners ways.*[32]

Their characteristics include the following:

- Used to **customizing and individualizing** everything, from ring tones to their Facebook pages, when they move into a workplace, they translate these experiences into wanting to customize their environment and take responsibility for automating as many activities as possible.

- **Creative, collaborative, and with little or no patience** for established lines of authority, Millennials won't want to wait for IT to get to the bottom of the application development priority stack. For this generation, a situational application approach to building systems seems natural. Many will have taken programming classes in middle or high school and college. They know what can be done, and they won't think it's a big deal to write a system to meet the needs of their job. With the right tools, they can do it themselves.

- They **live and breathe innovation**, constantly looking for ways to do things better, and expect constant change. Unafraid of the technology, they are constantly trying to push it to the next level.

- Unafraid of technology, they are accustomed to **figuring things out on their own**, and skilled at acquiring knowledge they may need but do not have. The key to discovering the hidden doors and

32 Don Tapscott, *Grown Up Digital: How the Net Generation is Changing Your World*, McGraw-Hill Books, 2009

winning video games is persistence in trial and error. Reading the manual is not considered an option.

- **The ultimate "now" generation** views the world as 24/7 and demands real-time and fast processing – the idea of waiting weeks for a response is just not in their worldview.

- **Millennials will automate their work themselves whether management likes it or not.** Therefore, it's much better to facilitate these efforts than try to sweep them under the carpet. These are opportunities that should be taken advantage of!

By the same token, companies that force their employees to go through IT to get systems built are simply not going to attract the best and the brightest. The reverse will be true – providing an environment that the younger members of the workforce can thrive in will **be a magnet for the best employees.**

> *It's the dilemma of managing a smart group of people anywhere, which is that it's very difficult to keep them from walking out the door if they don't like their work environment. If you have identical salaries for a terrible job and a good job, you aren't going to have any trouble attracting people to the good job.* [33]

---

[33] Clay Shirky, "How the Enterprise Moves to 2.0," April 27, 2008, http://www.cioinsight.com/ c/a/Foreward/Shirky-Enterprise-Web-20

Figure 23: This generation [of Millennials] is exceptionally curious, self-reliant, contrarian, smart, focused, able to adapt, high in self-esteem, and globally oriented. These attributes combined with [their] ease with digital tools spell trouble for the traditional manager. This generation will create huge pressures for radical changes in existing companies. – Don Tapscott, *Growing Up Digital*

The following is a great summary of how each generation thinks:

	Tradition-alist (55 - 65)	Boomers (45 – 55)	Gen X (30 – 45)	Millennials (18 – 30)
Training	The hard way	Too much and I'll leave	Required to keep me	Continuous and expected
Learning style	Classroom	Facilitated	Independent	Collaborative and networked
Communication style	Top-down	Guarded	Hub and spoke	Collaborative
Problem-solving	Hierarchical	Horizontal	Independent	Collaborative
Decision-making	Seeks approval	Team informed	Team included	Team decided
Leadership style	Command and control	Get out of the way	Coach	Partner
Feedback	No news is good news	Once per year	Weekly/Daily	On Demand
Technology use	Uncomfortable	Unsure	Unable to work without it	Expected to be intuitive
Job changing	Unwise	Sets me back	Necessary	Part of my daily routine

Figure 23: Source: Capgemini white paper, "People; Process and Real-Time Data; the battle cry of the new and future technology!" October, 2011

Web Services: The API Revolution

Enterprises want everything to work with everything else. That's precisely what these new APIs provide. Users can automatically route their applications to any other remote service as they need, with minimal preparation.

Application development obviously goes much faster if the developer can take advantage of pre-fabricated components and pre-packaged services. The problem has always been the ease (or lack of it) with which integration takes place. The universal adoption of application programming interfaces (APIs) solves this problem. An API is basically a standard specification that can be used as an interface by software components to communicate with each other.

A Standard Interface

The advent of web services and standard APIs is somewhat akin to the development of the RCA jack in the home electronics industry. Before RCA's introduction of its device for connecting radio receivers with other devices, stereo systems were closed, monolithic cabinet systems. As more manufacturers began to adopt the RCA jack, stereo components could interoperate without regard to vendor. Consumers benefited from a wealth of choices that they could simply plug in.

On the Internet, web services are equivalent to the stereo components, and the standard application programming interface is an RCA jack for connecting your applications. An API is a well-defined interface that allows other parties to interact with your data and services, in a highly controlled fashion, using a particular set of rules and  specifications that software programs can follow to communicate with each other.

When building an application requires existing data or logic, the application can access that data or logic through an API. Imposing a set of standards for the construction of any services assures they'll play nicely with all the other services that are being developed, and is key to making this "on the fly" development process work.

Here's a simple example of a web service provided through an API:

I am writing an application that needs to know the distance between two zip codes. I simply point to a service that provides this information. I tell it which two zip codes I'm interested in, and I get the answer in my application. The service has access to whatever data and logic it needs. I see it as a highly abstracted black box.

APIs tell the outside world what functions they perform, how they can be accessed, and what kinds of data they require. Their functionality is wrapped in a well-defined interface that "abstracts" the service they provide. The "wrapping" layer hides the intricacies of the application – the language it's written in, the platform it's running on, the database it's accessing. The only thing that matters is the interface, that is, the description of the service.

Using APIs, developers don't have to start from scratch every time they write applications. Instead of building one core application that tries to do *everything*, the same application can contract out certain responsibilities to remote software that does it better.

An API is also a new distribution channel for your digital assets, whether they are data, content, technology, or services. They have the power to unlock your assets and enable you to expand beyond your web site and to make your data, content, or services ubiquitous.

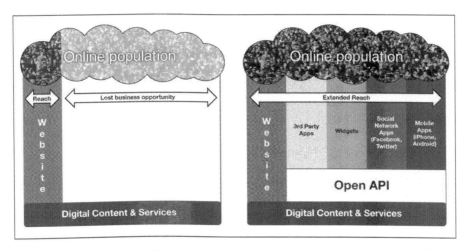

Figure 24: An open API significantly extends the reach of the organization's digital capital.
Source: Dion Hinchcliffe, blogs.zdnet.com/Hinchcliffe

Self-Service APIs

An API is essentially a turnkey partnering program: partners onboard themselves through an automated sign-up, licensing, integration, testing, and payment process. Self-service APIs make possible very lightweight integration where the partner does virtually all the work to integrate with your system. Because APIs can be used without a lengthy company-to-company negotiation and partnership process, it is possible to acquire partners more quickly and cost-effectively than otherwise possible.

APIs are rapidly becoming an important new business channel in the same vein as storefronts, the telephone, and even web sites were in years past.[34]

APIs and Mashups

Much like the concept of a musical mashup, where pieces of completely different original works are woven together to create a completely new original work, software mashups leverage data from

---

[34] Dion Hinchcliffe, "Open APIs Mature Into a Next-Generation Business Model," *ebizQ*, December, 2009

separate sources to create altogether new applications. APIs play a key part in enabling mashups, allowing users of a web site to see data presented from various sources, and integrated to deliver value when presented together.

A basic example of a mashup targeting a consumer is the way a real estate site might use APIs to call on various applications to present real estate listings, while using other APIs to render map details related to a particular listing so that it appears next to the listing. Similarly, a weather web site might call on various sources of incoming weather data, and APIs would enable the web site to reference and present that data all in one place for the web site visitor. The user of the web site may not know (and doesn't necessarily need to know) that the data is being aggregated from various sources.

In the enterprise, a mashup allows richer applications to call on internal and external data with the intent of presenting information for better and more collaborative decision making.

For example, when you buy movie tickets online and enter your credit card information, the ticketing web site uses an API to send your credit card information to a remote application that verifies whether your information is correct. Once payment is confirmed, the remote application sends a response back to the movie ticket web site saying it's okay to issue the tickets.

As a user, you only see one interface – the movie ticket web site – but behind the scenes, many applications are working together using APIs.

Accelerating Innovation with APIs

Web services accelerate innovation in the cloud. Opening and launching APIs offers rapid entry to new markets via the cloud as well as a quick way to monetize your digital assets, data and content, and provides gateways to web services and mobile apps.

"Opening an API" today means creating new business models that were not possible without an API. Serving as the "glue" between different software programs, APIs are gateways that allow businesses to transfer, track, and monetize valuable calls to their data (think of the potential of billions of tracked and monetized calls), while connecting with partners and expanding distribution.

...The big change in mindset is to recognize that data and services – the company's digital assets – must be unlocked from the confines of a web site. Once they are free, and can be accessed from anywhere, then the potential to grow the business can be realized.[35]

The API explosion means that it is feasible to create products that meet customers' expectations and desires more accurately. It may be to meet a need in a small market niche, to have access to data in a unique context, or to meet their preference to interact from a smartphone device. Ultimately it provides companies with the flexibility to design completely new business models.

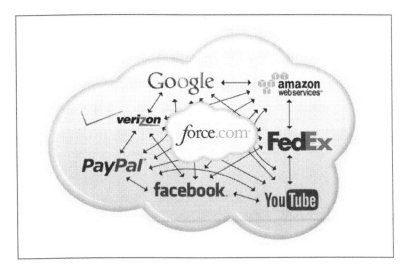

Figure 25: APIs allow developers (and increasingly users) to build solutions by "mashing up" services through standard APIs.

---

[35] Mark Cheshire, "API 2.0: Potential to Radically Reshape Value Chains for Business Development in the Cloud," SandHill.com, June 2011

Most of the benefits of APIs are still limited to serving developers with the programming skills necessary to write the required code. But APIs provide higher levels of abstraction and will help get us closer to the point where users themselves can "plug" web services into their applications.

APIs are opening up a new chapter for the Internet. Content and services are the digital assets that are the core of any business. An API can open up new distribution and solution options and therefore capture more value from an organization's assets. Unlocking the value of a firm's digital assets allows reach to explode well beyond the web site to mobile apps, partners, developers and more.

This greater reach allows partnerships to be leveraged and creates a multiplier effect for key assets, bringing the opportunity to innovate with completely new business models. Competitors are left standing still, while your customers can access content and services exactly the way they want.

A Streaming API = Real-Time Data

force.com now offers a "streaming" API. This allows an application to subscribe to a topic (e.g., "new orders") as they happen in real time. This is a big improvement over polling for changes, which was quite inefficient – the program had to poll continuously to see if changes had been made. Getting application data in real-time will change the dynamics of the applications you build.

How it works

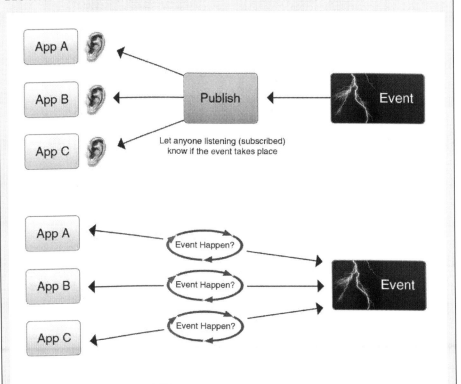

It works like this: any number of programs can "subscribe" to a particular event, such as "New account record created," or "Opportunities with a deal size greater than $1M." The system will "publish" a message to the client which will be received by any subscribing program. That program, which can be on any device, including mobile, can then send an alert, update a different database in another cloud, send to the Chatter feed, etc. It can also be used to do near-real-time synchronization with other cloud systems.

Complex Events

Complex events, comprised of related individual events, traditionally go undetected because they have multiple application characteristics and may occur at different times spanning geographic locations. More sophisticated applications can subscribe to multiple events and can immediately respond to opportunities and problems as they occur.

This takes us a step further to the real-time organization.

The Internet of Things

The streaming API is also important as the "Internet of Things" – the connection of inanimate objects like sensors, cameras, etc. to the Internet – takes off. This is a huge growth area, just now in its infancy.

Clicks and Code, by Steve Wood

Steve Wood is the Vice President of Platform Business Development at salesforce.com.

> *Turing Tar Pit: "Beware of the Turing Tar Pit, in which everything is possible, but nothing of interest is easy."*

> *The Inverse of the Turing Tar Pit: "Beware of the over-specialized system, where operations are easy, but little of interest is possible."*

Why clicks?

One of the most exciting trends in software today is that many non-technical people are creating their own software applications. Traditionally, software has been specified by a business and created by an IT person, but that model is changing, and with the change, we need to rethink the roles of business and IT. We also need to be very clear about the tools the business user can employ to build their software and how those tools work with coding development practices. Traditionally, the message to software vendors has been "build with clicks, not code." The force.com platform takes a slightly different approach: build with clicks *and* code. The code developer shouldn't be excluded from building software, but we want to make sure they own the right part of the solution. In this chapter, we'll look at some of the core concepts behind building an application with clicks, as well as a glimpse into the future of where salesforce.com is hoping to take the platform.

Types of applications

At the highest level, we can think about apps in two categories: technical innovation and business innovation.

Technical Innovation

Technically innovative applications create new end-user experiences or new capabilities that are quite distinct from existing applications. For example, when the very first 3D games such as "Doom" and "Castle Wolfenstein" came out, creating point-and-click tooling to build these games would have been extremely difficult. The creators were really blazing a trail in desktop computer gaming with new high levels of interaction (with other players, and even artificial players) and immersive 3D experiences not previously seen. The developers also created new ways of displaying graphics and navigating the user around a virtual 3D space, a big jump from Pac-Man! To build the new games, developers needed complete control of the underlying systems, which required using code.

Equally technically innovative are such applications as email, and more recently, collaboration tools such as Chatter. In both cases, technology has enabled new forms of communication and fundamentally shifted the way we engage with technology. Interestingly, both email and modern collaboration tools are technical innovations that have had a profound impact on business innovation, adding to the business developers' arsenal for creating applications. This demonstrates the power of software developers and the dramatic influence their technical innovations can have on business.

Business Innovation

Business innovative applications, rather than creating new user experiences, exist for solving business problems. In many cases, the business innovator will be thinking less about "apps" and more about business processes that can be simplified with the right software. For example, in retailing, applications focus on sales and order management. In telecommunications, the purpose of the applications is generally to provision new users and provide case management and technical support. Many of the standard business innovative apps are provided as packaged applications by third-party companies. This is largely because many business innovations, and the value derived from them, are universal across all businesses (or verticals, or segments, etc.), such as managing sales and pipeline (sales force automation), managing cases (customer service and support), managing projects, and so on.

These business innovation applications (also called "line of business" apps) go a long way towards meet our end goal, but we often need a fair amount of customization capability to make them work well for us. For example, a system may allow us to enter customer cases, but we have also our own workflow or escalation rules that need to be managed as part of our business's service level agreements. Having an SLA is pretty universal, but "our" SLA is unique to our company. Much of this leads to a simple conclusion. In the business innovation space, template applications that represent common business processes are extremely helpful when getting started. But once we get to the heart of what makes our business innovative, we must be able to customize on the template to make it work specifically to support our business processes.

The force.com platform clearly focuses on the business innovation side, as opposed to technical innovation. It will also be no surprise that many force.com platform users initially take advantage of CRM offerings to help in sales and service and then begin to use the underlying force.com platform, as their needs for configuration and extension grow. Because configuration and customization are keys to success in business application platforms, to really support businesses in their innovations, force.com cannot "productize" everything, but instead provides the ability for its customers to create products or apps themselves.

Brief history of force.com

Initially, Salesforce.com's goal was to become the CRM leader for Software as a Service – SaaS – much as it envisions itself next as the leader in cloud applications. The company's success began with salesforce automation, the focus of which is improving the interaction between an organization and its customers.

Focused primarily on the business processes that improve sales engagement, organizational visibility, and data and document management, the product comes with the best practice sales methodologies built right in, so it was easy for sales managers to quickly improve their top line. It also means that our customers can more easily organize their sales operations around these best-of-breed sales methodologies rather than having to re-invent the wheel. Salesforce.com then launched a customer service and support capability, to help improve the interaction between its customers' service and support organization and their customers. Again, we focused on and bundled best practice around case management, knowledge management, customer portals, etc., so it was easy for customer service and support managers to quickly improve their bottom line.

In many respects, we took the customer conversation deeper into the organization, first with how customers interact with sales, then further with how they interact with service and support – through multiple channels including telephone, portal, chat, etc. As customers deepened the conversation with *their* customers, a need arose to heavily customize the product to meet their business processes. With that came the birth of the force.com platform, and a fundamental switch in approach. Rather than embedding best practice in business processes or building apps to serve additional markets beyond sales and service, force.com gave customers the flexibility to create their own. No longer were we looking to build applications to serve additional markets beyond sales and service, but rather create an application exchange for customers and partners to distribute their own (either freely or for a license fee). The result is that customers and partners no longer need to wait for salesforce.com to create new systems for their business; they can create their own and drive forward amazing business innovation as a result.

What makes the force.com platform so powerful, particularly for business innovative or line of business applications, is that you get many of the benefits of an application approach (template, pre-built capabilities, security model, architecture, etc.) with the additional benefits of an application platform (tools, customization, coding, application lifecycle management, scalability, etc.). All of this means that you can focus considerably more time on what makes your business innovative and the business processes that support that, and less time on the technical infrastructure required to deliver truly scalable applications within your organization. The result is that you can deliver new applications much faster than ever before and the value of that is simple: you can adapt to business change more effectively and innovate your business faster.

The rise of business developers

At the core of the business innovative application is the need to solve a specific business problem. Business developers tend to think procedurally, more in the language of the business process they're trying to automate, less in a layered architecture that can be re-used generically through extensions and enhancements. Business developers tend to be concrete, tend not to think of layers of abstraction, and are not often comfortable with basic application development concepts such as object orientation and class hierarchies.

A code developer, on the other hand, is always looking for classifications to guide architecture in order to make applications flexible for future requirements. In software, if a developer were looking at a time management application, they might see a Task as a type of Activity, which is a type of Work Item, which is a type of Action, which is a type of Step, which is a type of Object. A Calendar Event would be similar as a type of Activity, which is a type of Work Item, etc. The developer would work through this hierarchy and decide where common concepts apply. For example, both a Task and an Event have a date – that should probably be something that's part of the underlying Activity. However, a Task has status (completed, in progress, etc.) where as an Event does not (it just happens!), so that should not be shared. This process continues and if done correctly, can make applications incredibly flexible to future requirements. A business developer would see a need for a list of Tasks and Calendar Events as part of their time management application, and define their specific management application needs and build exactly that – no further analysis required!

Business developers are becoming more common. When Millennials can't configure software to their needs, they often decide it's not worth having – personalization and customization are a basic expectation, not a luxury to be amazed over. As a result, platforms that can support this demand are becoming increasingly important. With that explosion of business applications comes the need for some kind of governance, the lack of which may result in inconsistent work practices, lost data, and ultimately, unhappy customers who cannot rely on consistent delivery.

Evolution of a line of business app

Understanding the evolution of LOB applications highlights the importance of roles in delivering software. It also helps explain the issues that can sometimes block businesses from embracing new approaches to software development – primarily approaches that allow the business to build their own applications with little or no code and without guidance from IT.

Applications that businesses have built to run their companies vary enormously. Some are created in development languages such as Ruby, PHP, ASP, or even .NET and Java. Others are locked away in Microsoft Excel spreadsheets or Lotus Notes applications. Many (if not most) are poorly architected, usually not officially supported by the organization, and expose the organization by introducing compliance concerns, data back-up issues, security violations, or simply a maintenance overhead for the IT department.

Business developers who create the line of business apps come from varied backgrounds. Some are more technical, some not very technical at all. What usually unites these people is that they have a business problem they want to solve with software. They tend to build their applications using the tools they're most familiar with, which are often the tools on their desktop. This shouldn't come as a surprise for those who have used Microsoft Office products or Lotus Notes. Once you become a regular user, you quickly start building or "hacking" useful macros and spreadsheets that speed up repetitive tasks.

In the software industry, this phenomenon is also well understood. The good news is that these tools – like Word and Excel (which started as apps and evolved more into application platforms) – allow you to do amazing things with software, with little to no formal IT training. The bad news is that these tools allow you to do amazing things with software, with little to no formal IT training! It all depends on your perspective. From the business perspective, this is a huge enabler. From the IT perspective, this appears to be a huge risk. IT has spent the last fifty years developing techniques and disciplines to effectively deliver software, often referred to as application lifecycle management. Without some understanding of those disciplines, software development can look a bit like the Wild West. The reality is that it often does without some controls and governance built into the application platform.

The evolution of a line of a business application usually starts with a comment in a meeting like, "Hey, we should put that into a shared spreadsheet so we can track it."

Imagine we're running professional services in a small software company. We have a small team of five implementation consultants and we need to track their time sheets to invoice customers correctly. We might go out and buy an application to meet this need, or like most organizations, we might shortcut the procurement process and simply start recording the timesheet in Microsoft Excel.

However, as we begin using the spreadsheet, our requirements start to change. Rather than simply showing billable time, we may see the need for basic resource planning to make sure we have the people available for fulfillment. As a result, we'll need to start sharing the spreadsheet, aggregating data, and providing basic reports. From there we may want to get a view on our forward resource pipeline, to make sure we're hiring in time to meet future demand, doing project planning effectively, and so on.

To make all this work, we'll need to create some complicated formulas and macros for the projections as well as standard reports for our weekly planning meetings. We may want to incorporate data from other systems, such as customer information, software release information, case management, and so on.

It's around this time that our spreadsheet has really outgrown its "spreadsheet-ness." We're now running our services organization on it, and it has become a critical application. With this realization often comes a need to engage with internal IT to look at a software solution more holistically. In many ways, the business innovation emerged from its scrappy teenage years, matured and became successful, and now needs to be taken seriously. We may go out to the software market to look at pre-built solutions, or we may look to re-build the application and have it updated and managed by IT (using their formal application lifecycle management approaches). We may even find we already own an existing application that does a lot of what our self-built application does, and choose to bolt this on as an additionally supported business process.

We can see a few common themes emerging from the evolution of this business application:

1. From the start, the app was never conceived as an app – it got there through the evolution of business needs.

2. Managing an app becomes incrementally harder as it scales to meet additional needs; it was built to solve one specific problem, not the future problems it extended to.

3. Usability of these applications is generally quite low and the quality of the applications is often equally low – sometimes resulting in simple annoyances from bugs, sometimes resulting in loss of data or incorrect application of company policy.

4. When the app is handed over to IT, it is frequently not their priority. If we're able to find a packaged application, it will likely be coupled with the organization needing to make big changes to the way we do business (which is sometimes a good thing, sometimes not).

5. The application went from being a simple enabler, to a critical part of business operations, so it needs to be managed with some rigor.

6. The larger the organization, the more likely it is that there are similar apps at varying stages of evolution, doing essentially the same thing and relying on the same data. In this example, there are likely many parts of the organization that do project delivery to customers.

There are countless variations of this story, but they all tend to share at least a few of these characteristics. In some ways line of business applications are a bit like company start-ups. Lots of people will have a similar idea, some of those ideas will have amazing success in up-take, and others will stay small and be used by very few. Over time, some will simply fade away. And just like competing start-ups, they will all vary in strengths and weaknesses. The apps are created in small, actionable steps, with very little holistic view – it's about getting it done, getting to market and iterating as we learn and need more. However, like start-ups, these apps drive much of the innovation that happens in business and they are the lifeblood of a healthy economy (or in the case of business applications, the lifeblood of your business). Therefore, this ecosystem should be treated with care.

What drives IT?

The evolution of business applications is not in alignment with a typical IT delivery process. As a result, it's easy to understand why IT departments are quite skeptical of the idea that business applications should be encouraged. Business apps are frequently badly constructed, there's often a wasteland of applications that never really work, there's repetition, and lots of "siloed" data is at risk of being lost.

When IT thinks about application delivery, they want a picture of the current business need and potential future needs, which drives how they plan out the product and architecture. With good application architecture, based on established design principles (often called design patterns), the ongoing development of the application is much easier. Perhaps even more importantly, the ability to extend an application into different areas of the business is easier and overall maintenance is much lower. In fact, from the perspective of application quality, it's very difficult to see why this isn't a far superior way of building all software applications.

The problem is that this rigor clashes with the evolution of a line of business application. The focus of a business app is to solve the business problem, not to solve underlying systems architecture quality and maintenance concerns. The rigor of the IT delivery approach assumes a holistic view from the start, so that we truly understand all of our needs, and so that we have the time and energy to justify their value. Just like any innovation, the business has to do significant amounts of discovery and iteration to evolve their application. However, to engage with IT, they need a much more holistic perspective and concrete understanding of the need.

To make the IT delivery approach work, what we really need are two very different methodologies for delivering software to come together, with very different priorities. The result? Well, just ask any business user how much they trust internal IT departments to deliver the applications they need – there's rarely a lot of love!

The power struggle for control

Many business developers may not even realize there is a struggle going on. To IT, the problem is obvious and their solution is often clear-cut but difficult to manage – stop the business from creating applications. However, to stop the creation of business applications is really to stop business innovation. Very few business developers are creating applications simply for the fun of it (which is more commonplace in IT). Even further, business platforms are everywhere – they exist in Microsoft

Office, Google Docs, Microsoft SharePoint, and Lotus Notes, to name just a few.

The issue and conflict continue, often revolving around a simple but ill-conceived principle: give IT control of the systems so they can ensure consistency, accuracy, and supportable implementation. It sounds good, but it just doesn't work. While IT often uses agile methodologies to manage projects between peers, these approaches are rarely inclusive of the business. In agile project management, software is managed using short iterations, with very little up-front specification. The team works closely together to ensure alignment and remain "agile" as new problems arise. What unites the team is an overarching vision – but that vision is often not particularly detailed. This contrasts with how IT works with business, often using "waterfall" style development, which contradicts the evolutionary nature of business applications. In waterfall, it is common to provide detailed specifications up-front, set delivery milestones against those specifications, and then manage variations with change requests. Change and iteration are exceptions in the process, whereas in agile project management they are core to the process. Interestingly, the way IT works with its peers is much more aligned with how business developers would wish to work with IT.

So, on detailed inspection, the two groups do actually share the belief that innovation is managed by building change and discovery into the process. The difference is that the business developer bases this on business innovation and IT bases this much more on technical innovation. For greater alignment in working practice, the key is to clearly distinguish between them, and that's the basis of the force.com approach.

In addition to methodology and management approaches, building software applications with inherent business flexibility is difficult, and very few internal IT teams have the resources to manage that uncertainty in their implementation. Simply put, it's difficult to build an application that meets the personalization and customization requirements of business users. As a result, IT staff often end up in the demoralizing position of making constant, incremental changes to applications for years. As time passes and IT staff change, these applications inevitably end up getting as badly implemented as their business developer equivalents, until no one is interested in the future of the application, and it becomes a big burden. The process of change becomes increasingly painful to the business users and the complexity of making the changes becomes increasingly risky due to unknowns to the IT developers.

The result is unusable internal software applications that EVERYONE hates. In reality, internal IT departments are not funded sufficiently to manage this kind of load due to legacy. The reason for this is simple: the economics simply don't make any sense. As a result, the backlog of applications internal IT has to implement, maintain, integrate and support becomes crippling. It's very rare for IT to have time for small implementations that don't have broad executive buy-in. The problem grows over time, and the solution gets more and more extreme as IT looks to "lock down" the business, and business looks to "rebel" against IT.

Rather than being a unique problem, it's somewhat common: as we saw in the graph in the Introduction, Gartner predicted that global IT debt totaled approximately $500 billion in 2010, with the potential to rise to $1 trillion by 2015.

The solution

The solution is surprisingly simple. Business must join the conversation when it comes to building software, and business needs a platform that will support organic growth of applications. Connectivity of data is essential, and the bridge between the role of IT and the role of business has to be patrolled intelligently. The solution is simple, but making it work in practice requires a rigorously disciplined approach. force.com created a platform that comes with a pre-architected technology stack to make IT happy, tight controls around code development, and business is empowered with easy-to-use tools to allow them to do many common customization and configuration operations.

All of this is wrapped in collaboration, a model of shared data, secure data policies to reduce silos and encourage connected applications across the enterprise. At the heart, IT maintains control of the IT architecture and the business maintains control of the business process. force.com manages the contract between parties to ensure neither side can break the other's work. The result is that both are free to be agile in how they work together. The essence of this is the reliance on patterns.

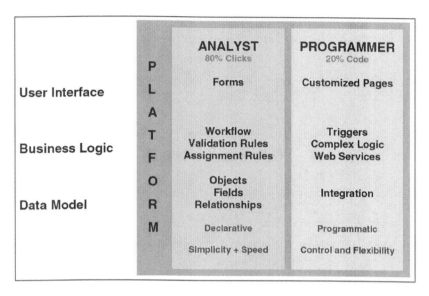

		ANALYST 80% Clicks	PROGRAMMER 20% Code
	P		
User Interface	**L**	Forms	Customized Pages
	A		
	T	Workflow	Triggers
Business Logic		Validation Rules	Complex Logic
	F	Assignment Rules	Web Services
	O	Objects	
		Fields	Integration
Data Model	**R**	Relationships	
	M	Declarative	Programmatic
		Simplicity + Speed	Control and Flexibility

Figure 24: The platform provides the bridge between the analyst and programmer. They can each take responsibility for what they are competent at, and work together towards a solution.

The power of patterns

One of the most important concepts to come out of IT was the idea of design patterns, a surprisingly simple concept, but very powerful when applied well. A design pattern is simply a repeatable way of doing things so that it can be re-used. For example, we know how to make bread. There are variations, but fundamentally, the basic process is the same. I don't need to re-invent how we do it – I just need to find out what it is, and perhaps contribute my own flair to add value.

This is indeed what happened in the field of 3D gaming, in which a technical innovation was the beginning. There are now numerous examples of gaming platforms that allow designers to create completely new plots and storylines for games with little to no programming. What was discovered is that all of these games followed a strikingly similar design

pattern (first person shooting, visually stunning landscapes and interiors, multiuser play, artificially intelligent enemies, etc.), and the thing that changed was the story and plot line – *that* was the innovation now, not the technology, but the story.

Recognizing the true value in this space of gaming, providers set about creating various tools to make it much easier for less technical people, who are more skilled at plots and stories, to become games developers. By creating a platform to support the development of new stories, they powered an explosion of amazing new games. The result? Incredible games that have inspired not only players, but have also elevated beyond gaming into feature-length films, books and music. This is what happens when you take experts in the core value of applications, and give them the tools to do it themselves, or at very least, join the conversation when building software. If you put the business into the beating heart of the application, so it can drive the purpose and value, truly amazing things can happen.

We already know how to build databases, workflow, security, and infrastructure to scale applications. We also know how to build forms, formulas, tables, and fields. So the question becomes: why re-invent the wheel? This is the power of patterns: using patterns dramatically increases the likelihood of success, radically shortens development time, and greatly improves confidence that things are being done correctly to represent true value. Fundamentally, the force.com platform is built on the principles of patterns, so users can very quickly leverage these benefits.

The force.com patterns

The platform has optimized around a number of common design patterns for applications: data-centric, process-centric, and content-centric. By leveraging these design patterns, the business developer and the IT developer are spared many of the common pitfalls of application development. Usability and accessibility, event handling, error handling and referential integrity, elastic scalability, security, re-use, deployment methodologies and distribution have all been subjected to great scrutiny. As a result, you can feel confident that the primary role of an app built on force.com is solving the business problem – and you can re-use Salesforce.com's knowledge of applications to ensure success. Not a bad deal: twelve years of cloud application development bundled directly into your business application. So where's the downside?

As powerful as patterns are, they do create one very recognized problem. When you are working within a pattern, it means assumptions have been made about how things are achieved. For example, if you're making a cake, knowledge of baking bread is helpful. If you're making soup, you probably don't need to spend much thinking about bread recipes! This idea follows with the platform – if you are building data-, process- or content-centric applications that are focused on business innovation, it's an excellent fit. If not, you might want to have a look at a platform more focused on technical innovation, such as Heroku. It's important to ensure the design of force.com meets your needs.

The force.com tools

With force.com tooling and products, the key is to articulate the tooling as closely as possible to the business need, whether the customer wants a web site, a database, or reporting forms, and whether the need is application-focused or market-focused. The great news is that all the tools come pre-integrated, so when the customer is more comfortable with software concepts and wants to build more apps, the platform makes it easy to switch between tools.

The next principle is that the platform does *not* seek to exclude IT or code, since it is often needed to complete a robust application.

Figure 25: An ever-increasing amount of an application can be built with clicks. When clicks are unable to provide the functionality required, code can be written and slotted into the application. The platform makes this seamless.force.com provides a point-and-click tooling experience that allows business developers to quickly build applications without code and also provides the APIs and language support necessary for developers to extend and enhance the platform with new services and capabilities that meet the specific needs of your business.

The idea of "the bridge" is simple – when you clarify the role of IT and the role of the business developer, and provide a clean line between the two roles, the platform acts as a bridge. This makes it much easier for the two groups to work together collaboratively to achieve their goals. This takes the principle of embedding the business user into applications even further. By allowing the business developer to drive the value and purpose of an app, amazing things do happen. If you surround that value with APIs that allow your developers to extend this business value with new services and capabilities, truly explosive things happen – we move into an age of revolutionary innovation. We can look at the structure of this in more detail.

- **Configuration**: Configuration operations are things like changing the contents of an email template, personalizing notification rules, or moving fields in a page layout. These are activities that require little conceptual knowledge and have low risk of causing the application to behave fundamentally differently from the way it was constructed to behave.

- **Customization**: Customization operations are things like modifying workflow, creating new page layouts or record types, or creating new fields of custom objects: activities that require conceptual understanding of the application and/or platform.

- **Code**: Code operations are often undertaken for the purpose of extending or enhancing the platform's capabilities to do new things or adopt new behavior or event patterns, and by definition, require actual coding knowledge to complete (in APEX/Visualforce or other languages).

Most people should be able to perform configuration operations, those more involved in the application in both business and IT should be capable of some form of customization, and the coding should be left to the professional developers. These distinctions are also made because it guides force.com product decisions so that configuration and customization operations will be done without any code, something that actually makes both business and IT happy:

- Business developers are not usually comfortable with component-based coding and patterns. For business developers that are more business than developer, the code will actually result in them not engaging in the tool. The sight of code is a clear indication to them that they're "not in Kansas anymore," and should vacate quickly and quietly!

- IT should be in control of component-based coding. They don't want untrained business developers inadvertently making changes to critical coding capabilities or integration touch-points with other systems.

The reality is that these lines are hard to draw in practice. Just because you can do something in clicks doesn't mean its business-developer-friendly. Having a user interface doesn't mean it's a business operation! For example, it doesn't matter how simple you make the consumption of a remote web service. Unless you're a fairly IT-savvy business developer, you may have no idea what a remote web service is or why you'd need to consume it! Conceptually, it's too far away. However, if IT were to give you a plug-in and say "use this plug-in to submit new orders to the system," that would be a lot easier to understand. Further, if IT provided clearly defined inputs and outputs (such as "order line item as the input and the order number as the output") that feels a lot more conceptually concrete. Business developers are often not familiar with the various layers of abstraction commonplace to developers; business developers are much more procedural and comfortable with concrete implementation concepts. As a result, the more concrete we can make the implementation, the more likely it is that a business developer will engage and make good judgments regarding usage.

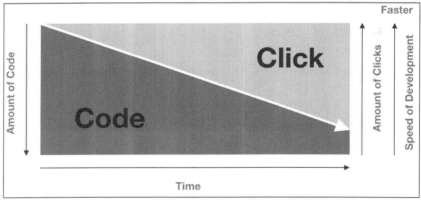

Figure 26: As clicks assume a bigger role (e.g., replacing hand-coding of screens with a drag-and-drop designer), the faster the speed of development proceeds.

143

Tooling up for the job

We try to align our tools as closely as possible to concrete problems:

- **Forms** – forms need to be created, and linked together with data. Forms have to capture critical business data, and also navigate clearly within that data. Forms can include logic and mash-ups of information from other systems.

- **Functions** – it's necessary to be able to create procedural logic as formulas to manipulate data, as well as validation rules to enforce policy.

- **Flows** – the ability to create workflows to enable more complex business processes is key. We want to enable business processes that are less about integration and much more about business operations.

- **Reports** – data is best presented in reports that are easily summarized and viewed by others.

- **Data** – the focus is entirely on the structure of your data, the access rights to it, and the relationships, rather than being about indexing or performance tuning as with traditional databases.

All of this is also wrapped in infrastructure services that include:

- **Collaboration** – your apps are immediately social and engaging for your end users.

- **Security** – ensures your data is safe and accessible only to those with the right privileges.

- **Change sets** – allow you to move changes from one environment to another to support your application lifecycle management requirements.

- **Packaging** – allows you to distribute applications between organizations, or even publish them for sale, using the app exchange.

- **Application containment** – permits you to group features and functions together into an identifiable application for distribution and management.

Eighty percent of the common IT work is done for you, so you can focus on the last twenty percent, which is what represents *the innovation that makes your business unique.*

Importance of social – the future

One of the big benefits of a point-and-click platform is openness. If the roles are clear and care is taken with complexity in the levels of the tooling (configuration, customization, and code), many people can join into the creation of software. Opening up the "language" of software, so that it's closer to a businessperson's conceptual understanding includes, a larger number of people in the conversation. And if we have a conversation across the organization, we have collaboration. As the force.com platform develops, you can expect to see Chatter leveraged much more, not just within the applications you create, but also in how you create them. In many ways, Chatter is a transparent, change management tool for business people. You don't just follow people and records, but you can follow page layouts, workflows, schemes, etc. If a change is made, you then have the opportunity to "like" it, comment and make suggestions for further improvement. Truly collaborative building will be a big step in the way organizations engage in the software creation process, and also in the way applications are managed through their lifecycles.

Imagine a future where everyone in your organization who's using an application could not only see how it was constructed, but also comment and contribute. Imagine if that application were as open to change as a wiki. Would it result in the "Wild West" of applications, or a new breed of applications based on the knowledge and contributions of the crowd?

Whatever your viewpoint, this is likely the future of application platforms. For too long, software has remained a closed language spoken only by a few people in the organization – who may be farthest from your customers. It's time the power of software development was unleashed to the masses.

An example of the power of clicks

Universal Containers is a rapidly growing international supplier of container products. It employs a diverse group of employees, including facilities and operations professionals, software and design engineers, financial accountants, and legal and human resources personnel.

Historically, HR has used Microsoft Word documents and Microsoft Excel spreadsheets as they manage the recruiting and hiring process of new employees. However, over the last two quarters it's become evident that unless this process is replaced by one that is more collaborative, reliable, and scalable, the department won't be able to meet its hiring goals for this fiscal year. Universal Containers needs a centralized application that can bring all of its recruiting and hiring processes together.

The new recruiting app needs to:

- Track positions in all stages of the process, from those that are open to those that have been filled or cancelled.

- Track all of the candidates who apply for a particular position, including the status of their application (whether they've had a phone screening, are scheduled for interviews, were rejected or hired, or declined an offer).

- Track the posting of jobs on external employment web sites such as Monster.com.

- Allow employees to post reviews for candidates they've interviewed.

- Provide security for recruiting data so that it's not mistakenly viewed, edited, or deleted by employees who shouldn't have access.

- Automatically inform the relevant recruiter about the next steps that should be taken when a decision has been made about an applicant.

- Automatically inform all employees of new positions that have been posted.

- Make sure that a new job opening has executive approval before it becomes active.

- Include reports that give users an overview of recruiting status.

- Allow recruiters to map the locations of all candidates applying for a position, to better understand relocation expenses.

- Make it easy to perform several similar tasks at once, such as rejecting multiple job applications.

- Automatically post open positions on Universal Containers' public web site.

Almost all the above functionality can be accomplished in force.com without writing any code – just clicks. There is some functionality where code is required, for example, the mapping of candidate locations and the posting of positions on Universal Containers' public jobs site. But the need for coding is a small part of the total application.

A Paradigm Shift

The big payoff of the living systems point of view is that what is remote and unnatural within the traditional frame of reference becomes sensible and accessible within the complexity mindset. – Richard Pascale, Mark Tillemann, and Linda Gioja, *Surfing the Edge of Chaos*

There is nothing that is a more certain sign of insanity than to do the same thing over and over and expect the results to be different. – Albert Einstein

Paradigms are important because they determine not only how we understand things, but also how we deal with them. If your worldview included the belief that the Earth is flat, it would be highly unlikely you'd set off on an ocean voyage for fear of falling off the edge. Paradigms help us make sense of the world. And they help determine the way we approach building information systems.

A shift in our interpretation of how the world works is being accelerated by the need to operate on the global digital playing field, where new rivals are unencumbered by rigid policies and thinking, fueled by fast-growth economies and new technology, and where market risks and opportunities appear and disappear at an incredible pace.[36]

---

[36] *The New Digital Economy: How It Will Transform Business*, June 2011

A Clockwork Universe

The robustness and endurance of the machine as the predominant metaphor of 20th century management practice is nothing short of amazing given the mounting evidence that it simply doesn't work. – John Hagel, *Out of the Box*

Until the early twentieth century, classical mechanics, as first formulated by Isaac Newton, was seen as the foundation for science as a whole. Other disciplines, such as biology, psychology, economics – and information technology – adopted a general mechanistic or Newtonian methodology and world view. This influence was so great, that most people with a basic notion of science still implicitly equate "scientific" thinking with "Newtonian" thinking.

The reason for this pervasive influence is that the mechanistic paradigm is compelling in its simplicity, coherence and apparent completeness. Moreover, it was not only very successful in its scientific applications, but largely in agreement with intuition and common sense. Later theories of mechanics, such as relativity theory and quantum mechanics, while at least as successful in the realm of applications, lacked this simplicity and intuitive appeal, and are still plagued by paradoxes, confusions and multiple interpretations.

The best known principle of Newtonian science, reductionism, was actually formulated by the philosopher-scientist Descartes well before Newton. Reductionism is the idea that in order to understand any complex phenomenon, you need to take it apart, i.e., reduce it to its individual components. If these are still complex, you need to take your analysis one step further, and look at their components.

So until fairly recently, the world was primarily seen as a machine – a clockwork mechanism where, with ever more knowledge, more efficiency, and more hierarchical command and control, we could pull a lever at one place and get a precise result at another, and know with certainty which lever to pull for which result. Cause and effect were simple relationships. Everything could be known. Organizations and people could be engineered into efficient solutions.

For centuries, we've been designing and pulling those levers, all the while hammering at people to behave in the compliant, subordinate manner one expects from a well-trained horse. Rarely have we gotten the expected result.

This image of ourselves as operators of an enormous machine has remained unquestioned until relatively recently. It continues to haunt the way we try to improve efficiency in our organizations. Consider the concept of "re-engineering." The term alone, says John Hagel, "attests to the depth to which mechanistic thinking has become embedded in our corporate psyches." Since the goal was to make an organization run like a "well-oiled machine," when it didn't, it meant looking for another solution to impose on the organization. This is reflected in the terms "jumpstart," "shift gears," and "out of sync."

But why would we want an organization to behave like a machine? Machines have no inherent intelligence; they follow the instructions given to them. They only work in the specific conditions predicted by their engineers. Changes in their environment wreak havoc because they have no capacity to adapt.

The influence of Newton is deeply felt in IT: if we get those specifications right, everything will work like, well, clockwork.

This mindset still serves us well when we need to achieve efficiency and economies of scale in an organization. If conditions stay the same long enough to churn out large numbers of predefined products and services, it is the best way to deliver them at the lowest cost.

But what happens when conditions change, and people no longer want standard products and services? What happens when product life cycles are measured in months instead of years? That lack of predictability throws a monkey wrench into the gears of the industrial efficiency model.

Newton's seventeenth century laws were simple, neat, and described a world that could ultimately be controlled. They no longer match the reality of the twenty-first century. The needs of the digitized business are quite different:

The Old Economy	The Digital Economy
Planning	Experimentation
Predictability	Uncertainty
Stability	Change
Justification	Responsiveness

Complex Adaptive Systems

We are sailors on a sea of change and organizations are part of the ships we sail. We cannot sail against the prevailing winds, but we can learn to work with the wind and the waves and harness their energy to arrive at the destinations we aspire to reach. – Michael Hugos, *Business Agility: Sustainable Prosperity in a Relentlessly Competitive World*

Change is the organizing force, not a problematic intrusion. – Margaret J. Wheatley, *Finding Our Way: Leadership for an Uncertain Time*

More than sixty years ago, scientists knew that Newton's model was incomplete. It turns out that we do not live in an even remotely linear world; in fact, our world should be categorized as nonlinear. But despite the fact that the machine metaphor has been all but abandoned by twenty-first century science, IT continues to clutch tightly the reassuring image of the clockwork organization. We have to come to grips with the fact that we are not cogs in a timepiece, but integral participants in a distinctly living, growing, and ever-changing whole being – what scientists call a complex adaptive system (CAS).

Today, we want organizations to be adaptive, flexible, self-renewing, resilient, learning, and intelligent. These are attributes found only in living systems, and we want our organizations to be regarded as, and behave as, living systems.

All living systems have the capacity to self-organize, sustain themselves, and move towards greater complexity and order as needed. They can respond intelligently to the need for change. They organize (and then reorganize) themselves into adaptive patterns and structures without any externally imposed plan or direction.

A CAS is a system of semiautonomous agents with the freedom to act according to a set of simple rules in order to maximize a specific goal. A CAS is a highly adaptive, self-organizing, interrelated, interdependent, interconnected entity that behaves as a unified whole. It learns from experience and doesn't simply react, but adjusts to changes in the environment.

Complex adaptive systems are all around us – the weather, ant colonies, the stock market, our immune systems, neighborhoods, governments, sporting events, and, most important, the organizations in which we work. The "participants" in every system exist in total ignorance of the concept but that does not impede their contribution to the system. And every individual agent in a CAS is a CAS itself: a tree is a CAS within a larger CAS (a forest), which exists in a still larger CAS (an ecosystem).

Properties of a Complex Adaptive System

To see the world ... as a ceaselessly complex and adaptive system requires a revolution. It involves changing the role we imagine for ourselves, from architects of a system we can control and manage to gardeners in a living, shifting ecosystem. – Joshua Cooper Ramo, *The Age of the Unthinkable*

While the Newtonian "machine" is a metaphor, the organization as a living organism is not a metaphor: the organization *is* a living organism, whether we want it to be or not. Viewing it as such will help us build better information systems. Here are some examples.

- We accept that it is impossible to fully understand and anticipate everything, so we know that our attempts at "nailing down the requirements" are doomed to failure. Complexity science suggests that we would be better off producing minimum specifications and a general sense of direction. The rest is left to the flexibility, adaptability, and creativity of individual agents as the context continually changes.

- Complex adaptive systems thrive on a constantly changing border between stability and chaos that has been dubbed "the edge of chaos." An organization with too *much* order atrophies and dies. If it lives in chaos, it loses control and ceases to function as a system.

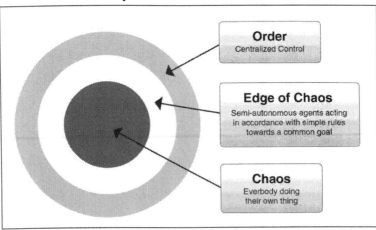

Figure 28: The Edge of Chaos. Systems need to balance between chaos and order to survive and adapt.

- In a CAS, there is a tenuous connection between causes and effects. Small changes can have huge effects.[37] Alternatively, large changes may have little effect. Does a more sophisticated system result in greater efficiency? The opposite may be true. Therefore, systems should evolve based on how people use them, rather than being imposed from the top down.

- Machine efficiency does not govern most life processes, which are fuzzy, redundant, and messy. Many solutions are sought in parallel, and many individuals are involved in experimentation about the same dilemma. There is no straight line of logic or process that leads to a perfect solution. Instead, there is a great deal of tinkering until someone discovers something that works (for now). The messy processes and fuzzy logic lead to orderly solutions because it is the nature of life to evolve towards more complex and effective systems. Life is attracted to order, but it uses chaos to get there.

- All systems exist within their own environment, and they are also part of that environment, existing in a feedback loop with their environment. Therefore, as the environment changes, s system must co-evolve – change to ensure a best fit. But because the system is a part of its environment, when the system changes, the system's response then causes a change in the environment, and as the environment changes in response, the system needs to change again; and so it goes in a continuous process. That's why the most successful systems are, paradoxically enough, those that need to change most often.

- A CAS does not have to be perfect in order to thrive within its environment. A solution doesn't have to be ideal – it just has

---

[37] This is like the *butterfly effect*, the best example of which is the Arab Spring, which began in the small Tunisian town of Sidi Bouzid (population: 40,000), when a policewoman slapped a fruit vendor, and the result was the toppling of three tyrants in eleven months.

to work. When it stops working, agents tinker their way into another solution. Once it has reached the state of being good enough, a complex adaptive system will trade off increased efficiency every time in favor of greater effectiveness. Yet we spend an inordinate amount of time trying to get the details right – when it is unlikely to matter very much.

- Complex adaptive systems are not complicated. Emerging  patterns may have a rich variety, but the rules governing the function of the system are quite simple. The flocking behavior of geese (flying in a V-formation) is a popular illustration of this concept. Geese appear to follow a simple set of rules when flying in formation: don't bump into each other; match the speed of the geese flying nearby; replace the lead goose when it gets tired; always remain with the group. From these few simple rules emerges a complex and efficient flying pattern. This is in sharp contrast to how we build systems, where our goal is to impose as many rules as possible, so that "exceptions" are kept to a minimum.

- Complex adaptive systems are inherently self-organizing. In a social enterprise, people close to the problem find it natural to form teams, and they are much more likely to be effective than if their group was imposed from higher up. Order is an inherent property of the system – it does not need to be imposed from the outside.

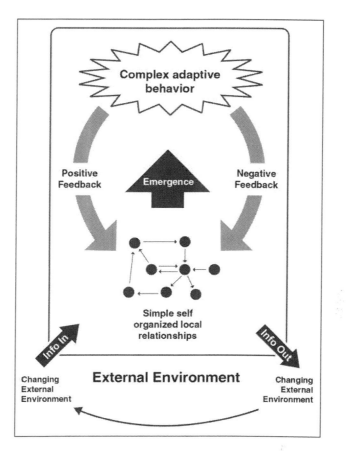

Figure 27:Behavior "emerges" as a result of feedback, relationships and the external environment. In the same way, an application emerges through usage, constant feedback, and ever-changing requirements.

Efficiency versus Responsiveness

> *It is not necessary to change. Survival is not mandatory* – W. Edwards Deming

Building systems to make an organization more efficient is quite different from building systems that make an organization more responsive. Thinking of the organization as a machine makes sense when efficiency is the goal. When responsiveness is the goal, the complex adaptive system paradigm makes much more sense.

Efficiency	Responsiveness
Limited, fixed responses to known situations	Chaordic (a mixture of chaos and order), adaptable
Unchanging	Always changing
Constant, uniform	Variable, complex
Focuses on doing the work in the correct manner	Focuses on the desired result
Seeks to avoid failure	Seeks success
Oriented towards keeping the current system going	Oriented towards strategy and keeping priorities
Concerned with maintaining the status quo	Attempts to find new ways to perform tasks better
Reacts to change	Anticipates change
Inflexible – determined to carry out plans regardless of change	Flexible when change is required
Disallows slack time – no place for creativity	Allows down-time – provides time for creativity
Comfortable with keeping things as they are	Motivated towards growth

Self-Organization

Why is change so uncomfortable in human organizations?

Margaret Wheatley explains: [38]

"Self-organizing systems have what all leaders crave: the capacity to respond continuously to change. In these systems, change is the organizing force, not a problematic intrusion. Structures and solutions are temporary. Resources and people come together to create new initiatives, to respond to new regulations, to shift the organization's processes. Leaders emerge from the needs of the moment. There are far fewer levels of management. Experimentation is the norm. Local solutions predominate but are kept local, not elevated to models for the whole organization. Involvement and participation constantly deepen. These organizations are experts at the process of change. They understand their organization as a process of continuous organizing...

"Whether it be birds, termites, or humans, the conditions that create organization are the same. Individuals are similarly focused, and members develop connections with one another. Each determines its behavior based on information about what its neighbors are doing and what the collective purpose is. From such simple conditions, working communities emerge, self-organizing from local connections into global patterns and processes. Nothing is preplanned; patterns of behavior emerge that could not be predicted from observing individuals.

"While self-organization calls us to very different ideas and forms of organizing, how else can we create the resilient, intelligent, fast, and flexible organizations that we require? How else can we succeed in organizing in the accelerating pace of our times except by realizing

---

[38] Margaret J. Wheatley and Myron Kellner-Rogers, *The Irresistible Future of Organizing,* July/August 1996

that organizations are living systems? This is not an easy shift, changing one's model of the way the world organizes."

Shifting the paradigm

The attitude that we're shifting into is viewing the world as chaotic. You're never going to understand it. You're never going to control it. Instead, you have to be responsive. You have to make sure that when an opportunity arises you can take advantage of it. - Danny Hillis, founder of Applied Minds, quoted in *What's Next? Exploring the New Terrain for Business* by Eamonn Kelly and Peter Leyden

Figure 28: A slight shift in perspective can have a dramatic effect. This well-known example effectively makes the point. (Do you see a young girl or old lady? Or both?)

Our Newtonian worldview has led us to focus our efforts on how to get the machine called an organization to work efficiently. But machines are exactly the wrong metaphor for what we need, since machines have no intelligence.

But if we change our thought paradigm, we will start asking a different set of questions and think of different kinds of solutions. If organizations are living systems, then they have many innate capacities, and we need to learn to harness them.

Ordered World	Complex World
Cause and effect can be precisely determined.	Cause and effect are intertwined and cannot be determined in advance.
Certain parties have control.	All parties have influence.
There is only one way ahead.	There are many possibilities for progress.
Large effects require enormous coordinated efforts.	Large effects come from small starts and positive feedback.
The future can be planned.	The future *emerges* from the combined actions of the players.
Top down.	Bottom up.
Complexity to simplicity.	Simplicity to complexity.

Figure 30: Different starting points for looking at the world.

The Linux example

The development of the Linux operating system is an elegant illustration of a distributed, complex adaptive system. The operating system was developed as freeware and soon attracted the attention of more and more programmers, who contributed their own ideas and improvements. The Linux community grew steadily, soon encompassing thousands of people around the world, all sharing work freely with one another. Soon, this loose, informal group, working without managers, and connected mainly through the Internet, turned Linux into one of the best operating systems ever created.

In contrast, how would such a software development project have been organized by one of today's major software companies, or in a typical organization? Decisions and funds would have been filtered through layers of managers. Formal teams of programmers, quality assurance testers, database administrators, and technical writers would have been established and assigned tasks. Customer surveys and focus groups would have been conducted, their findings documented in thick reports. There would have been budgets, milestones, deadlines, status meetings, performance reviews, and approvals. There would have been turf wars, burnouts, overruns and delays. The project would have cost an enormous amount of money, taken much longer to complete, and quite possibly have produced a system less valuable to users than Linux.[39]

The Lesson for IT

IT often acts as though it is not subject to the laws of chaos. It pretends it can predict what will happen in the course of each day, and can therefore ascertain the best course of action for any circumstance that may occur. Hence, the never-ending hunt to track down and kill exceptions.

This flies in the face of our understanding of organizations and living systems. The attempt to build bigger and more complex systems is *exactly the opposite of what is needed* to meet the challenges we face.

---

[39] T.W. Malone and R.J. Laubacher, "The Dawn of the E-lance Economy," *Harvard Business Review*, Sep/Oct 1998

The end of the change float

Not too long ago, a check would take a couple of weeks to find its way through the banking system. This "float" was used by many customers to their advantage. Today, of course, money can move through the system instantaneously, resulting in significant impacts on the world of finance.

Similarly, we've witnessed the disappearance of "information float." It used to take significant amounts of time for information to travel. It took centuries for information about the smelting of ore to cross a single continent and bring about the Iron Age. During the time of sailing ships, it took years for that which was known to become that which was shared. It took decades for the steam engine and automobile to attain universal acceptance. It took years, too, for radio and TV to become pervasive. Today, countless devices leap virtually overnight into, and throughout, the

world. This endless compression of float, the time between what was and what is to be, between past and future, has had an enormous impact on everything – except the way IT builds systems.

Our techniques are very much in line with how Newtonian science viewed "change" – as the movement from one equilibrium state (water) to another (ice). Newtonian understandings cannot cope with the random, near-chaotic messiness of the actual transition itself.

Information technologists similarly favor equilibrium conditions, because our techniques do not handle transition states (a necessary messiness) very well. But if change is constant, and there is no float anymore, we need to adapt accordingly.

We are getting closer to being able to do this. Today, there's no delay waiting for applications to go live, since they're already running in the cloud. Development work is done in short bursts, so results are delivered quickly and feedback is instant.[40] Equilibrium states are becoming shorter and shorter. Change is changing.[41]

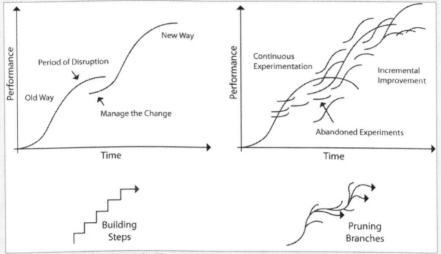

Source: Dave Gray, "Change is Changing," Dachis Group

Figure 31: Change is no longer a transition between two states. It's something that is happening all the time. This requires the ability to adapt and evolve on a continual basis, recover quickly from failures, and move on.

[40] Phil Wainewright, "Who Needs an IT Dept Anymore?" ZDNet, October 12, 2011

[41] Dave Gray, "Change is Changing," Dachis Group, blog post, October 26th, 2011, http://www.dachisgroup.com/2011/10/change-is-changing/

A quantum leap forward

With these prerequisites in place, we can take a quantum leap forward in application development productivity.

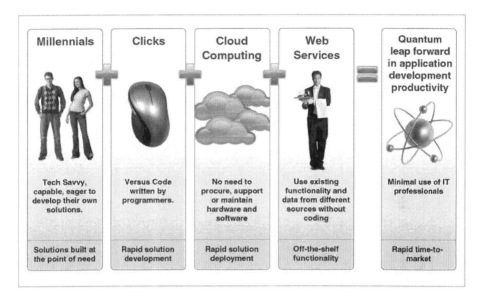

Foundation

Tools shape the solution. No one knew they needed a spreadsheet before Visicalc, or a home page before the World Wide Web. —Jeff Tash, *Flashmap Systems*

Unlike traditional application development, which we earlier compared to railroad construction, the digital economy calls for a dynamic business environment, which is more closely reflected in the process that taxicab companies use to respond to demand.

In a typical U.S. city, cabs cruise the streets with only flexible strategies, allowing response to demand to unfold as required. Decisions are made in real time, as closely as possible to the time when action must be taken. The driver makes decisions on the spot, consistent with the needs of passengers, whose plans are unknown most of the time.

With railroads, of course, the organization plans in advance and passengers must arrange their plans accordingly. The flexible approach requires organizations to embrace uncertainty, dynamic demand, and some degree of chaos, and to learn to thrive on it.

The rest is left to the flexibility, adaptability, and creativity of the individual agents as the context continually changes.

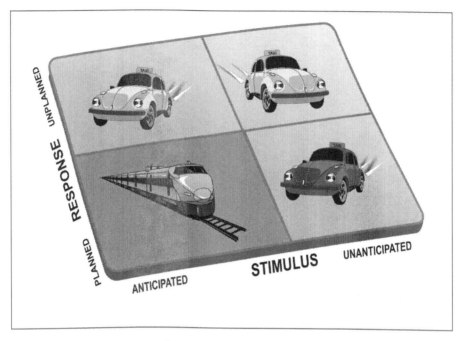

Figure 32: Railway systems require careful planning and the results are predetermined. Running taxicabs requires little planning and the results are completely unpredictable.

Taxicabs can do this because the foundation is already in place – roads, traffic lights, gas stations, electric cabling, telephone lines, and so on. This is a vast, interconnected, and mostly unnoticed network that operates to support the business activity.

For taxicabs, it's just a matter of getting the car on the road and getting going.

Building railways, on the other hand, requires an infrastructure to be built before trains can even think of getting going.

With force.com, all the underlying infrastructure, both hardware and software, is already in place. A framework is provided to make sure that the user can focus on building the logic specific to their needs.

Taxicabs only have to worry about their business. They don't have to be concerned with building and repairing roads and bridges, installing traffic lights, or monitoring that no one is abusing limits put in place to protect all users. They don't have to provide the services  necessary to make it all work, such as traffic cops or gas stations.

To decisively change the application development paradigm, all the infrastructure and supporting services must be able to be taken for granted.

The foundation of a digital business platform includes the following pillars:

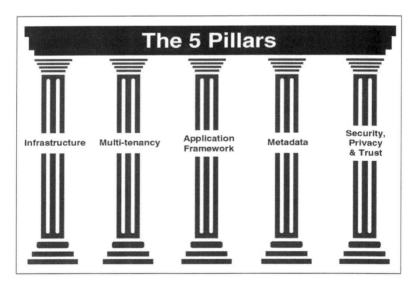

Infrastructure[42]

The force.com service delivery infrastructure consists of advanced and highly managed data center and security technologies. It currently powers more than 400 million transactions a day and supports more than 2 million subscribers. It is this same infrastructure that delivers all cloud applications developed and deployed by its customers, as well as the Salesforce CRM applications.

Redundancy

The force.com infrastructure consists of three geographically separated production data centers (with more to come) and a production-class lab facility that uses near-real-time replication to mirror the data at each location. A comprehensive disaster recovery plan ensures the platform will remain available for applications regardless of the situation. There is no single point of failure.

Security

All data centers are certified (SAS 70 Type II, SysTrust, and ISO 27001). Each facility's security team monitors site perimeters 24/365, and five levels of biometric scanning and other technologies encapsulate internal operations centers to ensure that only authorized personnel have system access. To protect data in transit between data centers, the system uses secure point-to-point data replication.

Salesforce.com performs both internal and external vulnerability assessments on a regular basis to further ensure system security.

---

[42] This section on infrastructure is adapted from the Salesforce.com White Paper force.com: *A Comprehensive Look at the World's Premier Cloud-Computing Platform.*

Scalability

force.com's infrastructure design can scale both vertically and horizontally due to its unique pod architecture. A pod is a set of industry-standard resources (high-performance database, web, application, search, email, storage, backup servers, load balancers, etc.) that work together to serve the needs of a limited collection of organizations and applications. To prevent demand overload of any one pod's resources, salesforce.com provisions a new pod when existing pods are nearing predefined capacity thresholds.

Monitoring

A collection of systems management tools closely monitors force.com's health and performance 24/7 and alerts the platform's team of specialized engineers to potential problems and resolutions.

Change Management

Salesforce.com thoroughly tests and manages new releases of force.com to ensure both quality and the transparency of changes to existing platform applications.

Multi-tenancy[43]

The application service provider (ASP) model of the 1990s delivered a traditional, on-premises application from its data center to a remote customer over a network, managing all the application's operational aspects. The customer was responsible for purchasing and maintaining a conventional perpetual software license, and the ASP charged a fee for managing the entire process. However, cost inefficiencies of deploying and

---

[43] The chapter on multi-tenancy is partially adapted from the Salesforce.com white paper force.com: *A Comprehensive Look at the World's Premier Cloud-Computing Platform.*

maintaining a dedicated hardware and software suite or ensemble for each customer (or tenant) doomed the ASP model to failure.

Modern cloud-based applications are much more cost-efficient than their single-tenant counterparts, thanks to a new application development approach that's at the heart of the force.com platform – multi-tenancy.

The easiest way to grasp the concept of multi-tenancy is by comparing it to an apartment building. An apartment building allows all the tenants to share the lobby, the swimming pool, the roof, the power, the fitness center, and so on. But each individual tenant can do whatever they like in their apartment without impacting any other tenant – paint the walls, put in their own furniture, etc. One tenant can't enter another tenant's apartment.

Multi-tenancy ensures that every customer is on the same version of the software. CIOs don't need to put off upgrades for months (or sometimes years) because of resource constraints or complexity. As a result, no customer is left behind when the software is updated to include new features and innovations.

Single version

Only one version of the force.com platform is in production. The same platform is used to deliver applications of all sizes and shapes, used by 1 to 100,000 users, running everything from dog-grooming businesses to the Japanese national postal system.

Continuous, zero-cost improvements

When force.com is upgraded to include new features or bug fixes, the upgrade is enabled in every customer's logical environment with zero to minimal effort required.

Salesforce can roll out new releases with confidence because it maintains a single version of its infrastructure and can achieve broad test coverage by leveraging tests, code, and configurations from their production environment.

Metadata

Why Metadata?

Multi-tenancy is practical only when it can support applications that are reliable, customizable, upgradeable, secure, and fast. But how can just one instance of a multi-tenant application let each tenant create custom extensions to standard data objects and new custom data objects? How will tenant-specific data be kept secure in a shared database so one tenant can't invade another tenant's data? How can one tenant customize the application's interface and business logic in real time without affecting the functionality or availability of the application for all other tenants?

How can the core application's code base be patched or upgraded without breaking tenant-specific customizations? And how will the application's response time scale, as tens of thousands of tenants subscribe to the service? It's difficult (if not impossible) to create a statically compiled application executable that can meet these and other unique challenges of multi-tenancy.

For those reasons, multi-tenant application designs have evolved to use a runtime engine that generates application components from metadata – data about the application itself. In force.com's metadata-driven architecture, there's a clear separation of the compiled runtime engine (kernel), application data, the metadata that describes the base functionality of an application, and the metadata that corresponds to each tenant's customizations. These distinct boundaries make it possible to independently update the system kernel, modify the core application, or customize tenant-specific components all in real time, with no risk of one update affecting the other components.

How it works

In force.com, everything exposed to developers and application users is internally represented as metadata. Forms, reports, work flows, user access privileges, tenant-specific customizations and business logic, and even the definitions of underlying data objects and indexes are all abstract constructs that exist merely as metadata. For example, when a developer builds a new custom application and defines a custom table, lays out a data entry form, or writes some procedural code, force.com does not create a table in a database or compile any code. Instead, force.com simply stores metadata that the platform's engine uses to generate the "virtual" application components at runtime. When a user wants to modify or customize the application, all that's required is a simple, non-blocking update to the corresponding metadata. When a user works with the application, force.com's runtime application generator uses metadata to render the application components in the interface.

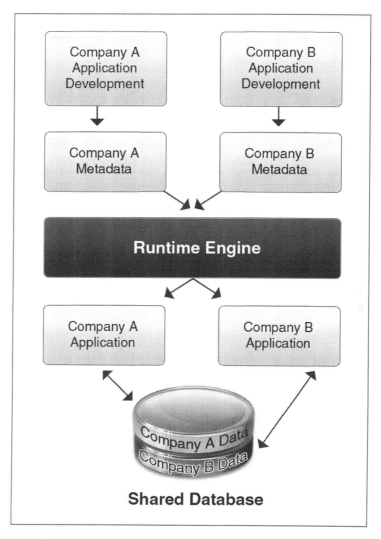

Figure 33: Each application is stored as metadata, which is then interpreted at runtime.

force.com's metadata architecture is scalable. Because metadata is a key ingredient of force.com applications, the platform's runtime engine optimizes access to metadata.

force.com also uses a metadata-driven development model to help app developers become more productive in putting together basic apps. The basic functionality of an app is stored as metadata in a database rather than being hard-coded in a programming language. When a user accesses an app through the force.com platform, it renders the app's metadata into the interface the user experiences. As a result of metadata-driven development, force.com app developers work at a much higher level of abstraction than if they developed applications using Java or C#, and are shielded from having to worry about low-level system details that the platform handles automatically. At the same time, force.com developers can also leverage advanced features that the platform provides by default.

Although at first glance metadata-driven development may seem somewhat esoteric, it's exactly the same model for how web browsers work. Instead of hard-coding the definition of a web page in a free-form programming language, a web page author first defines the page as HTML, which is itself a kind of metadata. When the page is requested by a user, the web browser renders the page using the metadata provided in the HTML tags. Even though the HTML/browser combination does not allow authors as much formatting power as they might get in a regular publishing tool, it simplifies the work of publishing content to a wide audience and increases the web page author's overall productivity. Likewise, even though force.com also does not allow app developers as much power as they might get from free-form coding in Java or .NET, it vastly simplifies the work of building an app and increases a developer's overall productivity response times.

In addition, without doing a single thing or writing a single line of code, every force.com application inherits any new functionality that is added to the underlying platform. So for example, when force.com added Chatter to the platform, every app ever built on force.com was automatically chatterized (inheriting the features and capabilities of Chatter).

Application Framework

Frameworks provide a quick start for developing an application. The closer the framework is to the finished application the better, reducing the effort needed to build the application. If you were building a house, a prefab framework that provides the foundations, walls, and roof is a quick start to finishing the house.

A software framework provides agility, lower risk, higher predictability and stability, and greater productivity.

The force.com application framework provides the functionality commonly needed for any business application, customizable for the unique requirements of each business through a combination of code and configuration. This framework, and the infrastructure that supports it, is delivered to you as a service in the cloud.

Most business applications are made up of features that are implemented in every new application – security, user identity, logging, profiling, integration, data storage, transactions, workflow, and reporting. You have to build all these things before you can even start thinking about the actual business problem you're trying to solve. This is time-consuming and costly.

Frameworks always need to negotiate a fine line between doing too much, which limits flexibility, and too little, which reduces effectiveness. force.com does a fine job of providing a lot of built-in functionality, while at the same time allowing developers to extend the functionality as they need to.

Benefits of an Application Framework

Software development can be an expensive and imprecise undertaking: expensive because of the cost of the IT staff, hardware, and software involved, and imprecise because of the range of variables that influence development activities, such as the requirements definition and the developers' experience and skills. An application framework is a way to reduce costs and introduce a higher level of predictability into software development.

Frameworks reduce the software development effort

Software applications consist of code related to the business logic, and code related to the infrastructure that holds the application components together. When development projects include a framework, developers will spend less effort on the infrastructure and have more time to work on the business logic.

Frameworks provide generic services

Frameworks provide the generic services needed by most applications, such as logging, configuration, database, access, and caching. They include tools and methods that simplify development for event handling, user interface management, data exchange, and job processing. Infrastructure code is usually the most detailed and tedious code to write, requiring deep technical skills. Because developers are more prone to making errors when working in this context, using frameworks is a good idea to help avoid or minimize this situation.

Frameworks protect users from themselves

Frameworks can protect users from doing "bad" things. The key is to build constraints without affecting flexibility. Think about lounge areas in airports. You don't see any signs that say, "Don't talk too loudly," or "Don't move the chairs," or "Don't occupy more than one chair." It's through the invisible hand of good design that those bad things are encouraged not to happen. Seats are arranged so that people talk to others close by, and don't shout across the room. The armrests are fixed, so you don't see people sprawling across chairs. The seats are bolted together, so you can't pick them up and rearrange them. It looks like it "just happens," but the airport seating area has been designed to ensure certain types of behavior without ordering it.

Frameworks reduce complexity

Many of the design decisions that need to be made when starting development from scratch are already built into the framework, which includes the code to implement the decisions as well. Therefore, developers don't have to waste time reinventing the wheel. Less experienced developers will build better quality software by adding to a framework, rather than having to write all the code, and better quality software reduces potential for errors and the need for substantial ongoing maintenance efforts.

Frameworks improve productivity, quality, and consistency

Frameworks make the software development cycle a more predictable process by providing a standardized architecture and a standardized approach to building software. For example, developers work with pre-defined rules for coding and proven methodologies for building parts of an application. They also use a given set of development tools. Developers will more consistently produce high-quality software, and productivity improves, because individual developers no longer need to make decisions about fundamental architecture and design issues.

Frameworks ensure a minimal degree of quality

No doubt many people who patronize the do-it-yourself section of Home Depot return home to build less-than-perfect artifacts. But their creations no doubt serve their needs. Maybe the bookcase doesn't look great and will fall over if someone bumps into it – but it solves the immediate problem, and the budding carpenters feel a sense of empowerment having built it themselves.

But at some level, a minimum level of quality is assured by the "provider." The lumber is solid, the screws hold fast, and the paint is lead-free.

Application Development Services

The force.com framework is made up of a set of services.

These services are highly customizable with and without writing code. Although each service can be valued as an individual unit of functionality, there is tremendous value from their unification. All the features of force.com are designed, built, and maintained by a single responsible party, Salesforce. Salesforce provides support and training for its customers, and accountability for keeping things running smoothly. This is in contrast to many software projects that end up as a patchwork of open-source, best-of-breed tools and libraries glued together by you, the developer.

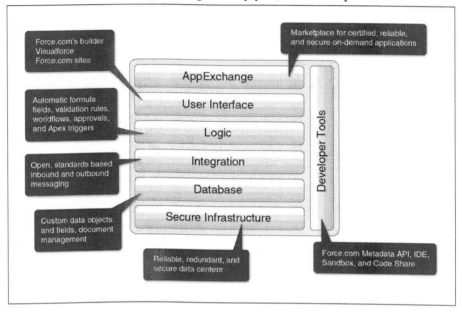

Database as a Service

The heart of force.com is the relational database provided as a service. The relational database is the most well-understood and widely used way to store and manage business data. Business applications typically require reporting, transactional integrity, summarization, and structured search, and implementing those on nonrelational data stores requires significant effort. force.com provides a relational database to each tenant, one that is tightly integrated with every other feature of the platform. There are no Oracle licenses to purchase, no tablespaces to configure, no JDBC drivers to install, no DDL to write, no queries to optimize, and no replication and backup strategies to implement.

The force.com database builds on the foundation of the force.com infrastructure to provide much of the platform's development power. Here you can create metadata that describes an application's custom database objects, such as tables and fields. There's no backup, no tuning, and no stream of upgrades for you to manage, because salesforce.com takes care of these tasks.

You can also declare metadata to establish relationships between data objects that are automatically implemented as master lookups and lists of related detail objects in force.com applications (for example, order headers and order line items). To ensure data integrity, you can declare data validation rules and use formulas to logically derive new data values. You can even audit database changes with the click of a mouse. The force.com database provides all these capabilities without the usual requirements for database maintenance and overhead.

Integration as a Service

Your cloud applications may have to fit into an existing environment that includes a variety of data sources and applications. The force.com platform provides the resources for integrating those applications into your current environment to access data in other systems, create mashups that combine data from multiple sources, or include external systems in your business processes.

At the core of these integration capabilities is the force.com Web Services API, which provides easy access to all the data stored in a force.com application through an open, standards-based Web service. This API is used by numerous environments, ranging from traditional development tools such as .NET, Java, and PHP to middleware and integration solutions such as BizTalk, Informatica, and Tibco. In addition, salesforce.com and third parties have used the API to create prepackaged connectors to many applications, including SAP R/3, Oracle Financials, and others. There are even prebuilt integration solutions that let organizations "connect the clouds" by integrating force.com applications with other cloud-based offerings such as Amazon Web Services, Facebook, and Google Apps.

Logic as a Service

The force.com platform makes it easy to automate a company's unique business processes and requirements. The workflow engine provides common, reusable process components such as task creation, record assignment, time-based actions, and even event-based system integration. With force.com, you can easily incorporate these components into your application's logic. For even greater flexibility, you can use APEX Code, salesforce.com's programming language, to extend your applications to include virtually any kind of business logic and functionality. Like a database-stored procedure, APEX can be used to create triggers that execute automatically in response to database operations. APEX can also access and invoke external web services. As an integral part of the force.com platform, APEX leverages the platform's multi-tenant architecture to ensure the scalability of any applications that run on it.

User Interface as a Service

force.com provides two options for creating and customizing the user interface of platform applications.

Through force.com's builder, a simple point-and-click/drag-and-drop interface lets you build and change the layout and the order of data fields on pages, rename and re-order tabs, create complex reports, and even create different views of the data for different users.

For more complete UI interface control, force.com includes Visualforce, a complete framework for creating and running virtually any UI, for any application, on any device. With Visualforce, developers can extend a cloud application's boundaries in almost any direction. Traditional web development technologies in conjunction with other force.com capabilities permit pixel-level control over the application's appearance and behavior.

force.com Sites allows you to harness Visualforce, which helps you transform current applications into public web sites and applications that run natively on the force.com platform, extending your reach to new users on intranets, external web sites, and online communities.

force.com Sites can reduce the cost and complexity of IT operations by securely and effortlessly building both internal and external-facing applications and web sites based on the same underlying database, without the need for separate systems and complicated integrations. For example, the same company database that manages products, customers, sales orders, and technical support requests on behalf of internal applications can also power the company's public web site with product catalogs, customer surveys, sales promotions, and knowledge bases. Data modifications such as price updates are immediately available to both internal and external users. There is no need for any type of data replication or transfer because the same centralized database serves the needs of both public and private applications.

---

force.com Sites

Visual Page Designer
- Point-and-click ease of pages
- Custom templates
- Pixel-perfect UI editor

Content Management
- Versioning
- Approvals
- Publishing

Widgets
- Out of the box CRM widgets
- Customizable UI
- Custom widget creation

Support for **mobile devices**

AppExchange

The force.com AppExchange is a marketplace connecting force.com commercial application developers with potential users. Customers or application providers wanting to share their applications can publish them on the AppExchange. Anyone who wants to use those applications can easily install them without any of the traditional software installation and configuration hassles. To date, over a thousand certified, reliable, secure, and interoperable applications are available via the AppExchange.

Security, Privacy and Trust[44]

To gain the trust of organizations, a cloud provider must deliver levels of security and privacy that meet or exceed what is achievable with on-premises solutions, including:

Security: a computing system's level of resistance to threats.

Privacy: protecting the digital collection, storage, and sharing of information and data, including transparency.

Trust: a reliably secure and private cloud computing system gives its users confidence in the system.

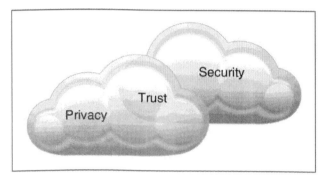

Salesforce.com's security and privacy infrastructure consists of many components. It includes a full staff of Certified Information Systems Security Professionals; a Global Privacy Counsel who is a Certified Information Privacy Professional (CIPP) with responsibility for helping to ensure compliance with global privacy laws; and regular internal and external vulnerability assessments.

---

[44] This section is adapted from the Salesforce.com 2010 white paper, "Secure, Private, and Trustworthy: Enterprise Cloud Computing with force.com."

Database Security

The force.com database, Database.com, has many layers of defense to resist various types of threats and achieve major security certifications like SAS 70 Type II.

At the operational layer, salesforce.com strictly manages access to its facilities and the work that operators can perform once inside a facility. Salesforce.com implements industry-accepted best practices to harden all underlying host computers that support the various software layers of the Database.com. The database protects customer passwords by storing them after applying high-level encryption.

Salesforce.com employs a number of sophisticated security tools that monitor system activity in real time to expose many types of malicious events, threats, and intrusion attempts.

Application Security

Application developers who design, build, and manage applications are provided with tools to ensure the ultimate security of the data their customers generate. Developers can implement security policies that govern exactly who, what, from where, when, and how users can access specific IT systems and data, along with related auditing requirements.

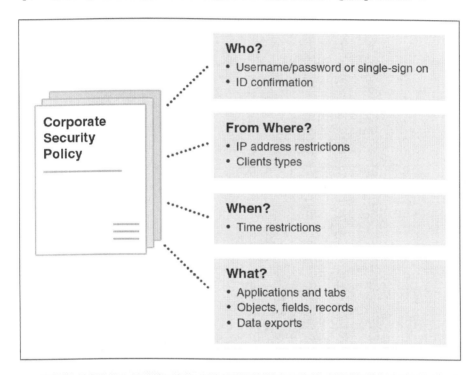

To enable users to do their jobs without exposing data they don't need to see, Database.com provides a flexible, layered sharing design that lets an organization expose specific application components and data sets to different sets of users.

This includes *user profiles,* which control the access users have by customizing profiles down to the field level; *sharing settings* that provide a baseline level of access for each object and let the organization extend that level of access using hierarchies or sharing rules; *sharing rules* that allow for exceptions to organization-wide default settings, and give additional users access to records they don't own; and a multitude of history-tracking and auditing features that provide valuable information about the use of an organization's applications and data, which in turn can be a critical tool in diagnosing potential or real security issues.

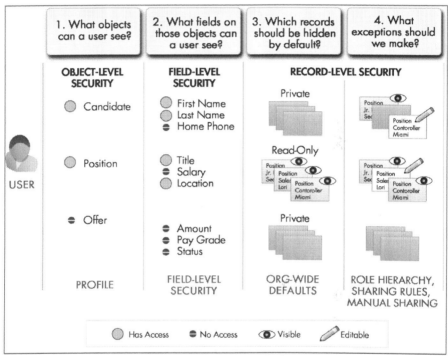

Figure 34: This chart shows how the force.com built-in database security works. (Source: *The force.com Fundamentals* workbook)

Database Privacy

Data privacy in the context of a cloud computing platform is somewhat unique in that the platform provider must address the privacy concerns of both its direct and indirect customers. For example, the data privacy of Database.com subscribers that build and deploy applications is just as important as the data privacy of end users who ultimately use those applications. Salesforce.com generally doesn't have a relationship with indirect customers, and therefore doesn't collect personal information on behalf of direct customers or determine how service providers use their data. Furthermore, salesforce.com's customer contracts generally prohibit salesforce.com from accessing or disclosing confidential customer data except under certain narrowly defined circumstances, such as when required by law.

And lastly, salesforce.com is transparent about security and privacy issues. Real-time system information is available at the company's "trust site" at http://trust.salesforce.com.

Summary

The force.com's substantial foundation consists of:

1. Infrastructure, including built-in redundancy, security, scalability, monitoring, and change management.

2. Multi-tenancy, so that only a single version of the software needs to be maintained, regardless of the number of users.

3. Metadata, so that platform changes can be made without impacting applications already written. Metadata also makes possible automatic enhancements to existing applications through advances in the platform.

4. An application framework, which takes care of the common functionality required by most business applications, such as security or database access.

5. Security, privacy and trust. These are safeguarded so that companies are comfortable entrusting their data to the platform.

With the foundation in place, the building blocks can be added next.

Building Blocks

We are at the beginning of a third wave in technology (the prior two were the commercialization of the microprocessor, followed 15 years later by the advent of the web), which is this convergence of mobile and social technologies made possible by the cloud. We will see the creation of multiple multi-billion-dollar businesses, and equally important, tens maybe hundreds of thousands of smaller companies. – John Doerr, Kleiner Perkins

According to Peter Sondergaard, SVP at Gartner and global head of research, the cloud, social, mobility and an explosion in information "are innovative and disruptive just taken on their own, but brought together, they are revolutionizing business and society. This nexus defines the next age of computing. To understand this change, you must appreciate each of the forces." force.com provides a set of building blocks that together form a powerful platform. The building blocks are designed to work together, each one enhancing the capability of the others, resulting in the whole being much greater than the sum of the parts.

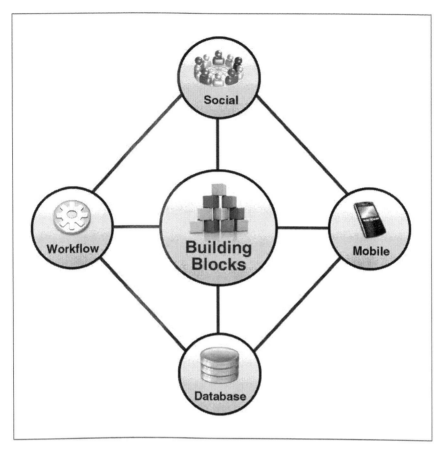

For example, the workflow building block can work directly with the database. Updates to the database can automatically be brought into the social conversation. Applications can be mobile-enabled without additional effort. There is no need to deal with different logins, different user interfaces, or integration when using any of the building blocks.

Not having to think about how to fit application building blocks together has enormous implications. It provides the user with a ready-to-go system, and eliminates the time and effort that would be necessary to construct solutions from disparate vendors working together.

For example, one of the building blocks is Chatter, which, with minimal effort, lets developers embed social networking functionality into an application. Chatter-enabled applications let end users collaborate privately and securely by "following" each other, data records, and groups, and by sharing files and status updates. Rather than building and maintaining all this complex logic yourself in your applications, you simply use Chatter when you want to integrate social functions into any of your applications.

Another building block integration example is mobile. The preferred user experience for a limited form factor device such as a smart phone or tablet is not forcing users to have to navigate complex user interfaces or type in search terms to find data of interest. Rather, it's letting users subscribe to data feeds of their choice and then pushing that data to the mobile app to consume the data in a meaningful way. To support this development pattern easily, mobile apps can leverage the integrated Chatter user, the record, and new feeds to publish information of interest to users (as indicated by their subscriptions).

An integrated set of building blocks is like a car in the sense that it's a complete unit of transportation. The user, of course, would rather buy a car than have to mix and match pieces of hardware to build her own car. Additionally, the superiority of an individual component – like a carburetor or transmission, in the case of a car – is of little use if the car doesn't have wheels or a dashboard. It takes many different working components to assemble a car, make it run, and keep it running, but a buyer doesn't need to know exactly what they are. They just have to be all there so the car can run and keep running over time. In the same way, having a fully integrated platform with all the building blocks needed to develop solutions is more important than relative power of the individual building blocks. Having one audio speaker is a lot better than having none – the difference between zero speakers and one speaker is infinitely greater than the difference between one speaker and twelve.

Most companies just need a small percentage of what's available for document management, the basic functions without the complexity. They need the equivalent of one speaker, and they wouldn't care about or maybe even hear the difference provided by twelve. The platform needs to provide at least one of each of the essentials to make the driving experience more of a pleasure and less of a chore.

An Example of Transformative Apps Combining Crowd, Cloud, Mobile, and Social

Traditionally, military intelligence was routed circuitously before it arrived at the places it would be most useful. According to *Forbes'* Roger Kay, one DARPA program manager who's working on "transformative apps" described conventional intelligence collection this way: When troops observed significant activity (perhaps persons thought to be harboring a wanted individual behaving suspiciously in their comings and goings at a secret compound), the troops would write up their findings, and then send it to their superiors. The higher-ups in the chain of command would determine the action that should be taken (should there be an airstrike, should ground troops be sent in?). Data and information moved up in the organization, not down, and the reporting soldiers might never be informed of the results of their intelligence.[45]

Things were different with the introduction of the Tactical Ground Reporting System (TIGR), a DARPA project deployed in Afghanistan and Iraq. TIGR is an advanced multimedia application that American soldiers use to plan patrols, file real-time reports, and stay connected on the ground. With many thousands of users, each of them evaluating and recording threats and opportunities, a crowd-based model of the front is rapidly disseminated via the soldiers' smart phones. The data from every image, sound, and video is time-stamped and geo-located, then sent to the cloud for rapid retrieval. Every soldier can know what every other one knows, along with where they are and what they are seeing and doing, completely innovating how replacement units enter a battlefield, while connecting elements previously unaware of one another. Only through those hand-held, connected devices can users, separated by space and function, collaborate on analysis and strategy. For example, the team approaching a target can watch the prisoner debriefing that yielded the

---

[45] Roger Kay, "Mobile, Social, Crowd, Cloud: Why These Concepts Matter," *Forbes*, October 19, 2011, http://finance.yahoo.com/news/Mobile-Social-Crowd-Cloud-Why-xfoftp-712286330.html

intelligence seconds before. The troops heading for a bridge can quickly redeploy when they see it's been blown up. Isolated reports are brought together to give a complex picture of what's happening in the field. General Peter Chiarelli, Vice Chief of Staff of the Army, put it this way: "Before, every soldier was a scout. Now every soldier is an intelligence asset."[46]

No one can deny that this new technology ensemble saves lives and wins battles. Combining mobile, social, crowd and cloud maximizes both responsiveness and effectiveness. It is easy to imagine comparable benefits for any business.

---

[46] Colin Clark, "Army Vice Touts TIGR: Success "in Spite of" System," DoD Buzz, Online Defense and Acquisition Journal, December 2, 2008, http://www.dodbuzz.com/2008/12/02/ army-vice-touts-tigr-success-in-spite-of-system/

Social

Many executives still do not understand the various uses of social media. Even worse, some think it is irrelevant to their business. This is a blind spot in the industrial world. – The New Digital Economy[47]

Just as the Internet changed the marketplace forever, the integration of social computing into enterprise design represents another enormous shift in the landscape. Organizations that successfully transform into a Social Business can potentially reap great benefits – among them the ability to deepen customer relationships, drive operational efficiencies and optimize the workforce... Increasingly, it is becoming clear that the traditional hierarchical enterprise, built on a structure of departments and a culture of compartmentalization, will give way to a socially synergistic enterprise built on continually evolving communities and a culture of sharing and innovation. – IBM, *The Social Business*

Enterprise social software is not merely another set of collaboration tools but **an emerging way to conduct business**.

The social building block is critical to situational solutions. Applications accommodate the need to automate tasks and replace human activity where possible, but solutions may need to be assembled or changed on the fly. Social software provides a way for the agents in the system to easily communicate with one another to reach that solution. This will increase operational efficiency and optimize the workforce.

The blind men are also deaf

This is like the parable of the blind men and the elephant, but this story assumes that these poor old guys are not only blind, they are also deaf. If

---

[47] *The New Digital Economy: How It Will Transform Business*, June 2011.

they weren't, as each individual announced his impressions of the elephant, the group would have discovered much more about what an elephant is.

The point is that the capabilities of the group emerge from the individuals who participate in it. The group can do more (see more, discover more, experiment more) than the individuals who are part of it. These individuals then benefit from the group, and in turn, these benefited individuals can contribute more to the group, which in turn …

Unstructured Communication

> *PCs are being replaced at the center of computing not by another type of device—though there's plenty of excitement about smart phones and tablets—but by new ideas about the role that computing can play in progress. These days, it's becoming clear that innovation flourishes best not on devices but in the social spaces between them, where people and ideas meet and interact. It is there that computing can have the most powerful impact on economy, society and people's lives.* – Mark Dean, Chief Technology Officer, *IBM Middle East and Africa*

Communication is a "messy" process – nonlinear, unpredictable, in-the-moment. By nature, people prefer to communicate in unstructured ways – holding discussions, debating issues, delegating tasks, seeking approval, solving problems, and changing rules. Things happen in the real world that can't possibly be anticipated by the system, especially because "the system" doesn't understand the vagaries of human thought. This is quite different from the world of enterprise systems aimed at efficiently automating transactions.

Self-organization

Information that flows openly through an organization often looks chaotic, but it is the nutrient of self-organization. As one utility chief executive aptly put it: "In our organization, information has gone from being the currency of exchange – we traded it for power and status – to being the medium of our organization. We can't live without it; everyone feeds off of it. It has to be everywhere in the organization to sustain us."[48]

Only when information belongs to everyone can people organize rapidly and effectively around shifts in customers, competitors, or environments. People need access to information that no one could have predicted they'd want to know. They themselves wouldn't have known they needed it until that very moment of need.

When information is available everywhere, different people see different things. Those with a strategic focus will see opportunities that others can't discern. Those on a production line will pick up on different information. There's a need for many more eyes and ears so that effective self-organization can occur. But it is information – unplanned, uncontrolled, abundant, and superfluous – that creates the conditions for the emergence of fast, well-integrated, effective responses.

In a social enterprise, teams can emerge from the people close to the problem, and are much more likely to be effective than if their group was imposed from higher up. In line with the observation that a complex adaptive system is inherently self-organizing, this is another example showing that order is an inherent property of the system – it does not need to be imposed from the outside.

Relationships

Relationships are the pathways to the intelligence of a system. Through relationships, information is created and transformed, an organization's identity expands to include more stakeholders, and the enterprise becomes wiser. The more access people have to one another, the more possibilities there are. Without connections, nothing happens. Organizations held at equilibrium by well-designed organization charts die. In self-organizing systems, people need access to everyone; they need to be free to reach anywhere in the organization to accomplish their work.

---

[48] Margaret J. Wheatley and Myron Kellner-Rogers, 1996

To respond with speed and effectiveness, people need access to the intelligence of the whole system. Who is available, what do they know, and how can they reach each other? People need opportunities to "bump up" against others in the system, making the unplanned connections that spawn new ventures or better integrated responses.

Where members of an organization have access to one another, the system expands to include more and more of them as stakeholders. It is astonishing to see how many of the behaviors we fear in one another dissipate in the presence of good relationships. Customers engaged in finding a solution become less insistent on perfection or detailed up-front specifications. Colleagues linked by a work project become more tolerant of one another's diverse lives. A community invited into a local chemical plant learns how a failure at the plant could create devastating environmental disasters, yet becomes more trusting of plant leadership.

The nature of knowledge

There are two basic types of knowledge: explicit and tacit. Explicit knowledge may be written down in FAQs, or stored in documents, and explicit knowledge is fine for dealing with similar requests that have relatively simple answers. Explicit knowledge is much less useful in business-critical situations that generate complicated discussions requiring a variety of expertise, with interactions that extend across multiple departments and possibly across multiple organizations. That's where tacit knowledge is imperative.

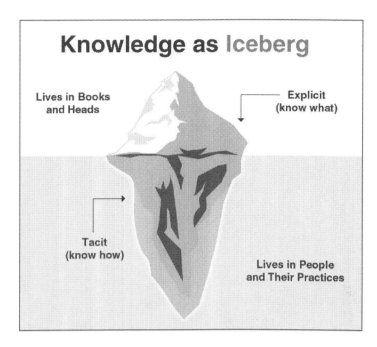

Figure 35: Explicit knowledge is just the tip of the iceberg. Finding a way to expose and harness tacit knowledge provides a critical edge.

Tacit knowledge is a treasure trove of intelligence gathered through experience. Relevant information that isn't written down but stored in a person's mind (such as the name of a key contacts assistant or the best way to deal with a difficult supplier), it remains largely untapped because it remains hidden. The difference between formal knowledge and tacit knowledge is the same as the difference between a clean, pristine, neatly organized (never opened) user manual, and a standard notebook that is highlighted, filled with scribbles, and annotated with notes and reminders. The latter is the type of knowledge you want to capture, so that the when a critical business situation occurs, knowledge workers can tap into time-saving relevant information to increase the quality of the resolution, and decrease the resolution time.

The importance of tacit knowledge is growing rapidly because all knowledge is time-sensitive – shelf life is limited because new technologies, products, services, regulations, etc., continually pour into the marketplace. Knowledge of yesterday's solutions "best practices" may not help with today's or tomorrow's problems. Rather than having explicit knowledge at your fingertips, it becomes much more important to know *who* knows something when you need to know it. In this environment, no one can hoard knowledge. People and organizations must constantly renew, replenish, expand, and create more knowledge.

This requires a radical overhaul of the old knowledge equation:

Knowledge = Power, so HOARD it.

The new knowledge equation is:

Knowledge = Power, so SHARE it.

Because change is so constant and so critical, without constant learning and sharing, today's guru will become tomorrow's loser.

We are fortunate that the pace of change has been matched by the speed at which people have become digitally connected.

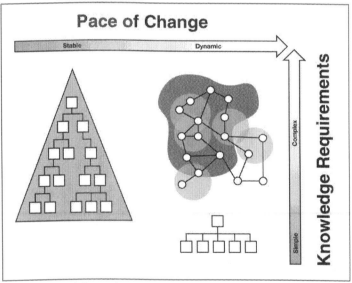

Figure 36: As the pace of change becomes more dynamic and knowledge requirements become more complex, the organizational structure and the tools to support it change dramatically. A command-and-control hierarchical structure is fine in a relatively stable environment, but a rapidly changing environment cannot afford to wait for information to traverse through the layers of the hierarchy.

The "Shadow" Organization

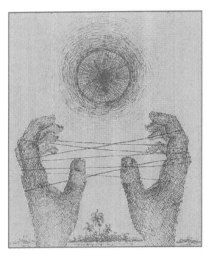

In *Cat's Cradle*, Kurt Vonnegut explains that the world is divided into two types of social organizations: the *karass* and the *granfalloon*. The karass is a spontaneously forming group joined by unpredictable links – that actually gets things done. A granfalloon, on the other hand, is a "false karass" – a bureaucratic structure that looks like a team but is meaningless in terms of the way things get done. Social software facilitates the formation of a karass wherever possible by providing the means for groups to form as needed to solve problems and take advantage of opportunities as they arise.

Challenges

An organization's data is found in its computer systems, but a company's intelligence is found in its biological and social systems. – Valdis Krebs

Some of the factors driving the social enterprise include:

201

Information Overload

It's now impossible to stay on top of everything. As a result, it's easy to miss crucial information, such as a new product update, or a requested delay for an order shipment when a critical customer update is missed.

Email

The problem with email is that the information it spawns is lost, buried, or out of context in the bowels of the email system. For example, an email exchange about a project may not be tied directly to the project, making any information the email contains difficult to find or reuse for similar projects.

Millennials

Steeped in a social culture of sharing and transparency, Millennials are entering the workforce in earnest. It's second nature to them to communicate their status, provide updates, and get feedback on their activities. They need the same types of tools in the enterprise as they use in their personal lives.

Geographic Distribution and Virtual Teams

As employees are dispersed across time and place, there is a growing need to work directly with suppliers, partners, and temporary workers, making communication, collaboration, and socialization tools that are online 24x7 critical. These tools, seamlessly deployed across all mobile devices, integrated into existing applications, and into the fabric of business culture, make a distributed workforce more productive.

The force.com Solution: Chatter

The killer apps of tomorrow will not be hardware or software, but social practices. Howard Rheingold, *Smart Mobs: The Next Social Revolution*

The force.com social building block is called Chatter. Chatter allows a person to tap into the collective brain power of co-workers immediately, find expertise and advice, make announcements that carry far across the organization, and get live feedback on planning and concepts. Chatter brings Facebook-like collaboration features and Twitter-style real-time status updates to the enterprise. For example, instead of having to log in to a system and run reports to get information, users can "follow" leads, opportunities, customers, projects, and people that are most important to them, and have the most relevant information brought to them.

Chatter is designed to bridge the gap between enterprise applications and the way people work. It does this by facilitating dynamic, informal, and shared communication across an expanding group of individuals.

Chatter is built into force.com at every level: any application built on force.com is automatically Chatter-enabled. This is another illustration of the power of being on the platform – as soon as Chatter came to life, any application that was already on the platform became Chatter-enabled.

Chatter is part of a broader social solution for enterprises that encompasses everything from what customers are doing on public social networks (Jigsaw/Data.com) to making internal processes social (Chatter/force.com) to listening (Radian6) and engaging with customers on public social networks (Heroku) to making one's own products social (force.com/Heroku).

System of record applications take part in the conversation

The breakthrough idea of Chatter is to allow system of record applications to participate in the discussion. This includes integration with enterprise systems utilized across a whole company, including transactions from custom systems and applications like Workday, Salesforce.com CRM, SAP, Oracle Expenses, and Microsoft SharePoint.

You and your colleagues can "chatter" just like you would on Facebook, sparking conversations and discussions with other colleagues. Your business applications can also "chatter." You can "follow" the parts of your business – people, projects, customers and financials – that are most important to you. When a part of your business changes, it can tell you... it can "chatter" about it in real-time by sending out a status update. With Chatter, you can instantly see important changes in your business and collaborate with the right people to take corrective action.

Imagine you're following an important implementation project. If one of the dependencies falters, you'll see that dependency "chatter" about the problem in your feed, along with your co-workers' chatter explaining what's wrong and what can be done to fix it. As soon as action is taken and the implementation plan is updated again, that will appear in your chatter feed as well – in stark contrast to waiting for a weekly status report, emailing the person responsible, and waiting for an update after corrective action is taken. Friction in communication is reduced, brings data and discussion come together, and an historical record is captured, which your company can learn from.

Bi-directional conversations provide work in context

Workers can close the loop on key business processes in their applications without leaving the context of their Chatter activity stream.

For example: a business process requires an approval. The request for approval surfaces in the appropriate person's Chatter stream. The worker can drill down to see all relevant information including any discussions that have taken place, and then click a button to approve or reject the request without leaving their Chatter stream. In this way, Chatter helps workers close the loop on business processes using social computing. The ability to stay in the context helps workers get their work done.

Reduce time to resolve issues

Chatter can be linked to business performance improvement. For example, time-to-issue-resolution is reduced because Chatter quickly cuts across departmental lines and brings together the relevant people to solve a problem, without having to wait for email. With Chatter, you can find out if someone is on line anywhere in the world, using any kind of device. This approach shifts the focus from the static content in an email to the source of the energy, creativity, and decision making that move a business forward: people. In a social business, people not only find what they need, but also discover valuable expertise and information they weren't even looking for, to solve problems in entirely new ways.

Features of Chatter

Chatter includes some unique capabilities:

1. **Chatter Social Graph** is built directly into the database. This makes it easy to follow user and data relationships.

2. **Chatter Security** ensures that any data you don't have explicit access to won't show up in your Chatter feed.

3. **Chatter Components** can be created by any developer and added to Chatter using point-and-click.

4. **Chatter Filtering** provides the ability to filter the activity stream as necessary.

5. **Chatter Integration** allows users to execute business processes from within the activity stream without having to toggle away to the application in question. It also allows users to upload a document to the activity stream and associate it with a particular activity.

6. **Chatter Live Collaboration** allows workers to shift from asynchronous communications to live ones. To facilitate

collaboration in real time, Chatter allows users to launch a video conference, instant message chat, or desktop share with colleagues, customers, and partners. Employees can leverage all these tools, as well as access playback recordings, right within the context of their relevant Chatter activity streams. This enables the type of impromptu collaborations that take place in real life, and ensures the collaborative conversation generated happens immediately, when it's fresh and relevant.

7. **Chatter Social Customer Profiles** allow companies to know what customers "like" on Facebook, what they're saying on Twitter, whom they are connected to on LinkedIn, and more. The social customer profile captures all of this publicly available information, empowering every employee to delight customers by knowing who they are and delivering the entirely new level of service possible in today's social world.

8. **Chatter Employee Social Networks** allow companies to connect their employees with the best information and experts within their own company. Similar to Facebook, employee social networks deliver information directly to users, rather than making users search for it themselves. This helps people at work rapidly collaborate across their company so they can engage, sell, and service their customers more effectively.

9. **Chatter Customer Social Networks and Product Social Networks** allow companies to build stronger relationships with their customers in an entirely new way on today's most popular social channels like Facebook and Twitter. With Salesforce Radian6, Heroku, and Database.com, companies can listen to, engage with, and analyze what people are saying about them and create apps so that customers can interact with their brands. These apps leverage cutting-edge social and mobile technology, can be location-aware, and can be accessed on any device. Companies can also bring their products into social networks so they can be part of the conversation, allowing consumers to not just "fan" a product, but become its "friend."

10. **Chatter Now** delivers real-time collaboration by enabling users to see when their colleagues are online, instantly chat with them in context and share their screen without leaving Chatter.

11. **Chatter Customer Groups** allow Chatter users to invite people outside of their organization into their Chatter network to collaborate. Chatter users can invite customers and partners to collaborate in private, secure groups, which will extend enterprise collaboration beyond the four walls of a company.

12. **Chatter Approvals** allow users to take action on any approval process from directly within their Chatter feed. Sales discounts, hiring decisions, vacation requests and more can all be approved without having to leave Chatter. Approval processes will have context, including comments and documents, helping to increase productivity, and helping users make informed decisions.

13. **Chatter Service** allows customers to ask questions in a familiar social feed and have the answer come to them in an instant – whether it's from the knowledge base, the community of experts, or a service agent. Chatter Service connects to public social networks such as Facebook, extending the community far beyond the boundaries of a traditional self-service portal.

14. **Chatter Mobile** allows companies and employees to connect socially through mobile devices. Touch.salesforce.com delivers an optimized experience of Salesforce apps and customizations for touch devices. Leveraging the open standard HTML5 technology, touch.salesforce.com will allow users to access salesforce.com from the most popular smart phones, tablet devices, and operating systems.

15. **Chatter Connect** makes other applications social by extending Chatter to custom and third-party applications. The Chatter REST API makes it easy for developers to integrate Chatter into other applications such as intranets and portals, custom mobile apps, and other enterprise apps. In addition, Chatter for SharePoint allows companies to make

SharePoint social. Companies will be able to embed Chatter feeds in a Sharepoint MySite or TeamSite and share documents from Sharepoint to Chatter.

Benefits

> *When we dream alone, it's just a dream. But when we dream together, it's the beginning of a new reality.* – Brazilian proverb

> *Social software reflects the "juice" that arises from people's personal interactions. It's not about control, it's about co-evolution: people in personal contact, interacting towards their own ends, influencing each other. But there isn't a single, clearly defined project, per se. It's a sprawling, tentacled world, where social dealings are inductive, going from individual, to a group, to many groups, and finally to the universe.* – Stowe Boyd, *Darwin Magazine,* May 2003

The focus is no longer on project plans, documents, and other temporary artifacts. Chatter rightfully shifts the focus to people: the source of the energy, creativity, and decision making that moves the business forward.

Creative problem solving

Chatter connects people to expertise. It enables individuals – customers, partners or employees – to form networks to generate new sources of innovation, foster creativity, and establish greater reach and exposure to new business opportunities. It establishes a foundational level of trust across these business networks and, thus, a willingness to openly share information. It empowers these networks with the collaborative and analytical tools members need to engage each other and creatively solve business challenges.

Transparency

Chatter removes unnecessary boundaries between experts inside the company and experts in the marketplace. It can capture knowledge and insight from many sources, and quickly sense changes in customer mood, employee sentiment, or process efficiencies. It utilizes analytics and social connections inside and outside the company to solve business problems and capture new business opportunities.

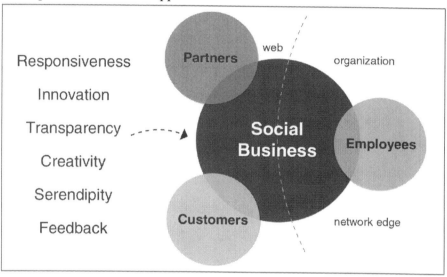

Figure 39: The social network brings together all the parties into an environment beyond the edge of the organization that facilitates responsiveness, innovation, etc. This is where "magic" happens.

Agility

Chatter can speed business up by providing real-time insight to enable quicker and better decisions. Ubiquitous access through mobile devices turns time and location from constraints into advantages. Business is free to occur when and where it delivers the greatest value, allowing the organization to adapt quickly to the changing marketplace.

Respond more efficiently to changing demands

Chatter provides the platform for scaling and amplifying connections and tapping into the knowledge flows within a company. This increases the knowledge of participants and results in sustained performance improvement to better meet customer needs.

Tap tacit knowledge

Chatter provides the ability to find, learn about, and connect with the right people, information, and other resources to address unanticipated needs, helping to tap the tacit knowledge available from people who may be scattered across departments and geographies. No organizational chart or directory is going to help you find the tacit knowledge you need.[49]

Capture informal conversations

Chatter allows a user to reach out to a large number of relevant participants and bring them into a virtual discussion around a specific problem or challenge, so tacit knowledge is shared and new knowledge is created. Social software also captures these informal conversations, and makes them searchable.

Amplify connections, increase serendipity

Chatter facilitates drawing out relevant people and resources – even some we're not aware of needing. We often don't know who or what will be valuable to our endeavors, or what to look for, but when we find it – that's called "serendipity." In the social context it means finding people and the knowledge they carry with them. The more Chatter is used in the organization, the more it becomes a platform for increasing serendipity. Users have more interactions and generate more detailed profiles of themselves as a by-product of their interactions – both their explicit

---

[49] John Hagel III and John Seely Brown, "The Enterprise Value of Social Software," *Harvard Business Review Blog Network*, September 30, 2010

knowledge and their expertise are exposed to others who need them but were not looking for them.[50]

Achieve sustained performance improvement

Chatter facilitates the blossoming of one-off interactions into long-term collaborative relationships that allow participants to tap into and create tacit knowledge. Companies won't be able to achieve sustained and extreme performance just by connecting workers to resources more efficiently in one-off situations. The real value comes when the one-off interactions develop into relationships and the relationships begin to facilitate sustained collaboration.

Facilitate innovation

Chatter provides a rapid feedback cycle, allowing teams to quickly bring diverse ideas together, develop innovations that improve products and processes, quickly spread them across the enterprise, and get immediate feedback. Ideas can be discovered, refined, expanded on, and turned into valuable products and services much more quickly.

Chatter facilitates the rapid formation of small focused teams to solve problems and innovate, unimpeded by organizational boundaries.

Reduce email

Email is a submerged, barely accessible content repository. Chatter provides a way to unlock information, contribute ideas, and find answers in near real time.

---

[50] ibid.

Shift from formal to informal learning

Chatter encourages just-in-time learning, allowing workers to leverage transparency. Workers are more likely to view unexpected challenges as positive opportunities for learning or problem solving if they feel they can quickly and easily reach out to find people who can help them in their quest.

Acquisition of knowledge in a fast-paced, complex world becomes less important than the ability to search, create, and manipulate information to generate knowledge on demand and just-in-time learning. The best way to conceive of this is to recall the movie *The Matrix,* in which revolutionaries trying to free an enslaved human race are hard-wired for data downloads. When in need, characters bark out their knowledge needs to colleagues who download the appropriate information – from driving directions to kung fu expertise – into disk drives connected to the recipient's brain.

Improve communication and responsiveness

You can accelerate and improve communication by facilitating direct, unfiltered, unmediated dialog within the organization, with suppliers and with customers and prospects. Improving the organization's responsiveness enhances reputation and prospects.

Reduce re-work

If you really want to avoid reinventing the wheel, the solution is not to build a warehouse of everything you ever knew about every wheel you ever invented.... You want to connect questions to answers or to people who can help you find the answers. – Thomas Stewart

In a study that analyzed where knowledge workers spent most of their time, Kit Sims Taylor found that creating what others have probably already created takes up a significant portion of the knowledge workers' day. Originality does not exclude the likelihood that someone else has had the same thought, used the same words, even put ideas together in the same way. Today, this makes little difference in the way we work because it's too difficult to leverage what others have done or thought, so we produce it ourselves. Chatter will allow workers to look up and borrow an idea that was already invented by a colleague for a similar product or project.

Capture content where it's created

We are all notoriously bad at documenting our knowledge. Usually there is just not enough time in the day, and even if we did find the time to create documentation, it would probably be too hard for others to find. So the answer is to capture content as it is created, through Chatter. Knowledge workers generate knowledge "packets" all the time – via Chatter correspondence with co-workers and business associates, via instant messenger with many of the same people, through presentations, documents, and recommendations, and with posts to Chatter groups. If the organization captured this content at the same time it was being created, rather than requiring extra software or numerous steps to publish it to a knowledge management system, the chances of that content being saved in an easily searchable way would greatly increase. For example, Chatter between two technical support reps outlining a fix to a common problem will automatically be available to any other technician who may be dealing with a similar problem. This technician doesn't have to know where to look or who to contact – the information will be easily found in the Chatter feed. Now that *fix*, that knowledge, is stored in a centralized location, and available to everyone else in the group.

Improve exception handling

Without Chatter, a customer calls with an issue that doesn't fit neatly into the categories of issues previously addressed, and a significant amount of time is wasted trying to identify the correct people required to help find an answer or determine whether an unusual request should be approved. In those situations, workers lack a single source of trusted answers to common questions and have difficulty finding the appropriate people to get involved in developing an answer. Similar problems occur repeatedly because the interactions with the customer and relevant functions are never formally documented. Chatter drives real value for the enterprise with exception handling.

Empower the socially inept

> No longer will you need to be charismatic, crazed or a hustler to connect with thousands of people. – Stowe Boyd, comment on blog

Social software provides a platform for those people whose social skills prevent them in one or more ways from contributing as much as they could to the informal intellectual capital of the organization.

There are many very smart people out there who have great trouble with social interaction. But their ability to communicate is greatly enhanced in indirect social situations – instant messaging, blogging, etc. What they would never bring themselves to express directly, they will have no problem doing when they're not face-to-face with others. In this way, they can increase their contributions to others without having to change their basic socially introverted nature.

The least socially adept people are often the ones with the most to contribute. Since they are not likely to congregate around the water cooler to share their knowledge, social software increases their contributions to the knowledge of the organization.

Use Chatter to drive production

Instead of using social software just to supplement "production" software (the world of automated transactions), we can use it to drive production.

For example, a buyer and supplier can start up a chat session in Chatter, and during that session create a process that consists of online forms to be completed and approved by several people in each organization. They can agree to the rules and terms right in the chat session – and everything is logged and available for future analysis and review. And during that session, the user could have access to any information that may be contextually relevant, such as knowledge about previous dealings with this particular supplier.

In this way, Chatter has the potential to completely reinvent the customer relationship, to one that is much more in-depth, seamless, and highly integrated. It gives the customer the ability to tap into the full resources of the service/product-providing firm and its supply chain.

In general

- Employees are more visible inside and outside the organization.

- Customers are more engaged through community participation, contributing content, and providing product feedback.

- Partners are more invested through increased recognition, support, and skill development.

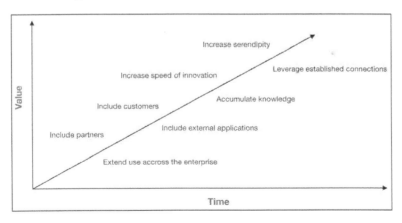

Figure 40: The value of social networking in the organization rapidly increases over time.

A SOCIAL Revolution

Marc Benioff, the founder of Salesforce.com, describes the social enterprise using a suitable acronym.[51]

S is for speed. Everything is now happening faster.

O is for open. If you don't have an open environment inside your company, these new tools will blow you wide open.

C is for collaboration. Social software enables people to organize themselves within companies and societies into loosely coupled teams to take on any kind of challenges – from designing a new product to taking down a government.

I is for individuals. Individuals are able to reach around the globe to start something or collaborate on something farther, faster, deeper, and cheaper than ever before – as individuals.

A is for alignment. The power of social media is that it is easier than ever to both articulate and reinforce the vision and values that create and inspire alignment.

L is for the leadership that does that. Leadership in a SOCIAL world has to be a mix of bottom-up and top-down. Leaders need to inspire, enable and empower everything coming up from below in a company or a social movement and then edit and sculpt it with a vision from above into a final product.

---

[51] Thomas L. Friedman, "One Country, Two Revolutions," *New York Times*, October 22, 2011

Mobile

The explosive growth of mobile telephony will open a huge market opportunity for companies in the years ahead. This is especially true in emerging markets, where the smart phone will allow many to move straight to the mobile Internet just as the cell phone leapfrogged fixed-line telephone connections. Remember these mobile digital consumers will in many cases be inaccessible through traditional, PC-based web environments.

This is not merely about creating a new app. Mobile marketing opens up an important revenue channel and helps firms penetrate a new set of emerging market customers...Mobility even promises new ways to connect to the physical world.[52]

The new generation of mobile devices is radically changing the way we access and use information. Location-aware, always-on and highly interactive, these devices are on track to replace the desktop as the default information source.

According to Gartner, by 2014, the number of mobile systems will exceed the number of PC-based systems.

"That's incredible change, not only for individuals. It requires IT to re-imagine the way it provides applications," says Gartner's Peter Sondergaard.

By 2014, private app stores will be deployed by 60 percent of IT organizations. The applications themselves will be redesigned – they will become context-enabled, understanding the user's intent automatically. Mobile computing is not just the desktop on a handheld device.

---

[52] *The New Digital Economy: How It Will Transform Business*, June 2011

The future of mobile computing is context-aware computing.

It is therefore imperative that every application has a mobile component.

Mobility has the ability to deliver reliable returns to business. Enterprise mobility can improve an organization's productivity, optimize logistics operations, enhance customer relationships, and streamline supply chain management. Mobile will have an enormous impact on the enterprise in ways we cannot yet imagine.

The value of mobility soars, however, when the mobile app transcends the boundaries of the enterprise to provide a user experience that combines real-time interaction with relevant, accurate, and timely information. This accelerates business processes, which impacts sales cycles and service response times; and it integrates social networking and location-based technologies to build a real feeling of being connected and empowered.

Mobile solutions make the best of what you already have. Investments in enterprise CRM and ERP systems, even legacy systems built in-house, can be leveraged – even reinvigorated – by simply mobilizing them and extending key business information to employees.

In addition to enhancing existing processes, mobile technology can drive innovation and can make current business processes more flexible, dynamic, and efficient. Indeed, mobility can introduce new business processes altogether and obviate the need for antiquated ones. With mobility, organizations can instantaneously personalize specific services used by customers, vendors, and employees, who can be individually identified and located through their mobile devices. Instead of forcing users to scroll through screen after screen, organizations can customize services to meet the different needs of different end users at different times. This power of mobile extends way beyond simply taking existing screens and putting them on a mobile device.

The Power of Composite Mobile Applications

Business value increases exponentially when companies implement mobility strategically across an entire organization, rather than as a one-off or point solution. The potential of mobile will be realized in a composite fashion because mobile applications will integrate multiple enterprise systems, legacy systems, and third-party content with inherent device capabilities (camera, phone, GPS) and unified communication (UC) technologies such as presence (knowing if someone is online and willing to communicate) and instant messaging (IM). Mobility brings everything together in a meaningful, relevant way and enables employees to work smarter and faster than ever before.

Mobile can have an explosive impact with context-aware composite applications and composite transactions, based on the notion that one mobile action can spawn myriad business reactions — yielding returns exponentially higher than the initial mobile investment.

For example:

1. A technician does an inspection of a building. The technician starts up an inspection application. There is no need to type in or select the building, since the application already knows where the technician is.

2. The technician walks around the building, using her iPhone to answer questions regarding each aspect of the building – heating, loading dock, mold, etc. She takes a photo with the phone to record the element they are answering.

3. The system automatically triggers a notification to the appropriate vendor to take care of any problems found, sending along all the information recorded, including the relevant photo.

4. If replacement equipment is needed, a purchase order is created and a notification is sent to the purchasing department.

5. At the end of the inspection, a list of outstanding problems is sent to the support desk for follow-up.

6. Once the inspection is complete (e.g., all questions have been answered), a notification is sent to the technician's manager for approval of the report. It's immediate, without any additional effort on the part of the technician or anyone else.

Challenges

Going mobile is complex, with challenges that include:

- **Time to market**: there's a need to quickly build and deploy mobile apps to keep up with ever-changing device technology and user trends.

- **Ease of deployment**: apps must be easily published and distributed, with flexibility and tight control.

- **Reliability**: can mobile apps be run with minimal disruption for all users and guarantee transactions in an occasionally connected environment, dealing with multiple potential security points-of-failure.

- **Scalability**: extending mobile apps to millions of users and transactions across the globe.

- **Support**: optimizing operations and mobile app usage.

- **Cost of ownership**: the burden on internal IT resources needs to be reduced and costs shifted to more strategic objectives.

- **Data feeds**: extracting data from a heterogeneous backend environment.

- **Performance**: optimizing application responsiveness and managing network latency.

The force.com Solution

force.com provides a set of services that shield the complexities of mobility from the enterprise, enabling developers to focus on quickly and easily delivering transformational mobile apps to customers, employees, and partners.

force.com brings together myriad disparate devices and back-end systems into a unified platform that is simple and manageable for customers. It enables companies to standardize on a common framework to ensure rapid deployment, consistent quality, and end-to-end security. On this platform enterprises can design, build, deploy, and manage their mobile applications across multiple organizations within a company.

force.com functionality includes:

- **Complete customization**. Users see only what they need to see.

- **Disconnected access**. Information is available on your device with or without network coverage.

- **Over-the-air management**. Users never have to plug in to update administrative information or receive automatic updates.

- **Centralized administration**. Manage users, applications, and devices from a central console.

- **One platform**. Develop and run mobile and desktop apps on a single on-demand platform.

- **Security and reliability**. force.com infrastructure gives you the best service delivery in the on-demand market.

- **Support for the leading devices**. Use Salesforce Mobile on BlackBerry, iPhone, and Android devices.

- **Support for Chatter collaboration:**

  - Receive updates about your groups, and the people and records you follow.

  - View and create posts and comments.

  - Post photos from your device.

221

- Find and follow people in your organization.

- Find and join groups in your organization.

- View your coworkers' profiles to see their contact information, bios, who they're following, and who's following them.

- Email, call, or text people directly from their Chatter profiles on devices with telephony.

Multiple Implementation Strategies

force.com supports both native mobile apps and browser-based mobile apps.

Mobile Web Applications

Mobile applications that run on a web server are accessed via the device's web browser using an Internet connection. These are not regular web sites, but rather purpose-built mobile applications that, when done right, provide the look and feel of native apps but require Internet connection to execute.

Mobile web applications provide the quickest way to get started with mobile. When compared with native apps, a mobile web app offers some very strong benefits:

- It isn't a whole new technology. If you're already doing web, the jump to mobile is much smaller than having to learn native. New devices deal very well with the most recent web standards such as HTML5 and CSS3. These standards are very powerful and can be used to build apps that provide a great user experience.

- You don't need to install the apps on users' devices: You just need to publish your app to the web server and you're done. There's no need to force all your users to install a new app, and when you release new versions, everyone stays up-to-date automatically.

- Because mobile web applications are based on standards, what you build once runs on a lot of devices. If you go native, however, you need to build and maintain different versions of your app for each device you plan to support.

- With mobile web apps, you get to be agile. Conversely, in order to publish your native app to the app store, you need to go through an approval process. The extra step means you can't deliver new versions of the app as quickly and often as you want, and you cannot be truly agile. With mobile web applications, all you have to do is publish to a central server and it is immediately available to all your users. There is no extra step preventing you from being agile.

This is what force.com provides out of the box, without any additional development needed.

Native Applications

These are mobile applications that you install on your device via an app store. Usually these apps provide a very rich user experience because they're built specifically for a particular device's hardware. On the downside, for each device you plan to support, you'll need to build a specific version of your app using a toolkit specific to the device.

	Mobile Web Apps	Mobile Native Apps
In general	Easily written in HTML5, CSS3 and published to a web server	App is downloaded to the device; syndicated through stores; uses the device OS
Cross-platform compatibility	One mobile app for many operating systems	An app OS needed for every targeted operating system
Syndication	Through web site or emailed link; one source to get the app	App store or marketplace search; app needs to be made available in multiple OS to support cross-platform syndication
Functionality	Can do most of what a native app can do; available in offline mode	Can use the OS API to enhance functionality (camera, GPS, etc.)
User interface	Look and feel not quite as good as native	Cleaner look and feel
Monetization	In app purchases; can monetize traffic	Sold in marketplaces; expensive to create for each OS
Development resources	Requires HTML, CSS and JavaScript, which are basic development tools	Requires specific knowledge of each OS

Hybrid Applications

Hybrid applications provide the advantages of both native and mobile web applications. This is achieved by building a very thin native shell around a mobile web application, and extending the mobile web application with capabilities that only native applications can access. By using this technology you can put your application in the app store, and you can use extended features of the phone such as the camera or gyroscope. You'll still need to build a specific version of this thin native shell for each supported device.

A Better Way: Touch

force.com recently announced a new technology designed specifically to work on touch screens. Using the open standard HTML5 technology, it allows you to access force.com from virtually any smart phone or tablet. Any customizations and recently accessed items travel seamlessly among all of your mobile devices, whether it's your laptop, smart phone or tablet. Touch brings many of the advantages of native applications, without the need to develop separate apps for each operating system.

What is HTML5, and why should you care?

HTML5 is the fifth generation of HyperText Markup Language, which is the coding language used to create web pages.

HTML5 promises to provide a standard way to build applications for any device on any platform supporting a browser, regardless of its shape or size.

This will radically change how mobile applications (actually, *any* application) will be built in the future. It will also be the pathway to much better tools for citizen developers.

force.com has fully embraced HTML5, and a new product called Salesforce Touch will be available in 2012.

Some of the many features of HTML5 include:

- **Offline capabilities** that let users interact with web apps even when they don't have an Internet connection.

- **Drag-and-drop capabilities** that allow (for example) the ability to instantly attach a file to an email message by simply dragging the file from the user's desktop computer into the browser window.

- **Richer user interface.** Web pages no longer need to look (and act) like traditional web pages. They can now look more like desktop applications. HTML5 replaces the need for Flash web pages.

- **Easy video.** Video and audio are easily added to a web page.

- **Content mashup.** Web pages no longer need to represent only one person's or one organization's content.

- **Display across different device types.** Web pages can function intelligently and easily across display devices. What works on a desktop browser will work on a phone.

- **Semantic tagging.** HTML5 introduces new tags intended to give semantic meaning to content. This will enable a human reader, and eventually a machine reader, to give context to the information in a page.

- **Validations.** Several new input elements (e.g., email, URL, number, range) all perform validation without the need for custom code.

Benefits of force.com mobile

> *Mobility forces us to think of new ways to approach the market, customers and our channel. The technology really enables new ways of operating. It allows us to think in new ways about different business models and about how to approach the customer.* - Bill Blausey, *Senior VP and CIO of Eaton Corporation*[53]

Time to market

force.com provides the ability to quickly build and deploy mobile apps to adapt to ever-changing device technology and user needs.

In this era of mobility, speed is crucial. Manufacturers are churning out new and more powerful devices faster and faster. While this is great for end users, for enterprises and developers the fragmentation becomes a nightmare to manage. The days of writing an app for one or two devices

---

[53] The Impact of Technology Mega-Trends on Corporate IT and Business Models, Glassmeyer/McNamee Center for Digital Strategies, Tuck School of Business at Dartmouth. 2012

and expecting it to last for three to five years are over – the shelf life of mobile apps these days gets shorter and shorter. Each platform also has its own versions and form factors (e.g., smart phone vs. tablets) that developers must contend with; and new OS's and devices are coming out faster than ever. Furthermore, developers not only have to worry about the various native device operating systems, but different types of device-side technologies such as HTML5, mobile web, and SMS-based apps.

force.com ensures your mobile solutions are "future-proofed" as the device landscape continues to change.

Ease of deployment

force.com provides the ability to easily publish and distribute mobile apps with greater flexibility and tighter control.

force.com allows companies to easily publish role-based apps to their customers, employees and partners.

Reliability

force.com provides the ability to run mobile apps with minimal service disruption for all users.

Mobility is all about getting data from point A to point B, and the main challenge lies in the nebulous middle area. The two end points are known (e.g., a backend host system and a smart phone device), but the in-between contains many unknowns, such as speed of connections, bandwidth, communications protocols, availability of networks, load balancing, and redundancy.

force.com makes mobile apps more reliable because all the idiosyncrasies of mobility are seamlessly processed and managed within a unified technology stack, rather than passing through an array of systems and data centers. Enterprises can simply plug into force.com to ensure that their apps have the greatest reliability and availability.

Scalability

force.com provides the ability to extend mobile apps to millions of users and transactions across the globe.

The mobile user population is vast, and continues to grow at a rapid pace. Any enterprise contemplating a mobile strategy has to think big.

Enterprises can leverage force.com to smoothly expand their mobile app roll-outs and deal with unexpected spikes in usage. Companies can easily add (or even subtract) users from the deployment without having to worry about the ramifications on the internal IT environment and resources. Moreover, force.com is built with overhead to accommodate spikes in transaction volumes and mobile app activity, so that any surge in the popularity or usage of an app can be handled without disruptions to service.

Database[54]

Reliable data must be available as a service somewhere for applications to pick it up. The database is where data is stored, combined in different ways, scrubbed, and made available to any kind of applications – mobile, the browser, and other applications consuming data.

Database technology is the persistence layer at the heart of all data-centric applications, the tier of software that's in charge of organizing, protecting, and managing shared database access reliably, securely, and efficiently.

In a just-in-time world, users can't wait around for the Database Administrator (DBA) to create a new database, find and clean the needed data, or add a field to an existing data object. The new social, workflow, and mobile applications need to have the right data quickly and easily accessible.

To address this, every organization needs **a way to enable broad and timely self-service access to business-critical information**. Organizations need unified methodologies for collecting, aggregating, matching, consolidating, quality-assuring, persisting, and distributing such data throughout an organization in order to ensure consistency and control over the use of that information. Critical business decisions are made based on such data, so having a single database of reliable information that can be used to build situational applications throughout the company is an essential building block. Ideally, every user should be able to go to one place for a holistic view of all the data they need to do their job.

To facilitate this, force.com provides a cloud database service called Database.com. Database.com can provide accurate and reliable database information on demand, and is management-free, automatically tuned and optimized, and highly scalable.

---

[54] This section is adapted from the Salesforce.com white paper, "The future of database technology is in the clouds."

Challenges

Database.com addresses many of the challenges faced by organizations today. Here are some of them:

1. On-premises database systems are difficult and time-consuming to manage, and complicated to configure and maintain. There are also different types of databases for each level of the organization: MS Access for desktop databases, MySQL for departmental databases and Oracle for enterprise databases. Expertise is needed for each layer.

2. On-premises database systems don't scale easily. They're not designed to automatically scale their workload elastically in response to varying demands at a moment's notice.

3. On-premises database systems aren't multi-tenant. They're inherently single-tenant systems, which require the set-up and management of multiple databases, sometimes for each application.

4. Most organizations have numerous databases spread around the organization, all of which must be managed, upgraded, and integrated. There is usually a great deal of overlap, with the same data being stored in multiple places. Building applications and reports across multiple databases is difficult and time-consuming.

5. Security and disaster recovery for desktop databases like MS Access are usually non-existent.

6. There is no single version of the truth. For example, there are likely to be multiple customer master files being used in desktop, departmental, and enterprise applications.

7. Data is often incomplete, missing, duplicated, or inaccurate. This makes many business processes inefficient, ineffective, and costly, increasing organizational risk.

The force.com Solution: Database.com

Database.com is a proven cloud database solution you can use to support the persistence needs for your apps. Following are some of the key features of Database.com:

- Database.com powers all of salesforce.com's products. It serves over 100,000 organizations and handles billions of transactions, all with an average request response time of less than 300ms and an average up-time of 99.9+ percent over many years.

- Database.com is built with the security and privacy of customer information in mind. Salesforce.com's infrastructure and corporate workplace meet all of the highest industry standards, including SAS 70 Type II, SysTrust, and ISO 27001 certifications.

- Database.com users, profiles, roles, groups, and row-level sharing rules help you build secure apps without the need to code, test, and maintain your own complicated security logic.

- With Database.com, it's easy to implement common application functionality without writing complicated and error-prone code. Features include declarative point-and-click configuration for workflows, encrypted/masked fields, validation rules, formula fields, roll-up summary fields, and cross-object validation rules.

- Database.com is "social" because it includes the Salesforce Chatter API, a built-in data model that apps can leverage to become instantly social and collaborative.

- Database.com's REST APIs, OAuth implementation for user authentication/authorization, data feeds, custom web services, embedded security model, and other features make it perfect to easily build secure, scalable mobile apps, either native or HTML5.

- Database.com's full complement of open APIs lets you build applications using the approach you choose. REST- and SOAP-based APIs are standards-based APIs that make Database.com open to whatever programming language you want to use. Using various APIs, your applications can create-read-update-delete (CRUD) business data, load a large number of records asynchronously, or take advantage of the Chatter API to provide collaboration and social networking capabilities to any application.

- Database.com provides a Data Residency Option that allows companies that have requirements, policies, or perceptions that prevent them from putting their data in the cloud to keep versions of sensitive data wherever they want, such as their in-house data center.

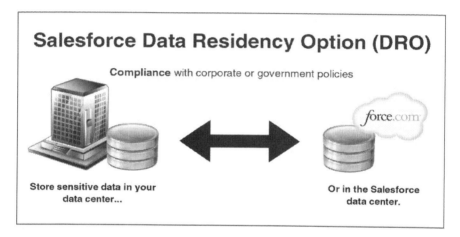

- Database.com can easily model complex data relationships between entities across every master data domain.

Benefits of Database.com

- Database.com is easy to use because IT professionals don't need to perform any low-level management such as patching, backups, or configuration.

- Database.com delivers performance that transparently scales according to varying application workloads.

- Database.com doesn't require any expensive up-front investments such as software licenses or hardware.

- Databases are instantly available to anyone who needs them with just a few mouse clicks; there's no waiting to provision databases.

- Reliable and secure, Database.com is constantly monitored and administered by dedicated professionals whose only job is to manage the database.

- Database.com takes care of backup and disaster recovery automatically.

- Declarative data security rules are isolated and managed independently from the rest of the application business logic.

- Rules can be assigned to users and groups of users (roles) and defined down to the row level (such as "user 1 can access inventory data for products A-M" and "user 2 can access inventory data for products N-Z").

- Rules are enforced automatically by the database for every query, freeing developers from having to code data security logic into each application they write against the database. This eliminates the need for each application to code, test, and maintain its complicated security logic.

- Access is granted to user profiles, groups, subscriptions to records and documents, social graph, and automatically generated data feeds while adhering to any security settings you have configured.

- All the infrastructure and corporate workplace industry standards, including SAS 70 Type II, SysTrust, and ISO 27001 certifications, are met.

- OAuth implementation for user authentication and authorization, data feeds, custom web services, and an embedded security model are supported.

- Backwards compatibility with APIs used for integration is maintained. You only have to integrate with the service once, and that integration will keep running, even as the platform is upgraded.

- Because new capabilities can be delivered without impacting applications already deployed, release cycles of new functionality can be delivered much faster, with no effort on the part of the developer.

- All levels of the organization are addressed. Some databases are critical to the survival of an organization while others are simply quick and dirty systems for ad hoc analysis. No matter how large or small the organization, databases are used at a variety of levels for a variety of reasons.

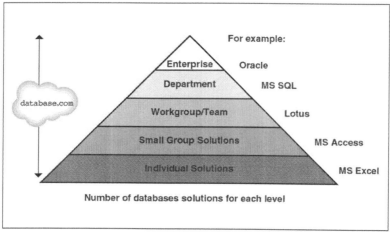

Figure 41: Database.com can be used effectively for most business applications at any level of the organization.

- Provides a "single source of truth" for the organization – for all applications.

- As each record is changed, that information becomes immediately available to everyone in the organization.

- New systems can be brought online quickly because they have immediate access to accurate and complete data in a single location, obviating the need to build new interfaces or cleanse data.

- Reports can be generated across many different areas of the business.

- Faster time-to-market is enabled by eliminating the steps to acquire, install, and maintain software.

- Users avoid wasted effort due to incomplete information or looking for information.

- Enhanced data visibility enables better decision making.

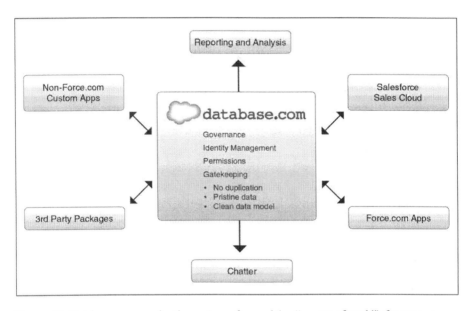

Figure 42: Database.com can be the system of record (or "source of truth") for many types of applications.

A Note on "Big Data"

With the digitization of everything, there is an unimaginably vast amount of digital information which is getting ever vaster ever more quickly. This makes it possible to do many things that previously could not be done: spot business trends, prevent diseases, combat crime, etc. This data can be used to unlock new sources of economic value and provide fresh insights.

The Enterprise Database under discussion in this book is completely separate from Big Data. For example, Big Data would be concerned with every cell phone call made by a customer, rather than just their monthly invoice total. In this example, the Big Data database stores billions of transactions, with the goal of running a business intelligence tool to slice and dice the data. The Enterprise Database would store a small fraction of this data in summarized form.

Big data requires exceptional technologies to efficiently process large quantities of data within tolerable elapsed times. Salesforce.com provides the ability to work with Big Data on a different platform, Heroku.

Workflow, by Steve Wood

Steve Wood is the Vice President of Platform Business Development at salesforce.com.

Workflow is a fundamental building block in any platform application stack, because workflow represents the way in which the organization gets things done. Getting work done effectively is, of course, one of the biggest drivers of business applications. The tasks, the approvals, and the data entry are what make up the day-to-day operations of a business. Workflow represents the tamed or reasonably well-understood processes within a business – often the processes that can be articulated using a flow diagram. However, just because the processes are understood or deemed "tame" does not mean that they will not change. For workflow to be truly successful, it's important that the ability to manage agility, iteration and change are built into the platform.

Workflow represents much of the logic of a user's applications. For example, an app can make sure your manager is notified if a purchase order is over a certain amount. It can follow through on an approval process for that purchase order, if it's required by your budget limit.

Rules, Roles and Routing

Workflow incorporates a few key concepts

Rules: Within workflow the ability exists to articulate your business rules – ideally without writing any code. Business rules are often used to check that information-gathering has been completed, to see that values are within a certain threshold, or any other number of other conditions (that have true/false answers) that help control the business' behavior

Roles: Workflow contains an understanding of the structure of your organization and your role within it. Your role within the organization often affects your ability to perform certain tasks. For example, it can dictate how escalations are handled: if I can only authorize payments under $10,000, then I should not be able to approve a purchase order for

$15,000. However, it's worth noting that as we embrace the "Social Enterprise," your role may become a much more dynamic concept based on skills, followers and influence as opposed to system-designated permissions.

Routing: Within workflow, the ability to route requests through to different parts of the process is often based on rules of events. Routing is often visualized in a flow diagram as the arrows connecting the steps – showing the different paths that will be followed based on the outcome of various actions in the flow. For example, if an insurance policy requires that I'm over 18 to complete, I would be routed to the first policy form if I'm over 18, but routed to a "Sorry, you can't have a policy" screen if I'm under 18.

Using these three concepts, you can see how workflow plays a foundational role in any situational or business application. Most of the capabilities of any of these applications fit within the above three concepts. What is most exciting about workflow is that it strives to visualize these concepts in a way that is immediately understandable. At salesforce.com, the goal is to make workflow a "shared language" between the business and IT. Making it possible to incorporate the rules, roles and routing behavior of your applications into a point-and-click flow allows IT and business to work together and iterate as business needs evolve.

Salesforce and BPM

To clarify the role of the force.com platform within business process management or BPM: force.com is not attempting to disrupt the BPM software industry with a cloud offering, but work with it. BPM systems tend to focus on integration, where the primary role of the business process is to link systems together as work is shunted from application to application. As a result, BPM tends to be associated with concepts such as Enterprise Service Buses (ESBs) or as part of a Service-Oriented Architecture (SOA) and is firmly in the IT domain. With force.com, the workflow tools are positioned in a way complementary to this traditional view. With force.com, the focus is on business processes that are "built for change" rather than "built to last," as is commonplace with traditional BPM.

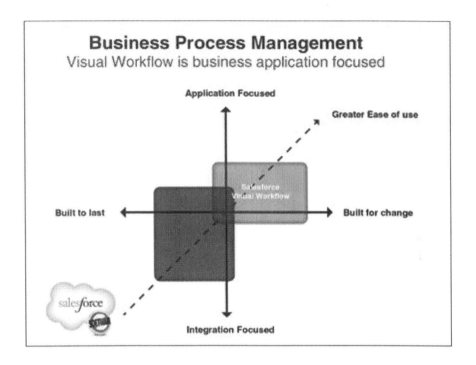

However, it may also be clear that this sells the concept of BPM short. BPM began with a very simple idea, something which sounds obvious now: If your business is aligned to your customer and your processes optimized around the customer – rather than your org chart – your business will be more successful. BPM is really about removing silos introduced by management and putting the goal of delighting customers at the heart of business operations. Sounds like a pretty good idea and a far grander one than being about systems integration. It also sounds suspiciously like the goal of many of the social technologies, and indeed, a newer industry has emerged called "Social BPM."

Social BPM

The idea of social BPM is that processes should be lightweight, agile, and designed by doing, rather than existing in a dark room away from the live business and active customers. Social BPM systems tend to be more human or people-centric and much less about systems interaction. In fact, with Social BPM the term "process" has taken on a much broader meaning, generally concerning the management of untamed activities as opposed to sequential sets of tasks. The focus of Social BPM is on enabling the end users to get their jobs done by removing many of the complexities introduced by policy, systems, applications, etc. Rather than attempting to control the untamed processes or communication and collaboration with colleagues and with customers, workflow should "get out of the way" and be the force for simplification and automation.

BPMN, BPEL or XPDL

Once we enter the world of business process management, we need to address a number of the standards that exist for articulating, persisting and executing business processes. force.com does not support BPMN (business process modeling notation), BPEL (business process execution language) or XPDL (XML process definition language), although force.com does support an open XML meta-data API for exporting and importing business processes.

It's important to understand the driving principles of the force.com workflow tools to understand the position with respect to standards. With force.com, the driving principle is that your workflow, either configured or drawn as a flow diagram, IS the application. There are no translation steps in between − what you draw is what is executed. This is not true of the BPMN standard, which was conceived of as a way of communicating business processes, but not executing them. Conversely, the BPEL standard was conceived as a way of executing business processes, but not communicating them. As you'd expect, business users and analysts use BPMN to write their processes, and IT uses BPEL as an execution language. However, these two standards are not naturally compatible and despite numerous attempts, translating BPMN to BPEL and vice versa is complex and error-prone. So the same business/IT divide we've seen before returns.

These standards were simply not meant to work together. One is about communication, and the other is about integration, and they are governed separately. Unfortunately, many vendors have recently tried to combine the two standards so that BPMN appears to be about communicating integration – which does not serve the business developer well.

At force.com this is considered an area in need of significant overhaul and innovation. Its old concepts and resultant problems are not suited to today's real-time, agile, adaptive needs. Therefore, force.com does not support BPMN, BPEL or XPDL. However, force.com does have an open API for process definitions and it is possible for these formats to be imported if they comply with the force.com workflow format.

.

The force.com Tools

force.com includes a powerful set of tools to add workflow and business process orchestration to your applications. These include simple workflow rules, multi-person approval processes, sophisticated business processes that span multiple data sources and backend systems, and cross-functional work relay.

Automating Business Processes

Workflow Rules
Automate specific actions

- Assign a task
- Send an email
- Update a field value
- Send an outbound message

Approval Processes
Automate approving a record

- Define steps for approval
- Assign approver for each step

Visual Workflow
Automate complex business processes

- Navigate users through screens
- Execute business rules
- Query and update Salesforce data

Work Relay
Automate cross-functional work flow

- Define a goal-specific unit of work
- Specify the cross-functional task sequence
- Automate the relay of work from function to function

Workflow and Approvals

Workflows are a simple way to extend the logical operations of your force.com applications. You specify the criteria that determine if a workflow is triggered by inserting or changing a data record, and you specify what action is to be performed.

As examples, a workflow can automatically:

- Assign follow-up tasks to someone a week after a record is updated;

- Send someone an email alert after a record is inserted;

- Change a record's Owner field at a specific date and time;

- Trigger an outbound message to an external application system to initiate a related business process managed by the external system.

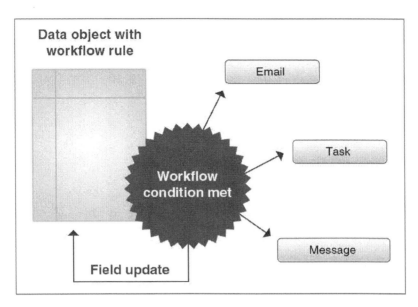

Figure 43: When a workflow condition has been met, the system can be instructed to take an action.

Workflow rules specify the criteria which determine if a workflow is triggered. A workflow can be triggered immediately, or set to operate at a subsequent interval after the triggering event. These outbound messages are one of the ways to send information from the force.com environment to external data stores and applications.

A specialized type of workflow called an "approval process" can route information to a series of people, each of whom can approve the information, send it on to the next recipient, or decline the approval.

An approval process specifies the steps necessary to approve a record, who must approve the process at each step, and the actions to take after each step. An approval process also supports the locking of an approved record to avoid changes after the approval is complete.

As with other force.com features, developers and non-developers alike can build even the most complex approval processes using the simple point-and-click designer that is part of the builder. No coding is necessary.

Visual Workflow

The Visual Workflow allows you to string together one or more UI screens, business rules, and calls to backend APIs to implement a complete business process without writing code. The role of this tool is to automate task-centric business processes. This tool is also likely to be the foundation of multi-user, work relay style processes as support for this improves.

Visual Workflow enables you to automate business processes across your organization, supporting such processes as call scripting for inbound or outbound call centers, diagnostics and troubleshooting guides, guided data entry processes to reduce errors and training costs, product configuration, sales quotations, guided selling with sales methodologies, employee on-boarding, and much more.

Visual Workflow is extremely useful in situations where data needs to be gathered in sequence and the user only needs to see the data entry fields that pertain specifically to their particular issue or inquiry. It allows you to ensure better data quality, to gather the right data every time, and ensure that mandatory paths are taken.

For example, a team of salespeople sells Medicare insurance to the public. Medicare has strict regulations about the exact scripts which must be used with new enrollees. With Visual Workflow, an analyst can design all the different paths and ensure that the exact data needed to enroll members is captured, along with their responses.

Without Visual Workflow, this type of application would have required a customized solution, such as using a programming tool like Adobe Flex Builder. Visual Workflow allows business users to design and deploy complex business processes on their own and adjust as quickly as their business changes.

Visual Workflow also includes an API so all processes created in Visual Workflow can be embedded in Visualforce and APEX. In addition, APEX developers can build new functions and capabilities by building APEX plug-ins, which appear in the toolbar for business users building business processes. This allows a clear separation of roles:

- **Flow builder**: Creates the sequence of steps, business rules, forms, data operations, actions and calculations required to fulfill the business process according to the business need.

- **Developer**: Embeds the flow into existing applications for web, desktop or any number of devices. Extends the flow with new business services that can act as integration points to other applications (e.g. SAP, Oracle Financials).

The person creating the flows can concentrate on the process and the developer can concentrate on the integration points and complex coding. The power of Visual Workflow is that complete process-centric applications can be completed without writing any code. IT can be engaged to embed or extend your flow, as your needs dictate.

Cross-functional work relay

There is a substantial class of workflows in many organizations that work like a relay race – work is passed like a baton from one area of responsibility to another, (including outside the organization) in order to reach a specific goal.

Unlike the Visual Workflow, which is focused primarily on either collecting data or employing data to guide the user, the focus of these types of workflows is on the roles involved and the sequence in which work is executed. How the work is completed in each step by each function is not relevant to the workflow. It separates the "who" and "when" from "what" and "how."

This satisfies the growing requirement to allow pieces of functionality to be completed outside the enterprise. The "what" and "how" are single-purpose applications (or services). These applications are strung together in a specified sequence to accomplish a specific business goal. They can change any time without affecting the flow, and the flow can change any time without affecting the applications. As an example, this approach also simplifies the need for solutions to adapt to local needs in different countries.

The best way to visualize cross-functional workflows is to use swim lane diagrams, like this:

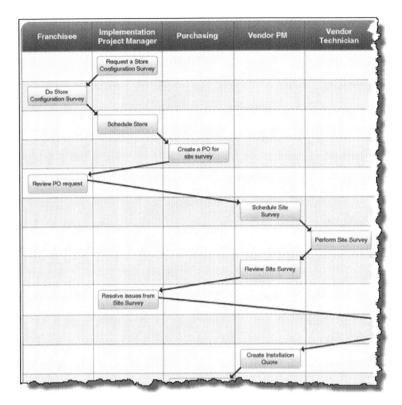

To help users with these types of workflows, SilverTree Systems has built a force.com workflow extension called Work-Relay that allows users to easily build swim lane diagrams, and implement them in force.com a simple way. The tool provides the following functionality:

- a simple drag-and-drop swim lane builder

- specification of rules governing the passing of the baton

- lanes within lanes for easy reusability

- Chatter integration

- ability to change the workflow mid-stream, including adding new tasks and changing execution rules

- a workflow tab for users to track all their workflows in one place

- expected and actual time duration between hand-offs

- ability to calculate expected hand-off dates given start or end date

- a visual depiction of where one or more instance(s) of a workflow is at any time

- ability for business users to associate screens, cloud flows or APEX functionality with specific tasks

- ability to easily include functions outside the enterprise (without licensing issues)

- ability to associate a workflow with a specific object, e.g., a Store, allowing workflows to be tracked by any object instance

Benefits

- Workflow permits people, information and computers to work together consistently and efficiently to produce the results the business needs.

- Abstracting workflow and visualizing the processes allows business decision makers to easily use this new vantage point to help determine and analyze their business process flows.

- Business analysts and policy makers can easily model and deploy business rules without the need for traditional programming. Dynamic business environments require constant adjustment to business rules, and users require simple ways to implement changes with both speed and accuracy. Reuse capabilities are valuable as a means of ensuring that rules can be written once and then applied across multiple applications and decision services.

- Business stakeholders can readily determine how effective and efficient the implemented process flows have been over time, by using analysis tools on top of the workflow database. They can answer questions like: What steps, resources, processes are bottlenecks to business delivery and success?

- Costs are reduced and employee productivity is increased by reducing approval cycles, minimizing processing errors and streamlining business processes.

- Minimal training is required for using the system so employees can begin using the processes immediately, and business analysts can quickly deploy and modify business processes without understanding programming or database systems.

Appexchange

The force.com AppExchange is a one-stop shop for cloud computing business applications and services. AppExchange allows you to easily find, test drive, and install hundreds of pre-integrated applications written by force.com partners.

The goal of AppExchange is to save you the time and effort of reinventing the wheel when a solution already exists. Instead of dedicating time and resources to build an in-house application, you can easily install one from the AppExchange, customize it for your business needs, and be up and running in almost no time.

In the AppExchange site you can easily find apps relevant to your business needs. You can also tap into the power of the force.com Community to see which applications are the most popular, read reviews from your peers, and help others by sharing your experiences.

Instead of engaging in lengthy pilots, the AppExchange makes it easy for you to quickly evaluate an application's functionality through a "test drive," which lets you interact with an application in one click to take it for a spin. This approach lets you see exactly how the application would work in your organization.

Summary

force.com provides a set of building blocks that makes it much easier to develop powerful solutions quickly.

The building blocks include:

1. Social networking, a critical component for success in today's environment

2. Mobile, to facilitate solution-building without having to deal directly with the rapidly evolving mobile technology.

3. A database in the cloud, eliminating an enormous amount of overhead associated with in-house databases.

4. Cloud-based workflow, including the inclusion of functions outside the enterprise in business processes.

5. An AppExchange, which provides easy access to an ever-growing number of solutions that, can be integrated in any force.com application, further reducing cost and time to market.

Implementation

The roots of great innovation are never just in the technology itself. They are always in the wider historical context. They require new ways of seeing. – David Brooks, *The Social Animal.* 2011

For this technology to be truly transformational, it isn't enough to simply start using force.com to build some applications using your existing business models and methodologies. This is a frequent phenomenon with emerging technologies. Phil Wainewright calls this the "horseless carriage syndrome," which he defines as "the propensity to interpret a new technology using familiar concepts from the existing world, rather than seeing it in its full, native potential."[55]

---

[55] Phil Wainewright, "The cloud is forked," ZDNet, January 22, 2012, http://www.zdnet.com/blog/saas/the-cloud-is-forked/1482

The Horseless Carriage Phase of Cloud Computing

When cars emerged in the early twentieth century, they were initially called "horseless carriages." As often happens with a paradigm shift, cars were viewed through the lens of the paradigm that had been dominant for centuries: the horse and carriage. In fact, the first cars also looked very similar to the horse and carriage (just without the horse). Engineers even kept designing the whip holder into the early models before realizing that it wasn't necessary anymore!

So initially there was a broad failure to fully comprehend the new paradigm. "The horse is here to stay but the automobile is only a novelty, a fad."[56] Even the early automobile pioneers car didn't fully grasp the potential impact their work could have on the world. When Daimler, arguably the inventor of the automobile, attempted to estimate the long-term auto market opportunity, he concluded there could never be more than 1 million cars, because of their high cost and the shortage of capable chauffeurs.[57] (Sound familiar?)

Understanding the possibilities of the new paradigm, such as

---

[56] President of the Michigan Savings Bank advising Horace Rackham (*Henry Ford's lawyer*) not to invest in the Ford Motor Company in 1903. Rackham ignored the advice and bought $5,000 worth of stock. He sold it several years later for $12,500,000!

[57] William Horton Consulting

building for higher speeds, or greater safety, took time. Even the early pioneers failed to realize that profound reductions in both the cost and complexity of operating cars along with a dramatic increase in its importance in daily life would overwhelm prior constraints and bring cars to the masses.

To get the most out of this new technology, you need to pair it with a different mindset and a different methodology.

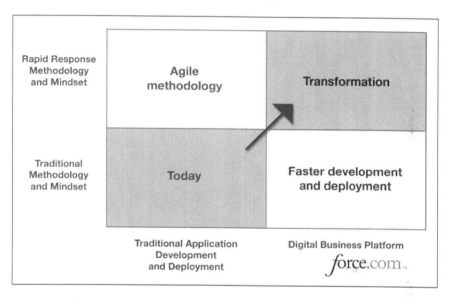

Figure 44: Simply replacing the development tool and deployment environment isn't enough. Transformation requires a new mindset and methodology as well.

Implementation therefore includes the following elements:

255

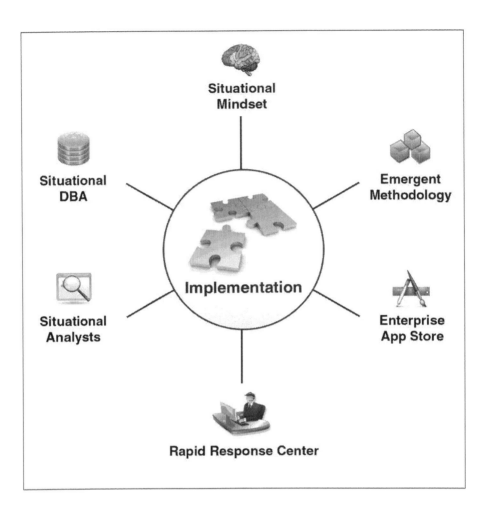

A Situational Mindset

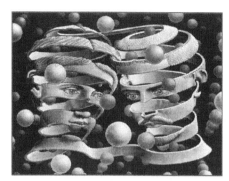

Mindset is everything. If that statement seems too strong, consider that we bring these basic assumptions to every decision and action we make. Left unexamined, they may unnecessarily restrict us or lead us in the wrong direction altogether. Perception may not truly be reality, but when it comes to how we approach challenges and opportunities, mindset determines the world we encounter and possibilities we apprehend.[58] – John Hagel III and John Seely Brown

The first thing to do is to adopt a new mindset. Without this, the ability to achieve all that's possible will be significantly weakened.

Key Elements of an Emergent Mindset

I have found that in nearly all situations I can view what is happening in Complex Adaptive Systems terms and that this opens up a variety of new options which give me more choice and more freedom.[59] – Peter Fryer, *Trojan Mice*

As discussed in an earlier chapter, one of the prerequisites for effectively leveraging the new wave of IT is to understand the properties of a complex adaptive system. One of the key elements of a CAS is the

---

[58] John Hagel III and John Seely Brown, "Do You Have a Growth Mindset?", Harvard Business Review Blog Network, Nov. 23, 1010

[59] Peter Fryer, "What Are Complex Adaptive Systems?", trojanmice.com

concept of emergence. The two critical elements of an emergent mindset are "good enough" and "closeness of fit."

What is "good enough?"

As we saw earlier, a complex adaptive system doesn't have to be perfect in order for it to thrive within its environment. A solution doesn't have to be ideal – it just has to work. Once it has reached the state of being good enough, a complex adaptive system will trade off increased efficiency every time in favor of greater effectiveness.

Yet we spend an inordinate amount of time trying to get the details right, when it is unlikely to matter very much.

Clay Shirky, author of *Here Comes Everybody: The Power of Organizing Without Organizations* and originator of the phrase "situated software" (from which "situational applications" is derived), describes a simple project undertaken by his students that very clearly illustrates the concept of "good enough" software. The WeBe application, a simple tool for enabling college students to coordinate and purchase things as a group, is an excellent example of why a situational application is so much less expensive and time-consuming to build.

Done is better than perfect.[60]

Because money is involved, the traditional approach would require a way of dealing with the threat of non-payment, using things like pre-pay or escrow accounts, or formal reputation systems. Instead, since all the users were part of the community, the decision was made that they would simply make it easy to track the deadbeats, with the threat of public broadcast of their names.

The solution was "good enough" – the application didn't have to take into account and deal with all the exceptions that might occur. This saved

---

[60] Sign in the Facebook corporate office. (Facebook uses force.com for all its internal applications.)

money and did not require any development at all – and possibly wouldn't ever have to be invoked, given the small scale involved. But the application had real value for the group it was intended to service, and would probably not have been built at all if this type of condition needed to be perfectly catered to by the application.

There are many times when building applications where asking the question "Is this good enough for now?" cuts time and cost without reducing the value and effectiveness of the solution.

What is "closeness of fit"?

> *Situated software isn't a technological strategy so much as an attitude about closeness of fit between software and its group of users, and a refusal to embrace scale, generality or completeness as unqualified virtues.*
> – Clay Shirky

The problem with traditional software is that often it's built for a generic user. Allowing a user to customize the interface of a web site might make it more useful, but it doesn't make it any more personal than the ATM putting your name on the screen while it delivers your money.

Situational applications, by contrast, don't need to be personalized – they are personal from inception. The application's lack of generality or completeness, in other words, communicates something positive: "We built this for you."

The following simple example puts closeness of fit into perspective: One of Shirky's students mentioned building a web application for his mother, a schoolteacher, to keep track of different aspects of her class. Making an application specifically for your mom is very different than writing an application that would satisfy the general and complete needs of schoolteachers everywhere.

The situational mindset resists the temptation to elevate a local solution to serve the whole organization or every client, every problem, etc.

Versus the traditional mindset

The big payoff of the living systems point of view is that what is remote and unnatural within the traditional frame of reference becomes sensible and accessible within the complexity mindset. – Richard Pascale, Mark Tillemann, and Linda Gioja, *Surfing the Edge of Chaos*

The following contrasts a situational mindset with a traditional mindset.

Mindset		
	Traditional applications	Situational applications
Embrace incrementalism	Because the overhead of starting up an IT project is so great, it only makes sense to tackle large projects with a significant payback.	A situational application is never going to have the impact of a single application, like ERP or CRM. But the incremental impact of a multitude of small force.com applications can result in geometric growth in productivity.
Embrace messiness	Messiness is the scourge of IT.	Act quickly, refine later. Highly adaptable systems may look sloppy. There is no point in wasting resources and energy trying to make something look beautiful if it's not going to be around for very long or if it's going to change all the time.
Use simplifying assumptions	Because of the time and cost involved, there is a need to anticipate the needs of "any" user and anticipate every contingency.	force.com applications are aimed at very specific target audiences. Assumptions that simplify the application can be made because it will be used by a small user community who know and trust each other.

Mindset

	Traditional applications	Situational applications
Get personal, don't personalize	A significant amount of time and effort is put into both making a system generic as well as providing a way to "personalize" it. This makes the application much more complex than if it were written for a specific use.	force.com applications don't need to be personalized – they are personal from inception. The application's lack of generality or complete-ness communicates that "this was built for you."
Re-think ROI	Because of the significant cost involved, calculating ROI is essential.	The cost of justifying the ROI for developing small services will, in many cases, be more costly than developing the service in the first place. For example, no one would do an ROI for a spreadsheet.
Embrace change	Great effort is made to limit the amount of change required once a system goes live. Users are discouraged from making changes once the code is written, because doing so is costly and time-consuming.	Solutions are recognized from the start to be temporary and are treated as such. The system can be made to respond to any situation. There are few negatives to implementing change.

Mindset

	Traditional applications	Situational applications
Underprescribe	The tendency in traditional development is to overprescribe – to think of all the possible exceptions and variations that might occur and cater to them when the system is written. This is important for applications where efficiency is key.	Most business processes involving edge workers are fluid and adaptable, so they cannot be too restrictive. This would also likely encourage rigidity due to a lack of desire to change the things needed to deal with exceptions. The goal is to keep force.com applications "elegantly minimal" – to create "elbow room" for local interpretations and innovations.
Be specific	To help justify the cost and to try to reduce the chance of changes later, every conceivable scenario needs to be considered.	Build for a very specific set of users and features.
Seek success	Traditional applications by their nature are focused on seeking to avoid failure and rely on "tried and true" solutions.	Easily adaptable, force.com applications are focused on seeking success and finding new, better ways to perform tasks.
Status quo	Because of the cost to change, there is a strong prejudice in favor of maintaining the status quo.	There is an impetus to find new ways to perform better.
Self-organize (start projects up at will)	Because of the number of people involved, and the cost and planning that need to take place to deliver a traditional application, self-organization is not an option.	One of the key determinants of force.com applications is the amount of leeway users have to "do their own thing."

Mindset

	Traditional applications	Situational applications
Start simple	Because of the high overhead associated with starting up a traditional application development project, it is difficult to justify taking on only a sub-set of an application.	Because applications can be built and abandoned quickly, they can be delivered informally, starting with a very crude first version, then iterated rapidly.
Re-think longevity	The assumption is that applications should work for long periods, in part because it costs so much to create them, and so much work has been done to anticipate future needs.	Once it's cheap and easy to throw together an application, longevity doesn't matter. The idea that software should be built for many users, or last for many years, are cultural assumptions that no longer pertain.

Figure 45: Situational applications require a different way of thinking.

Emergent Methodology

> *The traditional top-down style worked well when applied to complex, fixed functions — that is, human artifacts, such as aircraft, ships, buildings, computers .... However, it works poorly when applied to an equally wide variety of domains because they do not behave in a predictable way. The traditional approach ends up constraining the ability of an emergent domain to change because it is never possible to predict – and architect for – all the possible avenues of evolution.*[61] – Bruce Robertson, research vp at Gartner

Situational applications in the new digital economy require a new methodology if organizations are going to keep up with the demands of the business.

From Waterfall to Agile to Emergent

Traditional application development uses the "waterfall" methodology. In the waterfall methodology, user involvement brackets the start and end of a long process involving many players – analysts, architects, designers, database administrators, programmers, testers. In traditional application development, running projects using the waterfall methodology makes a lot of sense, given the amount of time it takes to move from phase to phase, and the huge expense in time and effort required to correct any (inevitable) changes that are required when the system goes live.

---

[61] Bruce Robertson, quoted in "Gartner Identifies New Approach for Enterprise Architecture," Gartner Newsroom, Aug. 11, 2009, http://www.gartner.com/it/page.jsp?id=1124112

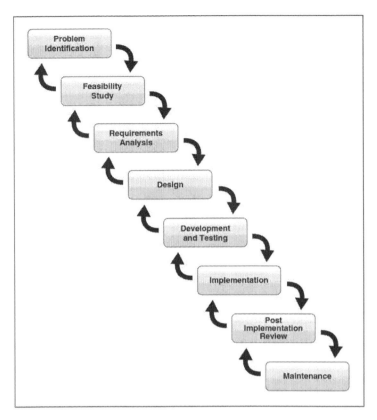

Figure 29: In the waterfall methodology, each step must be completed and signed off before the next phase can begin. Going back to a previous step is a usually time-consuming and painful process.

Over the years, many attempts were made to find ways to improve the waterfall methodology by developing better specification, design, and project management tools. The basic assumption was that we can write software more efficiently if we first define exactly what the user wants. This is the result of years of experience where finished applications did not fit the user's needs well, and changing the programs afterwards was extremely hard to do. The common sense solution seemed to be to spend more time on defining a more precise set of requirements. But while this is often true back-office systems like accounting or air traffic control, it is usually the wrong answer, because the requirements are *always* changing.

As the pace of change quickened, and the success of application development projects was seen as less than optimal, many IT organizations moved from the traditional waterfall methodology to agile methodology.

Instead of the big bang approach of waterfall methodology, which usually took months or years to produce a result, the agile methodology breaks projects into small increments lasting from one to four weeks. Each iteration involves a team working through a full software development cycle including planning, requirements, analysis, design, coding, unit testing and acceptance testing, resulting in a working product that is demonstrated to stakeholders. This minimizes overall risk and allows the project to adapt to changes quickly. An iteration might not add enough functionality to warrant a market release, but the goal is to have an available release (with minimal bugs) at the end of each iteration. Multiple iterations might be required to release a product or new features.

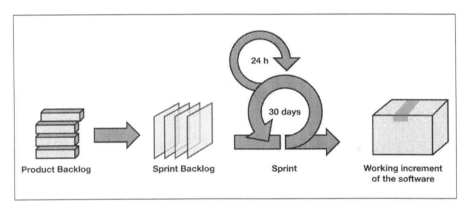

Figure 30: The users select the functionality they want added next from the backlog of requests. The number of requests depends on how many can be completed in the timeframe of a "sprint" (usually two to four weeks). Daily meetings help ensure everything remains on track. At the end of the sprint, a new version of the software is made available to users.

Team composition in an agile project is usually cross-functional and self-organizing, without consideration for any existing corporate hierarchy or the corporate roles of team members. Team members normally take responsibility for tasks that deliver the functionality an iteration requires. They decide individually how to meet an iteration's requirements.

267

Agile methods emphasize face-to-face communication over written documents when the team is all in the same location. Most agile teams work in a single open office, which facilitates such communication. Team size is typically small (5-9 people) to simplify team communication and team collaboration. Larger development efforts can be delivered by multiple teams working toward a common goal or on different parts of an effort. This might require a coordination of priorities across teams. When a team works in different locations, they maintain daily contact through videoconferencing, voice, e-mail, etc.[62]

But while agile methodology has undoubtedly led to a significant improvement in the speed and quality of application delivery, it is not responsive enough for the new digital economy. Fortunately, the combination of often code-less functionality, simple and instant deployment, and social networking (facilitating constant, real-time communication among all interested parties) makes it possible to dramatically shorten the iteration period in many cases, and simply use an ongoing flow of responsive development and deployment, resulting in a more emergent solution.

Situational versus traditional applications

Many of the factors dictating how to build traditional applications in a traditional environment change with the development of situational applications on a digital business platform.

---

[62] "Agile software development," Wikipedia, last updated February 8, 2012, http://en.wikipedia.org/wiki/Agile_software_development, retrieved February 14, 2012.

Methodology Characteristics

Factor	Traditional Application	Situational Application
Requirements definition	Requirements must be completely defined upfront, frozen, and signed off before development can start.	Because it's much easier to change the application, "freezing" requirements is unnecessary.
Feedback loop	Because a typical development team includes multiple people between the user and the person actually writing the code, the feedback between the programmer and user tends to be slow and subject to miscommunication.	The person developing the system (if it isn't the user) is usually in direct contact with the user, thereby significantly shortening the feedback loop, leading to faster, more accurate development.
The impact of change	Change creates a cascading effect across the various roles involved in the process.	The implementation of changes is much simpler – there are fewer people involved in the process and fewer components to impact (less brittle).
Team size	A typical development team contains multiple people, and also requires a team to take responsibility for the hardware and software implementation.	Because so much of the work has already been done by the platform, it's possible to have a much smaller team work on a project. In some cases, it just takes a business analyst to build – and deploy – a complete system.

Methodology Characteristics

Factor	Traditional Application	Situational Application
Coding standards and code walkthroughs	Because there are so many ways to program an application, it's critical for developers to follow the company standard. This has to be verified using code walkthroughs.	There is usually much less code to deal with, and when there is, it is in the context of the platform, standardizing it to a large extent.
Maintenance	Maintenance (e.g., bug fixing) often means digging deep into code. This is especially difficult when the programmer doing the maintenance is not the original coder.	Because there is much less code, changes are much easier to make. Anyone familiar with the platform will also find it easier to pick up where someone else left off.
Enhancements	Making enhancements to code is also difficult when the programmer is not the original coder.	Enhancements are easy to make because most enhancements are made without coding.
Training	In most environments, each new system works somewhat differently, so users need to be for each system.	All applications built on the platform work the same way, so that users have to learn only once.
Infrastructure procurement and implementation	Hardware, software, space, and implementation services must be procured. Software needs to be installed, patched, and tested.	No procurement or implementation other than signing up for the service is necessary.
Backup procedures and	The application must	The platform provides

Methodology Characteristics

Factor	Traditional Application	Situational Application
disaster recovery	have processes in place – and constantly monitor that they are in working order.	backup and disaster recovery automatically.
Scalability	The typical application has to be built to scale across multiple servers. When more power is needed, servers must be procured, installed, etc.	The platform guarantees unlimited scalability – both increased and decreased – with no effort required.
Time to market	Given the factors discussed above, the speed of implementation is by definition slow.	Given all the factors discussed above, the speed of implementation is significantly faster than traditional applications.

Building a situational application

> *Ideas for new solutions will spring from half-baked applications created by lay users who may start down the path toward a solution, but may lack the expertise to finish it.* – Andy Mulholland, Chris S. Thomas, and Paul Kurchina, *Mashup Corporations: The End of Business as Usual*

force.com empowers business users who are closest to the problems being solved to quickly build full-featured collaborative business applications online, and immediately deploy those applications to the appropriate people both inside and outside their organization.

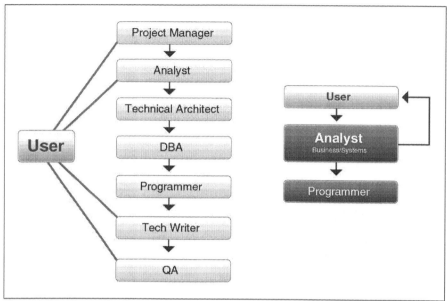

Figure 4631: The application development methodology changes completely. The analyst works closely with the user, building the application through configuration rather than coding. A programmer is used to create snippets of functionality only to supplement the platform where configuration falls short.

But when the solution to be developed is relatively sophisticated, the typical business user will not succeed in building the software entirely on their own. At the very least, there will be a need for someone with analysis and design skills to help frame the problem and model the solution for them. And in some cases, there will be a need to extend the platform and/or interface with external systems.

Therefore, the best way to build non-trivial applications using force.com is to split the workload into three parts, where each part is addressed by someone who is an expert in that area. So an Analyst helps the User to express what they want to achieve in "computer" terms, the User fills in the details that they know intimately, and a Developer provides any extensions or interfaces that may be needed.

The following describes the process in more detail.

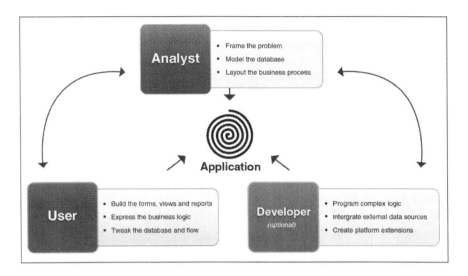

Role of the Analyst

Frame the problem

Most users have difficulty expressing their requirements in simple English. They need help doing this, especially when it comes to thinking about "fringe" cases and exceptions.

Model the database

Once the problem is understood, the database must be modeled. If this isn't done correctly, everything that follows will either fail or be miserably difficult to do.

Lay out the business process

If the application is designed to support a business process, the process needs to be laid out, and the primary actions need to be defined. For example, when a new lead is entered, a notification must be sent to the sales department.

Role of the User

Build the forms and views

The user understands what data needs to be collected, and how it is collected and viewed.

Express the business logic

The user expresses the business logic (calculations, validation rules, etc.) that make up any significant piece of software.

Tweak the database and flow

Once the database has been successfully modeled, it's easy for the user to add and delete fields and change the workflow.

Role of the Developer

Program complex business logic

A developer may be needed when the logic to be expressed is outside the capability of the platform, such as when complex mathematical functions that are not supported are required.

Integrate external databases

If data needs to be retrieved from existing data sources, a developer is usually required to put the necessary connections in place. The developer can make external data sources look like native force.com data sources to the user, thereby making it easy for the user to build applications regardless of the data's source.

Integrate web services

Developers are usually needed to integrate any external web services required by the application.

The limits of the citizen developer

In some cases, the analyst will need to take on more of the users responsibilities, because:

- Many users are simply not interested in building their own applications.

- Even those who are interested often won't do it because they don't want to spend the time on it.

- Users who try to build their own applications may never get to the "aha!" moment that often accompanies a breakthrough solution. The most common reason is that it's hard to understand database relationships.

The rise of the Situational Analyst

> *Solution development practices should not harbor old distinctions between business and IT. Instead, solution experimentation and creation should engage all individuals as part of in-flow business innovation. This will allow your organization to continuously explore and adapt based on an informed improvisation.* - Mike Rollings, "Citizen Development: Reinventing the Shadows of IT", *Gartner, Inc.*, February, 2012

In the situational application world, the analyst is king. The situational analyst's role goes well beyond that of a traditional analyst – they are actually responsible for building a substantial portion of the application. In addition to translating user requirements into system terms, these Situational Analysts model and build databases, develop screens, and implement business logic. The Situational Analyst also works with IT on behalf of users to secure access to corporate data as needed.

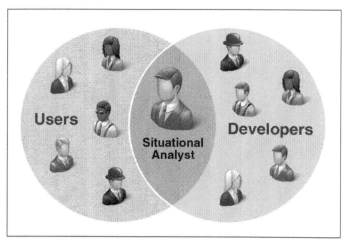

A Situational Analyst could start out as a power user, an analyst, or high-level developer. But the role of Situational Analyst could become more specifically defined in its own right as force.com applications start to take hold.

An Emergent Methodology

> *We must learn to cocreate the future and use an improvisational model for strategy that embraces uncertainty, emerges from execution, engages individual creativity and learns by testing many hypotheses.* - Mike Rollings, *"Citizen Development: Reinventing the Shadows of IT", Gartner, Inc.*, February, 2012

In the earlier discussion on Complex Adaptive Systems, we saw how behavior "emerges" as a result of feedback, relationships and the external environment. In the same way, an application emerges through usage, constant feedback, and ever-changing requirements.

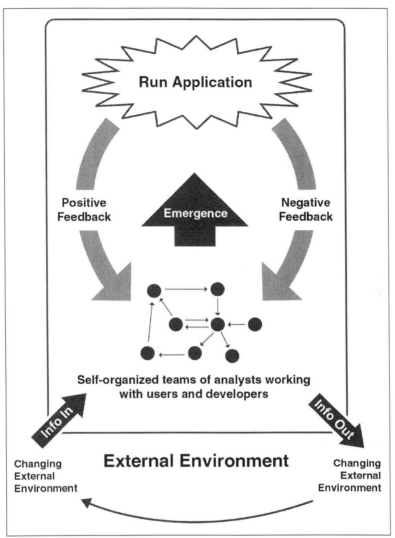

Figure 47: Users work with analysts, who work with developers when necessary, to build and continually tweak an application, which is tried out until ready to go live. The system itself changes the external environment, which adapts to the new system, and in turn may influence the new system in an ever-evolving process.

To be truly effective, it is not enough to adapt agile methodology to build situational applications on a digital business platform. We need a new methodology that exploits this new environment and mindset, and reflects the concept of emergence.

Emergent Methodology Rules

1	Don't fight the platform!	Not "going with the flow" of the platform will add significant time and complexity to your solution. So for example, use the default screens the platform generates for you instead of rebuilding them from scratch.
2	Have the user do as much as possible	The ultimate goal of emergent development is to get the user to take control of as much of the application as possible.
3	Coding is the last resort	The analyst must understand the platform well enough to ensure that coding is absolutely needed to get something done.
5	Constant feedback	Immediate feedback is critical to emergent development. A testing phase does not exist – testing is continuous, as functionality is completed.
6	No duplicate data	If the data already exists in the master database, it must be used instead of duplicated elsewhere.
7	No duplicate functionality	If the platform doesn't provide needed functionality, the analyst must check the Appstore, then check available web services in the cloud.
8	Put functionality that can be used by others in the Appstore	Be considerate to others – if you create functionality that could be used by others, make sure you put it in the Appstore.
9	Keep the system as simple as possible	Don't build anything that is not required *right now*.
10	Keep governance to a minimum	Don't add unnecessary red tape that prevents functionality from going live as fast as possible.
11	Have users use the system as quickly as possible	Start the system with the barest amount of functionality that provides benefit.
12	Limit programming to small increments	Provide programmers with the smallest bites of meaningful functionality possible.
13	Make it easy for users to give feedback on a continuous basis	Make extensive use of social networking so that feedback is easy to provide.

What is the difference between Agile and Emergent Methodology?

Agile	Emergent
Team is usually 5-10 people	Team is ideally 2-3 people
Focus is on functionality that can be delivered in a pre-determined time period	Focus is on continuous functionality delivery – time is not a factor
Time to live is usually 2-4 weeks	Time to live is usually hours or days
Users are passive participants	Users are active participants
Analysts do not build the application	Analysts build a substantial part of the application
Functionality is frozen for the duration of the "sprint" (development time box)	Functionality is never frozen – it evolves as it is developed
Estimation is an integral part of the methodology	Estimation is relatively meaningless - you want the requirements to emerge as the solution is developed
Feedback is periodic	Feedback is immediate
Formal status meeting are required	Because of the small team size, communication is constant, often through the social network

The Seed-Evolve-Reseed Cycle

An important aspect of the emergent methodology is the idea of seeding.

The Analyst would work with users in the following way:

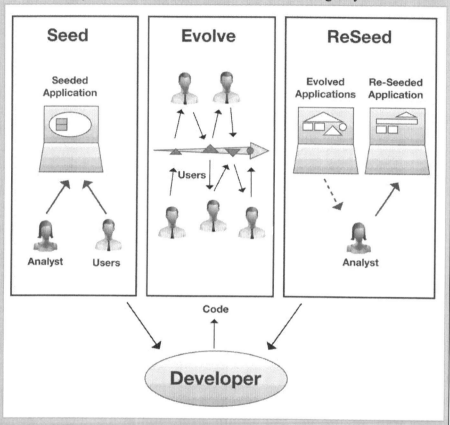

Figure 48: The Seed-Evolve-Reseed (SER) model ensures the application gets off to a good start, and then is kept on track as it evolves.

- The Analyst would basically **seed** the application with the user, helping the user put the first version in play.

- The user(s) would then **evolve** the application any way they like.

- There may be a point during this evolution where the Analyst needs to get involved once more to **reseed** the application. Reseeding is necessary when evolutionary growth is longer proceeding smoothly. It is also an opportunity to organize, formalize, and generalize information and application functionality created during the evolutionary growth phase so that it can be found and shared with others. [63]

The best solutions will ultimately emerge from these small steps forward, with the final step representing the sum total of accumulated reseedings.

An Example

It is possible to set up organizations so that when I am pursuing my own self-interest, I automatically benefit everyone else, whether I mean to or not. – Abraham Maslow

To understand the power of a situational approach to building solutions, let's take the following simple example. In it, each individual acts on his own to address their particular needs, and a comprehensive, adaptable application emerges. There is no central control, and very little coordination. Still, everyone is working towards the same goal.

---

[63]Daniela Fogli, Elisa Giaccardi, and Gerhard Fischer, "The Seeding, Evolutionary Growth, Reseeding Model," Center for Lifelong Learning and Design, UC Boulder, PowerPoint presentation, February 13, 2007, http://l3d.cs.colorado.edu/calendar/attachments/2008.02.13-fischer.pdf

Situation

An organization is running a series of seminars. People will register, pay, attend a seminar, and evaluate it. Registration can be handled online or over the phone.

There are a number of different parties involved:

- Marketing needs specific information to be collected during the registration process to help with fine-tuning the seminar agenda.

- The outbound sales team needs to be able to efficiently collect information when they register attendees.

- Management needs to monitor registration levels and analyze results.

- The billing department needs to track revenue and expenses, send invoices to attendees, and record payments.

- The seminar leader needs to communicate with registrants as soon as they register.

- The administrator needs to track who actually attends the seminar.

Conventionally, there have been two ways to approach this:

1. Use a mixture of Excel spreadsheets, email streams with (out-of-date) attachments, phone calls, lists, etc. There is no central database of information, and therefore no single record of everything related to the seminar. Status checking, searching for information, follow-up – all are performed manually, with lots of interruptions disrupting workers.

2. Have IT build an application. An analyst gathers requirements from each person involved, creates a requirements document, gets everyone to sign off, takes it to IT, which goes through its full development process. Eventually, the system is ready for

testing, and then the fun really starts. Of course, there will be numerous changes because users forgot things, or the requirements have been modified. Then, using the system causes more changes as it becomes more apparent what was forgotten earlier. Each change results in wasted time and money. Most importantly, IT cannot allocate resources in a timely manner.

Clearly, neither of these solutions is very appealing. This is where a situational application platform comes to the rescue.

Solution

Approach

Use force.com to progressively build the application as functionality is needed.

Skill set required

The type of users involved in this example are typical Millennials – they started working with MS Office back in elementary school, and have at least a basic understanding of what a database is.

Situational application scenario	
Who	**What**
Jane, Administrative Assistant	Jane is given the task of arranging seminars for clients. She wants to create a simple application to track seminar registrations.

Jane fires up force.com and starts a new application.

The first thing she does is specify the information she needs to track, by entering each data field she needs – name, address, etc. The system automatically gives her a complete data entry facility, along with the ability to give permission to other users who may need to access the application. She runs into a little difficulty in figuring out exactly how to structure her data, and calls on a Situational Analyst for a quick assist. |
| Sam, Outbound Sales | The outbound sales team is going to get clients registered. Sam will be the person responsible for making the calls and keying in the registrations.

Sam finds that the data entry screen Jane set up doesn't work well for taking registrations over the phone – the fields are in an awkward order, and there are too many screens to navigate through easily. So Sam opens the application created by Jane, and creates a different version of the data entry screen for himself using a drag-and-drop visual design tool. There is no need to ask Jane or anyone else to do it for him. |

Situational application scenario	
Who	**What**
Erica, Department Manager	Erica, the department manager, wants to track registrations as they are completed. She goes into the application, selects the data she's interested in, and generates a dashboard widget in the form of a gauge that shows the number of registrations in real time. She never has to ask Sam or Jane how many registrations have been completed at any time. She also wants to set up a workflow so that she can approve the registrations before they are accepted. She opens up the Visual Workflow Designer and adds a workflow that gets kicked off when a registration takes place. Other stakeholders will extend this workflow further down the process.
Frank, Seminar Leader	Frank wants to know when someone registers so he can contact them personally. He doesn't need to ask anyone to add this capability to the system for him. He just adds a simple workflow rule to the workflow Erica started that tells the system to update his Chatter feed (and/or send him an email) every time a registration record is added. He also decides he'd like Sam to collect an additional piece of information when he takes registrations, to help him plan his agenda. He adds the fields he needs, and Sam is automatically informed that this change has taken place in the system. Sam can then adjust his data entry screen as he sees fit.
Jane, Administrative Assistant	Jane needs people to register when they arrive for the seminar. She adds the additional fields so she can track this, and creates a simple registration screen. When attendees come to the seminar, they are asked to sign in using PCs provided. Their sign-ins are immediately registered in the system. No intervention is required by anyone else.

Situational application scenario	
Who	**What**
Frank, Seminar Leader	At the conclusion of the workshop, Frank wants to send out an evaluation form to be completed by each attendee on their mobile devices. He goes into the workflow designer and creates a questionnaire. He adds a workflow rule that emails the questionnaire to attendees at the end of the workshop. Their responses are recorded in the database and attached to their registration records.

When evaluations have been completed, Frank uses built-in reporting and visualization tools to analyze the results. He can add any response that he thinks others need to know to Chatter, and followers of the workshop can also add their comments through Chatter. |
| Frank, Seminar Leader | A week later, Frank decides to set up an email that will go out three months after the seminar to each attendee, following up on their post-seminar progress.

To do this, he goes back into the workflow designer and creates a notification event that associates an email message with the email addresses of the attendees. He specifies when he wants the email to go out. When that time arrives, the system will automatically send out the email. |

Figure 49: This describes how each person involved takes responsibility for building a small situational application to meet their specific needs. The ultimate application is fairly substantial, and would have taken a significant amount of time to build using traditional methods.

Chatter makes it easy for all involved to continuously discuss an application they are building together. Along the way, the Situational Analyst can assist and clean up as needed.

The next time the organization runs a seminar, they have a system ready to go.

Summary

In this example:

- Four different people have added their own functionality to the system with little effort;

- They were able to adjust the system themselves to work in ways that met their specific needs;

- They have collaborated, through Chatter, without even directly communicating;

- They have been able to build pieces of the system in their own time, at their own pace;

- They are committed to the success of the application – they own it.

From the self-serving actions of multiple individuals working towards a common goal using simple rules, a system emerges.

Caveats

1. Even though this is a relatively simple application, it could grow into quite a substantial one in the future. Therefore, a Situational Analyst should be involved from the start and Seed-Evolve-Reseed needs to be employed to keep the application manageable.

2. Some protection is necessary to ensure that other people don't disturb what you have done. This can be dealt with through a combination of permissions and guidelines. Remember, these are small applications, usually for a small group of people. It's not as though the application has to be protected from invading hordes of potentially damaging users.

3. While not needed in this particular situation, there is often a requirement for IT to provide external data for force.com applications. Plan A (the best option) is to get direct access to the data through the

platform so that the data looks native. Plan B is to import the data on a periodic basis. Plan C is to key it in manually (assuming the volume makes it feasible).

force.com can easily bring this scenario to life.

Now think about how much time and effort it would take to build a complete system like this using traditional IT methodology. It would never get done.

The complex adaptive system theory characteristics of this example include the following:

- The system is self-organizing.

- It is comprised of semi-autonomous agents.

- It behaves as a unified whole.

- There is no single point of control.

- A pattern (workflow) emerges.

- Communication/connection is built into the system.

- There is potential for unplanned creativity.

- The system evolves and adapts over time based on feedback from the environment.

- Agents act according to certain rules of interaction, that is, they work in the same system development platform, which prevents them from stepping on each other's toes.

- The system evolves to maximize "fitness" – in this case, efficiency.

- The system evolves historically – the experience of the agents determines the future trajectory of the system.

- The adaptability of the system can either be increased or decreased by the rules shaping their interaction (e.g., certain users can or cannot get access to certain data).

Supporting force.com in the Enterprise

Normal people can and will innovate of their own initiatives if enabling conditions are present. – A. Van de Ven, *The Innovation Journey*

The goal of situational applications is to eliminate as much IT overhead as possible. This needs to be balanced by ensuring that end users get the support they need to build their own solutions. Therefore, to get the most from your force.com investment, you need to provide the right kind of support for your universe of users.

The Rapid Response Center (R2C)

The first step is to create a Rapid Response Center (which I will refer to as the R2C). The R2C creates an ecosystem within an enterprise which would offer more autonomy to the lines of business (LOBs) by shifting some just-in-time business automation responsibilities from corporate IT to small teams and individuals.

The R2C facilitates:

- Collaboration—Help bring together a community of people who need a common solution to work on the application together, sharing it and improving it.

- Wide communication—As new applications and consumables are created, they are more likely to be exploited and reused if their existence is advertised widely outside of the primary community that created them.

- Feedback—Interested parties can comment on, suggest improvements, or even share their original work adaptations.

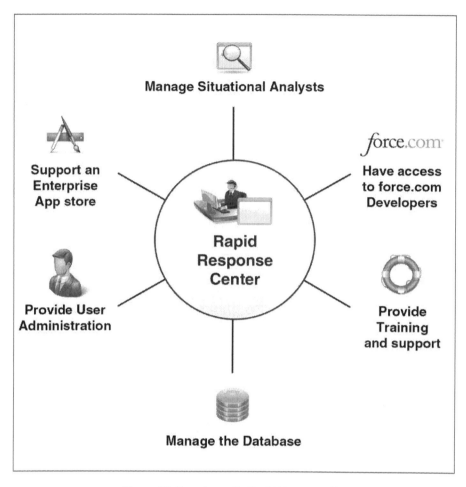

Figure 50: Functions of a Rapid Response Center.

The R2C would also be responsible for making applications available in an enterprise app store. Each app should be described, examples of how to use it provided, as well as contact information if questions arise. Users can comment on an entry and register details of their own usage examples. They can also add tags, and both the entries and tags can be rated on popularity and relevance. This helps drive the development of more functionality from actual usage.

Situational Analysts

The situational analyst (SA) has a critical role to play in the R2C.

Background

An SA will typically have a background as a:

- Power user who is currently building force.com applications in Excel and Access.

- Business analyst who is writing high-level specifications for IT.

- Soft core programmer who is writing applications in IT using languages like PHP.

Skills

The key skills an SA must possess include:

- **Communication skills.** The SA must be able to understand business users and help them express their needs. They must also be able to communicate with IT when there is a need for IT to provide access to data, or to extend the situational application platform.

- **Brainstorming skills.** The SA must be able to encourage users to think creatively in order to reach innovative solutions.

- **Database skills.** The SA must be able to help users translate their data needs to a database model.

- **Logic skills.** The SA must be able to help users translate their business logic needs into solid algorithms.

- **Process skills.** The SA must be able to help users express their process needs in workflows.

- **Platform skill.** The SA must be an expert in the situational application platform being used.

Situational Analyst Skill Set

Brainstorming

Communication

Process building

Platform expertise

Logic expression

Data modeling

Figure 32: The primary difference between a traditional business analyst and a situational analyst is that the situational analyst has a deep understanding of the digital business platform, and actually builds a good deal of the application themselves.

Responsibilities

The primary responsibilities of an SA will be to:

- **Model**. Understand a business situation and help model the database and business processes needed to support it.

- **Express**. Clearly express business logic without error.

- **Teach**. Teach users how to employ the platform most effectively in their jobs.

- **Seed and reseed**. Help users build force.com applications, first by ensuring the foundation of the application is sound, and later, after the application has been evolved by users, ensuring that the application remains solid and usable.

- **Specify**. Create specifications that tell a vendor, IT, or consultant exactly what extensions are needed to the platform so the users can do what they need.

- **Circumvent.** Find ways around any limitations in the platform without having to extend the platform.

- **Define.** Define what existing enterprise or departmental data is needed by users in order to effectively build their applications.

- **Suggest**. The SA should suggest and help implement links and re-use among force.com applications.

The Rapid Response Center Database Manager

Another important role to be played in the R2C is that of database manager.

This is not a database manager in the standard sense of a DBA – this database manager doesn't need to understand how to install, maintain, upgrade and tweak the database software, or SQL. The R2C database manager provides the following key services:

1. **Data modeling**. The database manager needs to understand how to build a data model and assist others in building their own data models.

2. **Protect enterprise data**. The database manager needs to balance the need to protect data in the database with the need to allow users to "do their own thing." One way to do this is to create different permissions for each level of the database. If an individual needs data from the departmental or enterprise level, they would need to have the appropriate permissions.

   In Database.com, this type of arrangement is easily implemented.

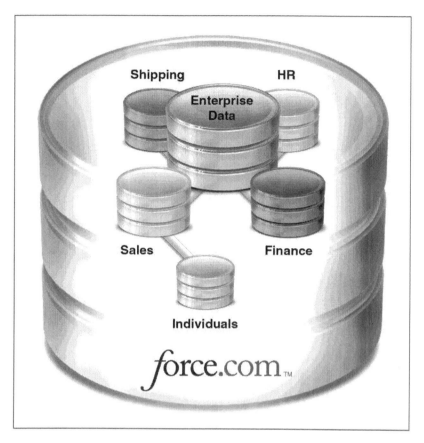

Figure 51: The goal is to make data that is shared available to those that need it, and at the same time, shield users from data that they are not interested in.

3. **Data integration.** The goal is to automate data integration tasks and maximize return on enterprise data by delivering relevant, trustworthy and timely data. This will reduce the cost with greater sharing and reusability.

4. **Data cleanliness, timeliness, and non-redundancy.** The database manager is responsible for ensuring that data from external systems is clean, timely, and non-redundant, before it is added to the database.

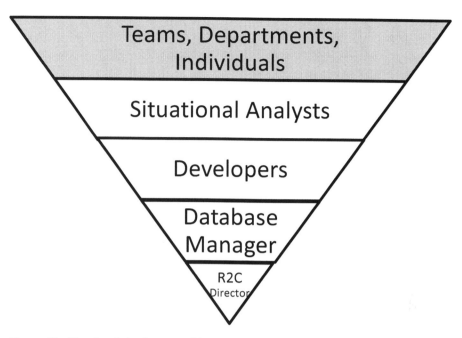

Figure 52: Situational Analysts would typically support multiple business units because many applications will be cross-functional. The developer pool (in-house or outsourced) supports the analysts as needed. The database manager serves analysts and developers, and the Rapid Response Center director allocates resources as needed.

Summary

Implementing force.com effectively requires more than simply signing up for licenses and starting to build applications.

Transforming the way in which solutions are built requires:

1. adopting a situational application mindset;

2. using an emergent methodology;

3. training situational analysts;

4. establishing a Rapid Response Center.

The Role of IT

The big thing [IT will] have to brace themselves for is that the functions that until now have accounted for most of their spending and most of their hiring are going to go away, such as all the administrative and maintenance jobs that were required to run complex equipment and applications on-site. This isn't going to happen overnight, but much of that is going to move out to the utility model over time. That doesn't mean IT shops won't continue to exist and have important functions – they might have even more important functions – but it does mean that their traditional roles are going to change....[64] – Nick Carr, author of *The Big Switch*

[I]t is imperative that technical professionals engage with in-flow business innovation and become a social collaborator with the citizen developer to maintain their business relevance. – Mike Rollings, "Citizen Development: Reinventing the Shadows of IT", *Gartner, Inc.*, February, 2012

Nothing is more difficult than to introduce a new order. Because the innovator has for enemies all those who have done well under the old conditions and lukewarm defenders in those who may do well under the new. – Niccolo Machiavelli, *The Prince*

The IT department has traditionally been the focal point of automation in the organization because it has the primary means of production (programmers, etc.) and the sole means of delivery (the data center). If workers wanted a system, they had to go to IT.

But both these factors are changing.

---

[64] Tom Sullivan, "Nick Carr: The Ways Cloud Computing will Disrupt IT," Computerworld, March 25, 2009, http://www.computerworld.com/s/article/9130441/Nick_Carr_The_ways_cloud_computing_will_disrupt_IT

With cloud computing and force.com, IT will gradually move from being the exclusive provider of enterprise systems to an enabler and facilitator of solutions built by self-reliant employees.[65]

This will accelerate the exploitation of new technology and help end users create competitive advantage and build closer links with their business peers.

By engaging with end users and helping them help themselves, IT can accelerate the exploitation of new technology and help end users create competitive advantage and build closer links with their business peers, while managing the risks of EUAD (End User Application Development). – Ian Finley, research vice president at Gartner

---

Like it or not, your organization needs to be ready for the do-it-yourself-ers. You can choose to ban this sort of work — and then be forced to do an about-face if an application gains a grassroots following — or you can provide a safety net for innovators within your organization who are looking for unique ways to differentiate your business.

force.com also provides the IT department with an "escape valve" for requests they don't have time for. IT can now say, "If you can't get it done through IT, here's a whole different way you can get it done. You can work on it yourself. Here are the tools. We'll help you make sure it's safe and secure and that it performs well. We'll help you make sure you're not creating a mess for yourself and for us, but you do the work."[66]

---

[65] "Changing the Corporate IT Development Model: Tapping the Power of Grassroots Computing," *IBM Systems Journal,* Vol. 46, Issue 4

[66] Shelley Porter, "Look out IT department - the citizen developers are taking over." silicon.com, July 15, 2011. http://www.silicon.com/ management/cio-insights/ 2011/07/ 15/look-out-it-department-the-citizen-developers-are-taking-over-39747704/

Facilitation

The value of IT groups within most organizations will no longer be measured by how well they operate information technology but how well they combine technology with business processes to create a stream of responsive and profitable products and services for their companies and customers. – Michael Hugos

IT provides frameworks, tools and environments for use by the citizen developer, and IT works with citizen developers to create cooperative relationships to safeguard and use data. - Gartner, Inc. *Citizen Development: Reinventing the Shadows of IT.* February 2012

Organizations are reluctant to really "set people free" to build and deploy their own solutions because it's perceived as being too difficult to control what people do, and too difficult to harness their efforts effectively for the good of the organization. Hence, we tend to create structures and strictures that end up limiting employees' freedom to perform – and thus contribute – at the highest possible levels.

But this perception is beginning to change. Information technology can now provide users the freedom and support to become self-reliant in ways that are compatible with the goals of the organization.

Unfortunately, this is still in the future for most companies: trapped in IT-centric development processes, the thought of giving business users the ability to do things themselves seems like a big leap. But in the same way that outsourcing a spreadsheet to IT today is absurd, so too will outsourcing many business applications in the future.

To facilitate situational application development in a number of different ways, IT can:

- Provide citizen developers with coaching on the best way to develop applications.

- Be responsive when users have questions, helping them along the way as an internal consultant.

- Provide access to enterprise data.

- Provide a way to share best practices.

- Work with teams to develop mutually-agreed upon guidelines.

- Encourage team members to collaborate, share what they've learned, and work out issues together.

- Recognize the importance of your citizen developers and reward their efforts. Providing proper training and certifications can go a long way in maximizing the business impact of their work.

- Ensure that your security parameters are well-defined. Maintain control over the ability to access, change, or share the data.

- Foster an environment in which workers can share their solutions with others.

- Support and supervise citizen developers to avoid a chaotic mess.

Seeding Data

> *All they [citizen developers] need are services that can supply them with data to feed these tools. IT can facilitate their efforts by supplying data services that virtualize complex data sources.* - Mike Rollings, "Citizen Development: Reinventing the Shadows of IT", *Gartner, Inc.*, February, 2012

force.com applications that rely on existing data can be built much more effectively and quickly when a base inventory of enterprise feeds is pre-established so the feeds can be consumed and mixed as needed for a given application.

Creating an inventory of data feeds allows IT to focus on how information needs to be delivered rather than how to find it. Establishing an inventory of feeds is a highly cost-effective and practical way for force.com applications to work with legacy systems, and can go a long way toward helping satisfy unmet LOB information access needs.

Define

- Find data

- Build the data model

- Govern information structure and content

- Understand data sources and relationships

- Define business rules to eliminate the risk of using bad data

Deliver Data

- Synchronize and make information available from all participating systems

- "Scrape" data off ancient applications (using screen scraping tools)

- Write code to extract data from packaged software

- Set up processes to refresh data as needed

Cleanse

- Standardize, merge, and correct information

- Create a single, comprehensive, accurate view of information by matching data across data sources

- Normalize data formats (for example, make sure all phone numbers and addresses use the same format)

- Replace missing values (e.g., insert defaults, look up zip codes for addresses)

- Standardize values (convert all measures to metric, prices to a common currency, part numbers to an industry standard, etc.)

- Map attributes (for example, parse the first name and last name from a contact-name field)

- Manage hierarchies – maintain data structures, such as bills for material, sales territories lists, etc., in a single place

Transform Data

- Combine and restructure information for new uses

- Mix and match information sources together to make them more useful, by filtering, merging, grouping, sorting, annotating, or augmenting

- Create new and purpose-built information feeds for the needs at hand

- Transform the format of cleansed data (such as addresses and phone numbers) into standards-based formats for consumption by force.com applications

Lightweight governance

End-user application development (EUAD) is nothing new, but the risks and opportunities it presents have become much greater in recent years… In the past, EUAD posed limited risks to the organization because it was typically limited to a single user or workgroup. However, end users can now build departmental, enterprise and even public applications. While this change enables organizations to empower end users and releases IT resources, it also heightens the risks of EUAD. – Ian Finley, Gartner research vp

Although each situational application is relatively simple, the enterprise IT environment will grow in heterogeneity and complexity. To shield users from these intricacies, the IT department can employ lightweight governance, which will also protect solutions from damage, prevent the accidental disclosing of protected assets, and enforce agreements with third-party asset providers.

A new opportunity for IT

To contend, IT must find new methods and structures to enable business growth and sustainable competitive advantage, as new opportunities and ways of working emerge. – "The Future of Work Has Arrived: Time to Re-Focus IT," *Cognizant,* February 2011

force.com offers new opportunities for IT to enhance its value and help the organization become more effective. Failure to take advantage of the possibilities would mean wasted resources, an inability to maximize the value of your company's collective candlepower, and lost opportunities.

- force.com creates opportunities for IT to service low-end, disenfranchised users.

- force.com provides effective ways to tackle high-value back-burner issues and alleviate the IT bottleneck.

- force.com can help restore the luster of many IT departments, because they will deliver "customized situational applications" that connect to a range of common and uncommon processes.

- force.com makes IT a business innovation partner delivering a competitive advantage to the business.

- force.com can move IT beyond being an operational cost center, into a business growth enabler.

- As succinctly put by Zapthink:

    IT no longer is seen as the entity that builds applications on behalf of the business, but rather provides the infrastructure, architecture, and governance by which the business units can meet their own needs.

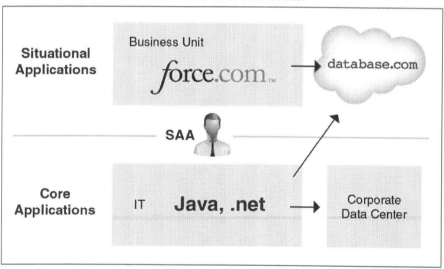

Figure 53: IT feeds enterprise data from core applications to database.com. IT can also start developing applications in the cloud by piggybacking on the business units embrace of database.com.

The Rapid Response Center

IT should spearhead the creation of the Rapid Response Center. This would be an excellent way to serve the needs of many more users, and allow IT to maintain a level of control over the DBP.

Situational Analysts

> *CIOs need to put an end to the stereotypical view of IT as a team of engineering-oriented specialists in specific technology domains who think only in linear and process-oriented models, far removed from the unpredictable marketplace in which businesses compete.* – "The Future of Work Has Arrived: Time to Re-Focus IT," Cognizant, February 2011

There will be an increasing need for situational analysts in IT's new role as facilitator (rather than provider). The R2C will foster an environment in which workers can share their solutions with others, help improve solutions through collaboration, and support the users continued building of solutions to meet new and evolving business needs.

Making the Transition

> *The business and IT must together find new ways of providing technology services more efficiently if IT is to enable new and more competitive business models and approaches...*

> *Clearly, it's time for IT to dramatically extend its capabilities and reinvent itself. No longer is it enough to just meet the current needs of the business; IT needs to position itself as the enabler for continual adaptation of the corporate operating model to ongoing waves of change.-* "The Future of Work Has Arrived: Time to Re-Focus IT," Cognizant, February 2011

Corporate IT will gradually move from being the exclusive provider of enterprise systems to an enabler and facilitator of solutions built by self-reliant employees.

Failure to do so will result in:

- reduced company competitiveness through missed opportunities;

- operational shortcomings resulting from a slew of uncoordinated, often dysfunctional, sub-optimal "solution-ettes";[67]

- a dramatic increase in the cost of technology support as a result of increases complexity, redundancy and the integration effort required.

CIOs have an important but challenging role: to change the enterprise culture to one that encourages and embraces innovative thinking and individual self-sufficiency. They need to actively remove existing technological and cultural barriers to support an entrepreneurial atmosphere. The Rapid Response Center is the start of an evolving experiment in enterprise-wide enablement and adoption of situational applications.

With or without IT's involvement, situational application development is happening – so IT can be part of the problem or part of the solution. It's their choice to step up to the plate and work cooperatively with the business to create opportunities in the cloud and lead their companies into the new world of cloud solutions.

To take advantage of this opportunity, IT needs to recognize force.com as a "good thing," with the understanding that there are capabilities outside the IT department that need to be used. This is nothing new, as exemplified by Excel spreadsheets and Access databases. Failure to embrace and support this "shadow IT" will result in significant lost opportunities.

---

[67] "We better have a Plan B for the 'Something about Services Era'", Bruce J. Rogow, Cognizanti, Volume 4 Issue 2 2011

Summary

IT leaders must be proactive in managing citizen developer initiatives by providing tools that enable transparency in monitoring, change control and analytics. Even if IT is not at the wheel, it should keep a close eye on the dashboard. - Eric Knipp, *Gartner research director*

Citizen developers are here to stay and will fundamentally change the future of IT work. How you embrace them will determine the future of IT within your organization and define the role IT plays in the creation of new innovative business practices. As a result, technical professionals must eliminate any resentful thinking inspired by shadow IT and see the partnership with citizen developers as an opportunity. They must rethink practices and processes to include these developers as full citizens within solution delivery, and create solution development infrastructure to support their unique needs. - Gartner, Inc. *Citizen Development: Reinventing the Shadows of IT.* February 2012

The role of IT in the enterprise is rapidly changing. The mix of IT resources and roles will change dramatically over the next few years. Rather than something negative, this should be seen as an opportunity to better serve the business.

In this brave new world, IT will be expected to:

1. Facilitate citizen developers to build their own solutions by establishing a Rapid Response Center, and providing Situational Analysts.

2. Seed data for the enterprise database by building mechanisms to exchange data with legacy applications and external databases, as well as ensure that data is cleansed and transformed as needed.

3. Provide lightweight governance to ensure developers don't step on each other's toes, and provide control where needed.

Migration

Almost every organization has at least some Excel, MS Access or Lotus Notes applications – some of them mission critical. These technologies are old, tired and inadequate, and need to be migrated to the cloud.

This is often the fastest way to get started with force.com.

Migration Drivers

Key drivers include:

- **Lack of business agility**. It's difficult to compete if you can't respond quickly to competitive pressures. For instance, the ability to deliver goods and services through emerging channels such as smart phones, tablets, and social media is a competitive advantage. But the outdated legacy systems were never architected with these newer technologies in mind.

- **High operational costs**. Every one of these older applications has to be individually dealt with in terms of backups, disaster recovery, support, etc. This eats up valuable resources, while important initiatives that could actually differentiate the business are not able to be developed.

- **Loss of system knowledge**. Every time an employee leaves the organization or retires, the knowledge contained in their spreadsheets or Access application flies out the window.

Migration Methodology

The objective is to first identify areas in the application portfolio where the biggest pain and biggest migration payoffs exist.

Evaluation Checklist

General

1. **User adoption**: How many users does this application serve? How effective do users find the application in meeting their needs?

2. **Maintenance costs**: What does it cost the organization to maintain this application?

3. **Value creation**: How much value is the application adding to the organization?

4. **Opportunity costs**: What opportunities are being lost by not migrating?

5. **Uniqueness to organization**: Does the application provide or could it potentially provide competitive advantage?

6. **Organizational fit**: How well does the current application meet the organization's current and emerging requirements?

7. **Business importance**: How critical is the application to the organization's operations (e.g., is the organization able to operate if this application is down)?

8. **Alignment to organizational drivers**: Is this application critical to the achievement of strategic organizational or program objectives?

9. **Technical value**: How stable and maintainable is the application?

10. **Complexity**: How complex is the application? How much effort will be required to understand the business logic?

11. **Fit for Force**: Is it a good candidate for force.com?

Security Risk

1. **Data Access:** When users download sensitive data to a local computer for use in a database, is the data still secure?

2. **Physical Access:** Can a desktop computer containing sensitive data or programs be physically accessed by other users?

3. **Network Share Access:** Can a user browse to another user's desktop and automatically gain access to unauthorized assets?

4. **Hardware Attrition:** Are there safeguards to remove confidential data from computers before they are rotated out of a department or organization?

5. **Audit Trails:** Does the data incorporate audit trails to track creation and modification information?

Data Integrity and Reliability

1. **Data Accuracy:** Is the data in the database possibly inaccurate?

2. **Backups:** Is the data part of an enterprise backup plan? Is there a defined policy for disaster recovery? Are there safeguards to prevent data loss when getting rid of old computers or passing them around within the organization?

3. **Sourcing:** Where is the data coming from? Is the data source reliable and accurate?

4. **Currency:** Is the data current? Is there a defined policy for data expiration? This is of special importance in environments of mandated data-sharing between and among organizations.

5. **Defects:** Does the program contain defects that yield incorrect results? If the program is connected to other programs or processes, how do they react to defects?

6. **Best Practices:** Does the application use best practices to ensure data and process correctness?

7. **Algorithms:** Does the application use organization-approved algorithms? The potential for data loss or loss of business due to inconsistent algorithms can be huge. What if two users have slightly different routines for calculating interest? What does the organization stand to lose?

8. **Viruses:** Is the program protected from viruses by up-to-date scanners?

Manageability

1. **Documentation:** What happens when the author of an Access application moves within or outside of an organization?

2. **Knowledge Transfer:** What is the cost of transferring knowledge of Access applications to new staff and computers?

3. **Inventory**: How many MS Access databases exist, and where are they located? Do they represent mission critical processes, or require secure data? How often are the files updated?

4. **Risk Assessment:** What is the organization's overall exposure to risk because of Access databases?

Migration Roadmap

After conducting a thorough investigation and analysis of your existing portfolio applications, disposition strategies need to be developed for each application.

> *Develop a plan for sequencing application migration.*
> *Time and cost considerations have to be balanced with*
> *urgency and user availability.*

Migration is generally an iterative process. Incrementally refining an initial approach into a roadmap that properly balances the organization's cloud migration vision with the disposition strategies and priorities assigned to specific applications allows for best outcomes.

Considerations include:

- Retiring aging, low-value, or redundant applications.

- Modernizing aging, high-value applications.

- Consolidating applications.

- Ranking by business importance.

- Logical predecessor/successor relationships – workflow and business process relationships need to be considered.

- Enterprise database – it may make sense to migrate applications that will provide core objects to be used by other applications when they are migrated.

- Evaluating what new technologies like mobile and social would bring to the application.

Migration Strategies

There are a number of different migration strategies that can be followed, depending on your needs.

Strategy 1: One-to-one

This strategy calls for simply migrating an application as-is to force.com.

The advantage is that the entire migration can be outsourced fairly easily, and can get an application completely out of Access/Excel quickly.

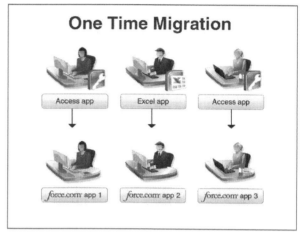

The disadvantage is that it initially perpetuates the data silo problem. Reengineering an application to take full advantage of force.com instead of simply replicating the functionality of the original may be a better idea.

Strategy 2: Data Only

This strategy calls for replicating the legacy database in force.com, and periodically refreshing it from the legacy system using a periodic refresh tool.

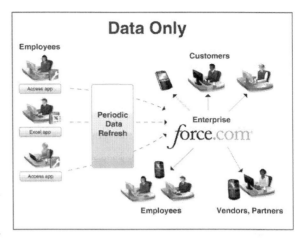

The organization can continue using the legacy application as is, but allows for force.com applications to be built using that data. Examples include making the data available to:

- customers, partners, and remote employees over the Internet

- mobile devices

- the social enterprise

- new force.com specific functionalities.

This is a quick way to start leveraging force.com without having to migrate the entire original application.

The disadvantage, at least initially, is that the original application remains in MS Access/Excel.

Strategy 3: Hybrid

This strategy moves the legacy database and switches data maintenance to force.com, and regularly refreshes the legacy system from force.com using the Access Migrator periodic refresh tool.

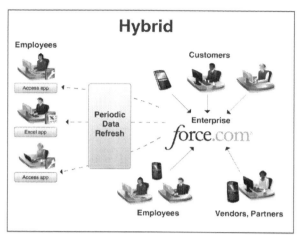

This will allow the organization to evolve the force.com version over time, while continuing to use legacy functionality, such as reporting.

The advantage of this strategy is that the legacy functionality can be migrated over time. The disadvantage is it requires keeping the legacy application up and running until it is fully migrated.

Strategy 4: Package Migration

It's possible that given the nature of the legacy application, it makes sense to replace it with one of the "packaged" applications provided by Salesforce.com, such as the Sales or Service Cloud, or by an application from AppExchange. Once

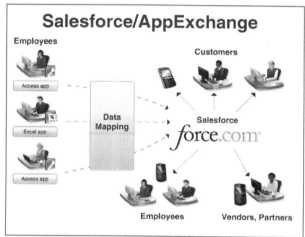

implemented, any needed customizations can be implemented using force.com.

Access Migrator can be used to map the data from Access to the packaged application.

Strategy 5: Rationalization

Over time, applications and databases are likely to contain duplicate and confusing data leading to business sub-optimization. Rationalization calls for a centralized initiative to consolidate data being used across multiple legacy applications into a single force.com database.

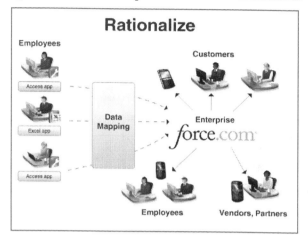

This strategy can be used in conjunction with the previous strategies, but requires more planning and control.

The advantage is that there will be no duplication of legacy data in force.com.

Migrating Lotus Notes, by Francois Koutchouk

Francois Koutchouk is the creator and President of EscapeNotes

Lotus Notes

A major Silicon Valley corporation started trying to remove Notes less than one year after a costly corporate-wide deployment. In one very large cosmetics company, it took five years to escape Notes. One of the most common first initiatives of a freshly hired CIO is kicking off a project to jettison Notes.

Some of the common reasons are:

- **Politics**: an attempt at regaining control over a close-knit Notes IS group.

- **Uncontrolled application and data growth**: large organizations have thousands of Notes applications developed and operating outside the control of central IS.

- **Misaligned technology**: the proprietary development and administrative technology of Notes requires skills that don't match the mainline corporate ERP or server strategy.

- **Application backlog**: "maintenance-only" investments in Notes led to a shortage of manpower to meet business requirements. The cost of failing to match ongoing business needs with application development is hard to measure, but is intuitively a "lost opportunity" for the corporation.

Technical issues with Notes fall into four categories:

Problems with Lotus Notes

Loss of Expertise and Institutional Knowledge

Most Notes applications have outlasted the job of the person who put them together, who took with them knowledge they failed to document.

Decentralized Data and Process Design

In contrast to a relational database, Notes is an object-oriented repository. No need to learn relational integrity: the world is seen as forms, responses, and files. This means that data is completely unstructured – the complete opposite of IT best practices. The practical consequence is that the business processes and data of Notes are hard for third parties to consume, without the cooperation of the original developer.

While Notes evolved as a tool to permit structured development though sophisticated inheritance of designs, those features are hardly used. The reason is the same: a business developer will not take the time and complexity required to locate, include, modify, and share objects.

Inconsistent Security Model

U.S. government agencies were key users of Notes in its infancy. Over the years security has remained intrinsic to the design of Notes, and applied properly by trained administrators, it has proven bulletproof over the last twenty-plus years.

Not all Notes system administrators have the skills or time to enforce security down to the remote corners of a Notes domain. More specifically, excessive rights are often granted to Notes business developers, allowing them to build parallel rather than strictly hierarchical privileges.

Practically this leads to an excess of groups, roles, and exception-based entitlements. Without native tools to spot those issues, data access swings like a pendulum, from stuck in a silo of former employees to excessively exposed.

New versions of Notes depart from the original intent

In an attempt to compete with other technologies, IBM has evolved Notes from an edge tool to an ERP-like platform, rendering it less and less accessible to its core constituents, the business developers.

Newer versions introduced the use of DB2 as a repository, Pages as a framework for development, and Eclipse as an Integrated Development Environment (IDE). This follows years of promoting Java over Lotus Script as a programming language. Those technologies are inaccessible to citizen developers – and require dedicated commitment to professionals.

The once vibrant third-party market building vertical applications (such as commercial property management, medical records management, or CRM) has moved on to more profitable platforms. The midlevel Notes developers switched to .Net, SAP or J2EE years ago, leaving only costly Notes experts and some offshore developers seeking a differentiator for their first job.

The combination of less accessible Notes development tools with a scarcity of skills leads to a stagnant environment unlikely to motivate significant investments.

Lotus Notes Migration Do's and Don'ts

First, what not to do:

Don't:

- ✓ Leave data behind
- ✓ Leave attachments behind
- ✓ Leave formatting behind
- ✓ Confuse users
- ✓ Suggest a big bang approach

Do:

Make sure you know what you have.

Do an in-depth discovery of what you have, including as many details as you can understand about it. Lotus Notes doesn't make this easy but there are resources and third-party tools to help you. You wouldn't plan for a major home renovation without knowing what was already there.

You need to identify key factors such as dependencies between Notes apps, access to external data, user activity (frequency, scope, etc.), security requirements, volume of data and files, and complexity.

Create a blueprint based on knowing what you have, and your specific business goals.

Some of the goals might be:

- Reduce the number of Domino servers

- Reduce the number of Domino apps that require a Lotus Notes client license

- Focus on one department first (e.g., sales)

- Deliver Notes apps currently unavailable to mobile workers

- Migrate apps that would benefit from real-time interaction rather than email back-and-forths (i.e., implement Chatter)

Rationalize, triage and migrate

The greatest return in migration is found in the rationalization step. Group Notes apps by finding duplicate designs or closely related "templates" or code. Merge Notes apps based on data siloed by region or functional role.

Add customized components

- Simplify and build upon the visual workflow tools of force.com, addressing first the backlog of Notes application development.

- Reduce the complexity of Notes views using the native force.com reporting tools.

- Normalize file attachments in a single repository (such as Content Libraries).

- Substitute "legacy" email and sequential workflows with real-time notification of Chatter.

Have a transparent transition plan

Some of us learned the hard way that a lack of planning can lead to three months of doing the dishes in the garage sink during a kitchen renovation. The sheer quantity of Notes apps and the number of users impacted requires building a calendar of events and respecting deadlines.

It's necessary to include basic training in what force.com looks like, how to find the Notes apps now in force.com, and what new functionality is available (Chatter, Content, etc.).

Users need a forum to request fixes to their Notes apps, as well as enhancements long overdue while their app was still in Notes. The team responsible for migrating Notes must retain sufficient bandwidth and show sufficient flexibility with "feature creep" to (within reason) deliver new value to the end user.

What force.com offers Lotus Notes users

Ray Ozzie, the father of Notes, showed the path it should have taken years ago: real-time and more ad hoc with Groove. He then evolved those concepts into cloud-based and deeply integrated with desktop applications while at Microsoft.

force.com is the closest cousin to Notes, intuitively making it the easiest platform to move to. The architectures are very similar:

force.com	Lotus Notes
App	Database
Custom Object	Form
View	View
Record	Document
Document	Page
Visualforce page	Agent, events
APEX class, triggers, validation	Shared elements
force.com IDE	Domino Designer/IDE
Formulas	Formulas
Buttons	Buttons
APEX2WSDL, web services API	Web Services
…	…

The similar architecture is not coincidental: the *intent* of force.com is to cater to the same needs that made Notes the most successful edge platform since Lotus 123.

force.com focuses on the same functionality but goes much further:

- Safe place to create, modify and deploy apps: but added the concept of sandboxes, code compliance, and consistent UI

- Agility: but removed the need for coding to put together a fully functional app, with UI

- Reporting: but added graphical tools that do not require understanding the data schema

- Workflow: but added visual tools to define, test, and run complex flows

force.com provides an opportunity to focus on building apps rather than worrying about the administration and delivery methods. It offers, for free, the following features over Notes:

- **Browser-ready**: force.com offers a consistent UI that eliminates the need to build "tricks" that complicate Notes code

- **Mobile-ready**: runs on iPad, iPhone, and other devices without additional code

- **Transparent platform upgrades**: no need to modify the app to handle new features on the server

- **Vibrant AppExchange**: third party apps are certified safe, easily integrated with existing apps and maintain a consistent look and feel

In Notes, an amateur could start with a free template provided by Lotus, change a few design features, and roll out the app. As the complexity of the requirements for the app grew, so did the need for Notes development skills, along a rather linear curve: learn the @formula language, learn view and form advanced formatting, learn LotusScript, learn how to integrate with outside data, learn JavaScript, etc.

As Notes did, force.com pushes the Rapid Application Development envelope along a smooth curve, without encountering the "wall" of alternative platforms. For instance, SharePoint provides smooth development while using standard templates, but anything beyond that requires a compiler and C# skills.

Those similarities of architecture, intent, and tools provide a unique career opportunity to business developers proficient in Notes. A few weeks are sufficient time to turn the Notes @formula and form-building skills into the comparable force.com skills.   More advanced Notes programmers will convert their LotusScript to APEX in less time they would need to learn Java and its frameworks.

Other considerations

- First-hand experience: when Lotus Notes was initially sold into large organizations, it was not a technical decision. Getting out is still not a technical decision – it's a business decision.

- Remove the politics: career paths can be reinvented, ownerships can be readjusted, and there is nothing religious about technology.

For those who have been involved for a long time with Notes, whether fighting for it or against it, here are the five stages of grief (with apologies to Kubler-Ross).

1. Denial and Isolation

    - Fighting against the political tide.

    - Producing and supporting many of the critical and non-critical but often used Notes applications in the organization, with a limited budget.

    - Supporting thousands of users and hundreds of apps on a Windows server that is seven years old, and a version of Domino out of support.

    - Being required to modify complex and undocumented Notes apps while hearing from management that "there has been no additional Notes development over the past few years – the users haven't really asked for any."

    - The best, after fifteen-plus years of continuous use: "Notes will die out on its own."

2. Anger

- "If we are doing all this on our own, why change it?"

- "By the way, if you put these apps in a new platform, make sure it is one that doesn't have to be touched for a few years."

- "If we migrate off Lotus Notes you need to prove you can migrate our biggest and most complex app for us, one hundred percent, seamlessly – in two days."

- While migrating is absolutely possible whether manually or with an automated engine, no consideration is really taken on what can be done better, or that it doesn't look the same as the average app in the organization, or that they have been building and refining the app for the past ten years.

3. Depression

- "If we go to the force.com platform, I'm going to lose my job." This is not the case as shown previously. The Notes skill set and platform structure is similar – going to the force.com platform is a great career move!

4. Acceptance

- "I've held on as long as I can. force.com is the new, better cousin of Lotus Notes."

- "I need help to migrate all those apps – I need a tool that can help me escape Notes through automation."

Conclusion

Migration should not be perceived as a sunk cost. It's an opportunity to adopt a new platform better aligned with current requirements for business agility:

- Reduce the IS application backlog by providing tools usable by those closest to the business requirements.

- Deliver apps in line with the growth of social and mobile business needs.

Migrating MS Access and MS Excel

The objective of SilverTree Systems' *Access Migrator* is to facilitate the orderly and expeditious migration of an organization's MS Access and MS Excel applications to the force.com platform.

Access Migrator is a combination of tools and services:

- An **analysis tool** that interrogates the Access application. It produces:

  - a complexity index based on an automated interrogation of the Access application;

  - an interactive report that provides a view of the logic of the application in an easy-to-understand format – this allows the migration of forms, reports and business logic to be done by force.com developers who are not familiar with MS Access functionality;

  - the forms and reports in HTML format, making it easier for developers to recreate them in force.com.

  - all the required information is on one page, eliminating the need for the developer to go to the properties of each form/report to get view the necessary code.

- A **migration tool** that migrates data and forms from Access to force.com.

- A **synchronization tool** that facilitates the ability to use functionality in both Access and force.com.

- A **migration factory** staffed by experts in both force.com and Microsoft technologies that are dedicated to migrating MS Access and Excel applications to force.com.

- A **Project Portfolio Management tool** to assist in managing multiple application migration projects.

Access Migrator facilitates the ability to quote projects on a fixed cost basis, which minimizes project risk and provides a clear timeline for project completion.

The SilverTree migration process is designed to result in a functional, fully-tested, enhanced cloud application that meets all client requirements and expectations.

Best Practices

1. A significant amount of functionality may be able to be recreated in force.com using the point-and-click workflow designer and report writer.
2. The real-time notification of Chatter can be substituted for "legacy" email and sequential workflows.
3. Multiple Access applications should be consolidated into a single force.com application where possible. Similarly, it is often possible to consolidate several Access forms into a single, well designed VisualForce page.

force.com vs. MS Access Cost Considerations

The Enterprise Value of force.com

The real value of force.com is fully realized when the entire organization (or as much of the organization as possible) is on the platform. Therefore, it's inappropriate to evaluate ROI for each individual Access application.

The reasons:

1. The cost of a force.com license needs to be spread among many applications.
2. Chatter has an enormous impact on productivity when used across the organization, allowing more to be done with fewer people, thereby reducing costs.
3. Multiple applications can share a single database. There are cost savings in not needing to create a database for each application, get data feeds, maintain the data, maintain backups, etc. New applications can be built faster because at least some of the database is likely to be already in place (e.g., Customer Master).

Cost Savings

- Eliminate hardware and software.

- Eliminate backups and disaster recovery.

- Eliminate operating system and Access upgrades.

- Eliminate the need to maintain multiple software versions.

- Eliminate client-side installation and support.

- Eliminate multiple data feeds to multiple applications.

- Eliminate the need to maintain redundant data in multiple applications.

- Decrease developer hours spent from design to deploy.

Productivity Improvements

- Eliminate up to 40% of email traffic with Chatter.

- Speed up problem resolution with Chatter.

- Make sure nothing falls through the cracks with workflow.

- Make the application accessible anytime by anyone with a browser.

- Single database immediately reusable across projects.

- Eliminate time spent ensuring that correct, clean, timely data is available.

- Workflow engine often eliminates the need to write any code.

- Many add-ins reduce development time.

- Easy integration with external systems.

- Better performance reduces time spent getting work done in applications.

Revenue Increases

Additional operational income resulting from improved:

- time to market

- application quality

- ability to deliver services through emerging channels such as smart phones, tablets, and social media.

A Comprehensive Enterprise Strategy

The ultimate goal is to create a single database with no duplication of data that can be used to build all situational applications in the organization. There would be one point of control, one system of record, and one place to get reliable, up-to-date data.

Lastly, having a single database makes migration faster to do.

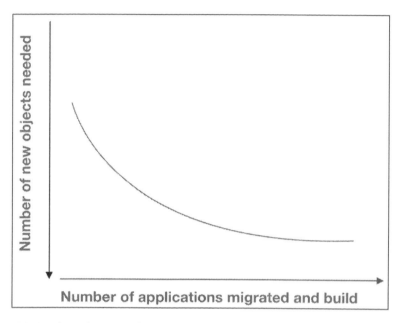

Figure 54: Another advantage of having a single database for situational applications: the more data objects are added, the more likely it is that the required data will already be available for new applications.

Case Studies

What follows are descriptions of the different ways that two enterprises – one, a division of a Fortune 500 conglomerate, and the other, a British not-for-profit – came to embrace force.com.

Case Study 1: Bottom-Up

Background

Like most organizations, this business – a chain with 6,000 stores – makes extensive use of MS Excel to build small ad hoc operational solutions. While Excel often works well for a single user with minimal needs, it becomes woefully inadequate as users are added and functionality requirements grow. As the number of applications grows, data is duplicated, isolated, and often unreliable and out of date.

The company's point-of-sale management technology implementation project started as a single spreadsheet and rapidly grew into a hodgepodge of many interrelated spreadsheets that were emailed around for data entry, cut-and-pasted, manually consolidated, and otherwise used well beyond the intended capabilities.

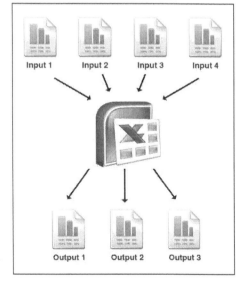

It became apparent that in order to meet the goals of the project without having to add an additional three or four resources, a much more effective system had to be put in place.

The company decided to use force.com to build the solution they needed. It addressed the needs for a relational database, workflow, reporting, task management, collaboration, and more. It also did not require any capital expenditure or any assistance from IT. force.com would allow the system to be built and deployed within a matter of a few weeks, at a relatively low cost.

With the execution of the point-of-sale management technology implementation project, the chain planted the seed for a comprehensive, enterprise-wide situational application environment that can be used by anyone in the organization to build solutions for their needs.

Scenario

- There are approximately 6,000 stores in the U.S., split between franchises and company-owned stores.

- The objective is to install a new PoS system in every store by the end of 2013.

- This requires coordinating multiple vendors and departments, integrating with internal and external systems, tracking a significant amount of information, reporting, and so on.

Current Solution

1. Master Spreadsheet

   - Contains 68 columns

   - Pulls data from 15 different "input files" which are updated on a weekly or daily basis

   - Input files are updated by different departments (IT, Help Desk, Training, Operations, HR, and others)

2. The Master Schedule is refreshed weekly

   - Six "output" files pull data from master schedule

- One file is distributed internally and five files are separated and sent to the appropriate vendors

Problems with current solutions

- Heavily reliant on email

- Important information falls through the cracks

- Redundant messages/notifications

- Flooded inboxes

- Redundant processes

- Data is managed in Excel makes finding information tedious

- Store tracking after installation

- No checks and balances system for missing information prior to install

- No easy way to provide an overview of project's progress

- Manual scheduling

- Manual workflow management

- No integration with other teams and departments

- Error-prone and time-consuming cutting and pasting spreadsheets

- Missed sending of notifications and updates

- Slow speed of huge spreadsheets

- No central repository of information (single source of truth)

- Need for backups and disaster recovery

Solution: force.com

- Centralized database provides a single, non-redundant source of truth

- Dashboard provides a snapshot of current status

- Workflow ensures that nothing falls through the cracks

- Elimination of cutting and pasting spreadsheets

- Automated notifications and updates

- Manages unlimited amount of data

- Guaranteed performance and uptime

- Automated integration

- No need for backups and disaster recovery

- Chatter allows all parties, both inside and outside the organization, to communicate in real-time, significantly reducing email traffic and speeding up problem resolution

- Chatter allows a knowledge base to be built organically, reducing the time required for future installation

- Mobile enablement allows technicians to complete checklists and register and assign issues immediately

Outcomes

- A complete force.com solution was built and deployed in six weeks

- No additional resources needed to be hired to complete the project in time

- The project was scheduled to be completed six months earlier than planned

- Beginning with 100+ users, it will eventually scale across the extended enterprise

- The solution has effectively addressed all the problems identified above

- The database created will be used as the basis for many other currently isolated applications

The future

- Other departments have been invited to take advantage of the database that has been created for the application. Having this core set of data available makes building new applications a lot faster.

- As more users get on to the platform, the network effect will kick in, and the company will be able to start using Chatter as an effective enterprise social network.

Case Study 2: Top-Down

"Salesforce as your strategic Cloud platform," by Katy Ring, Director at K2 Advisory[68]

What a growing number of CIOs are realising is that Cloud delivery makes it very much easier to develop, make available and consume application and business services.

This is part of a realisation that the evolution of Cloud platforms is potentially game-changing for CIOs, the IT service delivery they oversee and the organisations they serve.

---

[68] Katy Ring, "Salesforce as your strategic Cloud platform," www.BusinessCloud9. com, January 23, 2012. Reprinted with permission of Katy Ring and Sift Media. http://www.businesscloud9.com/content/salesforce-your-strategic-cloud-platform/7609

The key enabler for all this is the Cloud platform, which is the tool to enable the IT Department to act as an internal service broker for the organisation. Let's take the Salesforce application development platform Force.com as an example.

Until the acquisition of Heroku by Salesforce.com, it was a closed development environment with limited scalability, but now it has the potential to be a far more useful enterprise tool.

We've observed before that CIOs should re-think their view of Salesforce.com – it has much more to offer than web-based salesforce automation. At a recent Salesforce.com analyst event this was demonstrated by presentations from several customers, such as the Alzheimer's Society.

Phil Shoesmith, Head of Infrastructure at the Alzheimer's Society, runs a Microsoft shop with 1600 clients and 40 servers. However, he took the tactical decision in 2008 to use Salesforce.com for development work. As Shoesmith comments, "Security is a big issue for us. We need to be on top of the data protection issue, but we worked with the Cabinet Office and others regarding Cloud. And they have no issue in us using Salesforce.com from a data protection point of view."

From 2008 onwards the Society used Salesforce.com for more small projects, e.g.: tracking lobbying interactions with Members of Parliament, tracking properties, and health and safety. In 2009 Shoesmith set up a proper CRM system for healthcare contracts, which took two months to develop and is now used by 200 users.

Salesforce.com is now also used for managing tenders, tracking aid to 100,000 people each year, and is now the Alzheimer's Society's strategic platform for outward facing processes. It links into the HR system for users and locations, and Shoesmith is currently exploring migrating paper-based processes such as Expenses and PO management to the platform, using AppExchange to source solutions.

Shoesmith is pleased with Salesforce.com as a platform because of its quick development time, reliability, lack of on-premise software and infrastructure, as well as access to AppExchange to enable his team to piggyback on other's development work. For an organisation such as the Alzheimer's Society, Salesforce.com offers not for profit pricing, a not for profit community of users, and the ability to use an expanding portfolio that enables not for profit organizations to have access to significant technology developments they otherwise would not be able to access.

No relationship is ever perfect and Shoesmith is slightly concerned that the Salesforce.com licensing model is getting more complex, lacking clarity, for example, about whether an organisation needs to buy licences for external Chatter users. And there is still no information about when and where the Salesforce.com EU data centre will appear. Also Shoesmith notes that there is a skills shortage in Salesforce.com development in the UK, which makes use of external developers very expensive.

On the whole, Shoesmith is clear about the benefits that Salesforce.com brings:

- You make the business case once for development and then additional projects can be delivered much less expensively so that the Alzheimer's Society is able to do many more things than it could otherwise afford.

- It is rapidly becoming the enterprise data store for things outside finance and HR and having a central application for CRM reduces data protection risks as this is much more secure than having data scattered in different spreadsheets.

- Working with Salesforce.com enables a not for profit organisation to access technical innovation that it would not otherwise be able to access.

But is Force.com only a viable strategic Cloud platform if you are an SMB? The next challenge for Salesforce.com is fielding large enterprises that are prepared to use it as their strategic Cloud platform and talk about it.

What next?

There is nothing more difficult to take in hand, more perilous to conduct, or more uncertain in its success, than to take the lead in the introduction of a new order of things. – Machiavelli

To get maximum ROI as quickly as possible, implementing force.com should be tackled as an enterprise-wide endeavor. This will alleviate the problem of having to get licensing approval multiple times, and will thereby significantly speed up adoption. Of course, this is not always possible, so force.com will sometimes need to be introduced more gradually.

Who is the buyer of force.com?

When a major change arrives on the IT scene it's not always clear what the implications will be, if any, and so for large organizations a risk-managed wait-and-see attitude tends to prevail. Occasionally however some shifts offer cost savings, improvements to operations, or ways to tackle business problems that offer significant strategic advantage. The larger the benefit in one or more of these areas, then the more strategic the advance is and the greater potential it will impact the bottom line. – Dion Hinchcliffe

The case studies provided earlier represent two opposing approaches to bringing force.com into the organization.

The Fortune 500 company took a bottom-up approach, starting with a project manager looking for a better way to run his project. He understood the vision presented in this book, and methodically sold it up the chain of command, one level at a time, by demonstrating value that was easy for management to understand.

The not-for-profit company took a top-down approach, with upper management as the champions of change, deciding to try a different way to meet the needs of the organization.

Every company will, of course, take the approach that makes sense to them. The following table summarizes the pros and cons for each type of approach.

Who should implement force.com in the enterprise?

Position	Reason to implement	Benefits for the position	Drawbacks for the organization
CIO	• Provide service to underserved employees • Develop applications that could not be built cost-effectively before • Take a first step into the cloud • Provide a single database and toolset for situational applications for all departments across the enterprise • A single enterprise data integration point	• One decision for entire enterprise • Immediate ability to start building solutions across the enterprise • Shared implementation across departments • Best license pricing position • Fast ROI from the development of multiple applications • Enterprise-level governance from day one • Enterprise-wide data and function rationalization	• Potential restricted ability to make an enterprise-wide decision
Department Manager	• A single database and toolset for all departmental applications • Develop applications that could not be done before • Faster time to market and lower cost for application development • Eliminate duplicate silos of data and functionality in the department	• Everyone in the department can immediately take advantage of the platform • Fast ROI from the development of multiple applications • Good license pricing position	• Each department must subscribe separately • Likely continuation of departmental silos with duplicate data and functionality • Weaker pricing position vs. Enterprise • May need department-specific enterprise data integration • Hard to build and implement cross-function applications
Project Manager	• Fast development and deployment of a single project	• An immediate demand is satisfied • Can serve as a Proof of Concept for the rest of the department	• Limited license acquisition can restrict the effectiveness of individual solutions • No license pricing leverage • License must be justified for a single application • Can't take advantage of shared implementation • May need project-specific enterprise data integration • Hard to build and implement cross-function applications

347

Seven steps to get you going

Now that you're convinced force.com is a great idea, what do you need to do to get started?[69]

Regardless of who makes the buying decision, taking the following steps are a good place to start.

Step 1: Find a pilot project

Starting with a pilot project is critical in order to showcase the capabilities of force.com.

The application should have as many of these characteristics as possible:

1. Requires core enterprise data objects (e.g., customers, products, etc.)

    a. This will make the application more meaningful to a wider range of employees

    b. It can be shown as a starting point for an enterprise-wide central database for building situational applications across the organization

2. Includes workflow

3. Requires third-party integration

4. Includes social networking (use of Chatter)

5. Includes mobile access

---

[69] Also see "Cloud Strategy and Roadmap: The Path to an Agile Business" by Kamesh Pemmaraju, Sand Hill Group, May 11, 2011, http://sandhill.com/article/cloud-strategy-and-roadmap-the-path-to-an-agile-business/.

6. Includes both internal and external users, to allow a better understanding of Salesforce.com's licensing options

7. Will provide meaningful and understandable ROI

It will help tremendously if you use many of the advanced features of force.com in building this application. For example, create an iPad screen, build great looking dashboards, exploit Chatter, and implement workflow.

Candidates for a pilot can usually be found where workers are sending, sharing, and cutting and pasting Excel worksheets, or trying to get along using a totally inadequate MS Access application.

Step 2: Exhibit the pilot project

Once the pilot application is up and running, schedule short presentations for as many departments as possible. Explain the problem solved by the application, and demonstrate all the functionality delivered.

The presentation should make clear the elimination of hardware and software procurement and implementation, the speed of development and deployment, and the ease with which end users can build their own workflows, reports and dashboards.

Step 3: Look for Low-Hanging Fruit

There are millions of applications out there, some of which have become mission-critical, that are built on 20+ year old technology like Access, Lotus, and Excel. Many of these applications have to find their way to the cloud sooner rather than later.

Ask departments to analyze their application portfolio and backlog to identify the best candidates for an initial force.com implementation for their area of responsibility. Ask questions like:

- Can the application take immediate advantage of force.com functionality, like mobile and social?

- Will moving the application to force.com help drive innovation?

- Are there significant costs that can be eliminated by moving the application to force.com, like hardware/software?

- Is there anything you need that has been back-logged in IT?

With force.com, it is possible to develop a simple but meaningful application in less than a week. Once you have successfully completed these projects in much shorter time and with less effort than it would have normally taken, you can then push the results up the value chain and find new projects. Solving specific and tactical problems will provide the basis for further success.

Step 4: Experiment and Learn

Embracing any new technology involves learning. Conduct experiments to see how force.com meets the needs of the business. Through this process, you can become familiar with perceived constraints, issues, and benefits of the technology.

Step 5: Communicate a Vision

Make no small plans; they have no magic to stir men's souls. – Spencer W. Kimball

Educate employees in what a digital business platform built around force.com can do for the success of the business. Mobilize employees around a clear vision, and translate that vision into a set of measures and targets to drive the desired results.

Step 6: Make it Easier for Employees to Get on Board

The successful move to force.com as a transformative technology requires a willingness to adopt a new mindset and adapt to new approaches and technologies.

As Andy McAfee, a principal research scientist at MIT, puts it:

> *"It's difficult to underestimate the fondness of people and organizations for the status quo. While most managers may recognize that using new technologies will increase their ability to effect change within the company and change how people work, many don't really understand what this means for themselves or their company, and don't see where the innovations will come from. Sometimes they're unwilling to enter into a field they know little about. Sometimes they just don't think it's their job to take the initiative."[70]*

And then there is the fear factor:

1. Fear of the unknown

2. Fear of loss of control

3. Fear of job loss

4. Fear of taking risks

5. Fear of change

Communicating the vision, showing early successes, implementing the Rapid Response Center – all of these things should be deployed in the effort to get employees on board.

---

[70] "Transform to the Power of Digital," Capgemini, 2011

Step 7: Develop and Execute a Roadmap for IT

Think big, start small, and deliver quickly.

The starting point includes:

- Establishing and staffing a Rapid Response Center
- Training Situational Analysts
- Appointing an enterprise database manager
- Building an enterprise database
- Developing a migration strategy

Conclusion

How important is cloud computing? I would argue that it's a sea change—a deep and permanent shift in how computing power is generated and consumed. It's as inevitable and irreversible as the shift from steam to electric power in manufacturing, which was gaining momentum in America about a century ago. And just as that transition brought many benefits and opened up new possibilities to factory owners, so too will the cloud confer advantages on its adopters.— Andrew McAfee, MIT Sloan School of Management[71]

There's a warning for everyone that attempts to dismiss the cloud as a fad or as just another means of delivering IT. Those who really seize its potential are creating entirely new business opportunities — not only start-ups like Recruitment Genius but also big established firms like HSBC. And those initiatives are stealing business away from others that are slower to react to what's going on. As the cloud matures, resistance isn't merely futile; ignore the cloud and you could find your business has bought a one-way ticket to the scrapheap.- Phil Wainewright, "Why you can't afford to resist the cloud," ZDNet, January 27, 2012

In an era when change arrives without warning and threatens to eradicate entire companies and industries overnight, organizations can survive and prosper only by engaging the minds and emotions of all employees, providing them with the right tools and encouraging them to use their initiative to adapt the organization to the changes buffeting it.[72]

---

[71] Andrew McAfee, "What Every CEO Needs to Know about the Cloud," Harvard Business Review, The Magazine, *November 2011,* http://hbr.org/2011/11/what-every-ceo-needs-to-know-about-the-cloud/ar/1#.

[72] Thomas Petzinger Jr., *The New Pioneers: The Men And Women Who Are Transforming The Workplace And The Marketplace,* NY: Simon & Schuster, 1999

Empowering individuals and teams to take responsibility for building solutions will produce the flywheel affect – each small push, taken together over time, can have an enormous impact.

Imagine the level of innovation that can be achieved by enabling your employees to create applications that help them solve situational problems or take advantage of new business opportunities.

Indeed, force.com applications represent billions of dollars in potential productivity gains, higher customer satisfaction, new business opportunities, faster time to market and innovation.

To realize this potential will require a concerted effort that brings together all the necessary strands of platform, support, methodology, and mindset.

Once these are in place, you can set your employees free. The result will be a peak-performing, robust and sustainable organization – based on the shared efforts of thoroughly empowered, energized, self-reliant employees working with the most powerful tool ever created!

Need help?

My company, SilverTree Systems, focuses on implementing the ideas expressed in this book.

If you are looking for help getting started, please contact me at jon@silvertreesystems.com.

Figure 33: We can help you build your business in the cloud.

Appendix A: Best Practices

The following summary provides a handy reference guide when implementing and using force.com.

Management

Embrace the Citizen Developer

Citizen developers are here to stay, and how they are embraced will determine the future of IT in your organization.

Being on the front lines of your organization, citizen developers can help create new business opportunities and achieve new business outcomes. They will provide new solutions that are crucial to improving the organizations agility and responsiveness. It's time to bring them in from the shadows!

Make it overwhelmingly attractive for your users to select force.com

Users tend to do the easiest thing, so you need to establish an effective Rapid Response Center and offer easy access to force.com data, support, and training. You don't want to repeat the past, with users going off and doing their own thing because it's too hard to use the options sanctioned by the company.

Force first!

The goal should be to leverage force.com as much as possible. The more applications built on the platform, the greater your return on licensing. The database will become more complete over time, more applications can take advantage of existing external data integration, and it will build up a cadre of experts in the platform.

Fragmented solutions built on multiple platforms are expensive to maintain in aggregate. Siloed applications are harder to pull into an interconnected ecosystem.

Focus on new, not legacy

Peter Coffee puts it best:

> *Treat the toxic sludge of legacy apps the way you'd treat a Chernobyl in your basement. Put a concrete cube around it, feed power in and get data out, but don't go in there and try to innovate in it: instead, innovate in mobile experience delivery, and social community creation, with cloud platforms that are designed to integrate and add value instead of being built to wall out alien technology.*[73]

Don't create silos

Companies that implement force.com through multiple, separate and uncoordinated initiatives are doomed to create information silos, making it harder to connect the right people in the right ways to create and maximize value.

Leverage the network effect

The utility of social networks scales exponentially with the size of the network. Adding a single person to a social network doesn't simply increase the network by one – because they can now communicate with everyone already on the network, the number of nodes added is exponentially higher. The network effect applies to information generally – the utility of any information increases exponentially with the number of individuals accessing it.

---

[73] Peter Coffee, "Refuting Cloud 'Lock-in': Zero, One, Too", Cloudblog, Jan. 18, 2012, http://cloudblog.salesforce.com/2012/01/cloud-leverage-is-not-lock-in.html

There is therefore much more benefit to be derived by having everyone in the organization on the platform networking and sharing information with one another.

Embrace change

An organization's competitiveness is determined by the speed at which it adapts to change. Agile organizations capitalize on changes in the market by quickly adapting to them, resulting in a definite competitive edge. They do this by embracing the notion of continuous change, setting in place a mindset that allows for the rapid redefinition of business processes, reorganization of staff, and realignment of technology in support of new business goals.

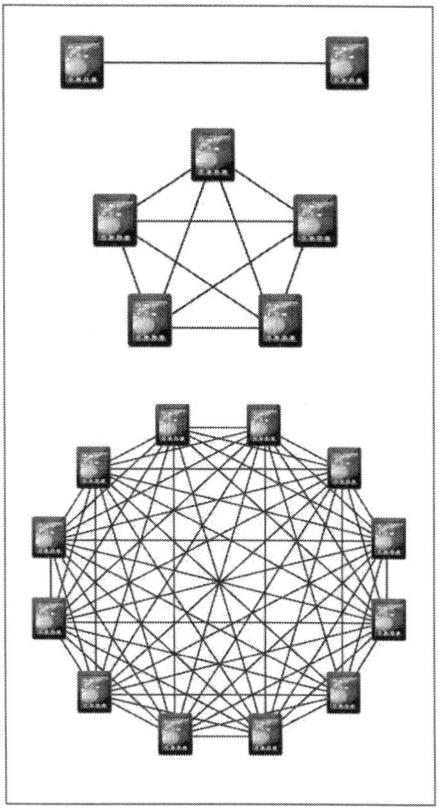

Figure 34: This diagram shows the network effect, the phenomenon whereby a service becomes more valuable as more people use it, thereby encouraging ever-increasing numbers of adopters. The lines represent the potential interaction between devices. For example, Facebook could add its second million users much faster than it first million because of the network effect.

The key to embracing change and developing into a technically agile enterprise lies in the development of adaptable business systems – systems that can change quickly in response to changes in either the processes or the organization they support.

force.com makes this much easier to do by significantly reducing the time and effort required to build and modify business applications.

Re-think ROI

Because of the significant cost involved, calculating ROI for *traditional* applications is essential. The cost of justifying the return on investment for developing situational applications will, in many cases, be more costly than developing the solution in the first place. No one would do an ROI analysis for a spreadsheet, for example.

Embrace incrementalism

Because the overhead of starting up an IT project is so great, it only makes sense to tackle large projects that offer significant payback. A single custom application may not have the immediate impact of a packaged application, like ERP. But the incremental impact of a multitude of small situational applications can result in geometric growth in productivity.

Use force.com as a platform, not a tool

With force.com, the whole is much greater than the sum of the parts. The real benefit comes from using the full force.com platform.

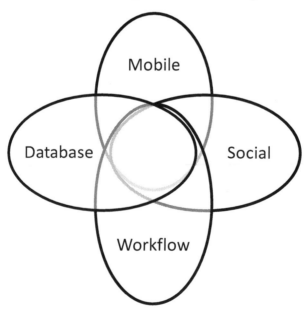

Be careful choosing your force.com developers

While it's true that an expert programmer is significantly better than a mediocre programmer, a mediocre force.com developer can be potentially much more costly still. Remember that you can end up doing much more work than necessary writing code if you're unaware that the platform can provide the functionality you need in just minutes.

Experiment and innovate

Because building new applications is relatively quick and easy, it becomes much more feasible to experiment with new solutions. Since the cost is relatively minor and there's no capital expenditure at all, it's easy to close a new project down if it doesn't work out. The risk of undertaking a new project is significantly reduced.

Stability versus agility

On one hand, you don't want Joe in shipping to be able to add or delete a new field in your Product Master. On the other hand, you don't want him to wait around for IT to create a table next week that he needs for an urgent project now. Have a gatekeeper to make sure enterprise data is protected, but allow users to add their own data as needed.

Resist the temptation to prematurely integrate situational applications into the core of your operations

When a situational application becomes mission critical, there's often a temptation to have IT take over and treat it like a traditional application. This may have the chilling effect of cutting off new innovations and making enhancements more difficult.

Outsource more effectively

Using a complete application development and deployment platform like force.com makes it easier and less risky to outsource application development, because all major architectural decisions have already been taken care of. If you need to extend the platform by adding more functionality, the task can be isolated and hooked into the platform with relatively ease.

Don't work alone

There are a lot of new ideas and new technology to absorb. While it's sometimes easy to lose sight of the big picture, it's also easy to miss critical details. Work with someone who can help you construct a vision that works for your organization, and join with an organization that can help you leverage your technology to the fullest extent possible.

Limit the number of people involved in projects

Typical applications involve veritable armies of participants, from analysts through network specialists. The ideal situation would be to eliminate many of the usual players involved in building an application – project manager database administrator, technical architect, QA, and so on, by having the user work directly with a Situational Analyst.

Database

Make sure there is a single source of truth

Users should be able to point to just one data object to get what they need, and there shouldn't be any duplication of data across all applications using force.com. For example, if you want to build an application that uses the list of Franchisees, simply point to the Franchisee object. There should be less and less need to add new data objects as the core enterprise database evolves over time.

Start building a centralized, controlled enterprise database as soon as possible

Don't wait for the Enterprise database to be built before starting to build applications. Instead, have the Enterprise database emerge as new applications are built and existing ones migrated.

Allow departments to control access to their databases

Allow departments and individuals to add their own data as needed to their own databases. If another department needs access to someone else's data, consider moving that data to the enterprise database.

Analysis

Exception handling

Building systems that can handle everything users may throw at them increases cost and complexity exponentially. Have people, not computers, handle rare exceptions and one-off occurrences, and develop systems to handle the routine, day-in and day-out transactions. Resist the temptation to build lots of complexity into new systems. Given the ease of adding functionality to a force.com application, sophisticated exception handling can easily be added over time, as necessary. Social networking will also increase the effectiveness and speed required to handle exceptions.

Develop what users need *right now*

Unlike traditional systems, where users try to think of everything they may ever need because they're afraid there won't be a "Phase 2," situational development is all about evolving the application. It makes sense to start with the bare necessities, go live, and evolve from there.

Because you focus only on the here and now, you can build a system very quickly – figure out what matters and leave the rest.

Design

Use the standard user interface

Wherever possible, use the standard force.com user interface. Because it requires no programming expertise, it saves significant time by eliminating hand coding, testing, maintenance, and adding enhancements.

Focus on "good enough"

With force.com, your goal is to produce something "good enough" of value as soon as possible, deploy it immediately, and refine it later if needed. The formal methodology of traditional applications, favoring a "big bang" approach – getting all the requirements, then programming – is unnecessary now.

Underprescribe

Keep solutions "elegantly minimal" so you can create "elbow room" for local interpretations and innovations. While the tendency in traditional development is to overprescribe – to think of all the possible exceptions and variations that might occur and cater for them when the system is written – now, underprescribing is what works best.

Get something real up and running quickly

Get users to start using the system as quickly as possible, even if it means starting with less functionality and taking shortcuts. There's no substitute for live software to put things in perspective.

Use simplifying assumptions

When you aim your applications at a very specific target audience, assumptions that simplify the application can be made. For example, you may be able to build an application without being concerned with permissions or approvals, because you know it will be used by a small community who know and trust each other.

Development

Don't fight the framework!

The power and development speed provided by force.com is derived substantially from the framework it's built on, which expects you to do things in a certain way. Don't get fancy and try to bypass the force.com framework, or try to draw outside the lines. Architect your application within the boundaries of the platform in order to retain all its possible advantages.

Get simple things done well, not complex things done too fast

The goal should be to find simple solutions to immediate problems, not cramming complex solutions into shorter development times. An elegantly simple solution (a robust 80% solution) doesn't do everything – just the most important things.[74] This will also limit the amount of code that needs to be written and maintained.

---

[74] Michael Hugos and Derek Hulitzky, *Business in the Cloud: What Every Business Needs to Know About Cloud Computing*

Don't write code if you don't have to

Writing code is not only time-consuming and error-prone; it also requires deep skill, extensive quality assurance, and longer time-to-market. Using a high-level point-and-click, drag-and-drop graphical interface to specify business logic, without coding wherever possible, significantly reduces the cost of development.

Provide early visibility through prototyping

force.com facilitates taking an incremental versus "big bang" approach to building systems. Companies can start small and grow by eliminating the need for costly and risky large-scale development projects. New ideas can be implemented without undue risks of jeopardizing the business at large.

Embrace messiness

Significant time has often been wasted getting an application to look like "packaged" software – but highly adaptable systems may just have to look a bit sloppy. There is no point in wasting resources and energy trying to make something look beautiful if it isn't going to be around very long or if it's going to keep changing. Of course, this doesn't apply to some customer-facing applications.

No documentation

In a constantly changing world, there's no time for writing documentation. force.com provides the ability to provide help in context, and Chatter will provide users with access to just-in-time answers.

Licensing

Use standard Salesforce.com functionality when needed

If you need functionality that is already provided by off-the-shelf Salesforce functionality (such as CRM), don't try to recreate it. Sure, license costs may be higher for those users requiring the functionality, but chances are you'll be better off in the long run (and in the short run, the functionality will be available immediately).

Use force.com licenses when possible

There is no reason to purchase licenses for Salesforce off-the-shelf functionality for users who won't need it. Purchase less expensive force.com licenses instead.

Use alternative force.com licenses for light users

force.com offers low-cost licenses for users (both internal and external) who will use the system in a limited way (e.g., for checking statuses, or occasional data updates). Make sure you understand what the options are at any time – they aren't set in stone, and can sometimes be negotiated for special circumstances.

Appendix B: Leveraging force.com

> *The slightest advantage of one being, at any age or during any season, over those with which it comes into competition, or better adaptation in however slight a degree to the surrounding physical conditions, will turn the balance.* – Charles Darwin, *In the Origin of Species* (1859)

> *As the second decade of the 21st century dawns, organizations worldwide are contending with four unrelenting and interrelated forces that were once peripheral but are now critical to their very existence. These forces — accelerating globalization, changing demographics, expanding virtualization and evolving cloud-enabled collaboration technologies — are causing organizations across industries to seriously re-think not only how they are organized and operate, but also how information technology should be utilized to unlock innovation that enables greater operational efficiency and business effectiveness.* – "The Future of Work Has Arrived: Time to Re-Focus IT," Cognizant, February 2011

force.com facilitates building many new types of applications. This appendix provides a good sampling of what is possible, and is aimed at stimulating thinking about how to leverage force.com to the fullest extent possible.

The potential impact of force.com

> *The effect of these continuous adjustments and enhancements to business operations can generate a steady stream of savings and new revenues that may sometimes seem insignificant from one month to the next,*

but as years go by, they become analogous to the growth of capital over time due to the humble but powerful effects of compound interest. The profits generated this way can be thought of as the agility dividend. – Michael Hugos

The days of market stability and competitive advantage from a single innovation are over. Today, companies must respond to new entrants in their industries that come from nowhere. And they must not just innovate, they must set the pace of innovation, gaining temporary advantage, one innovation at a time, and then move on to the next. – Peter Fingar, *Extreme Competition*

Organizations can find hundreds of ways to make small, continuous adjustments and provide value-added services that will increase their profits and decrease their costs every day, every week, every month.

force.com can provide many of these enhancements with out-of-the-box, or near out-of-the-box functionality.

Here are some examples:

Improve exception handling

When things "just come up" and disrupt someone's workflow, requiring special time and attention, routine work stops – and force.com can help.

- **Deaf ears.** Messages requesting action on an internal control issue languishing in email boxes and on voice mail systems can be dealt with by implementing Chatter.

- **Burnout**. Process owners grow weary of repeated requests to address exceptions, even as they are in the process resolving them. Eliminate this by providing an easy way to share and spread knowledge through Chatter.

- **Falling through the cracks**. What if the email alert for an exception goes to the inbox of an employee on vacation? Eliminate the chance of things from falling through the cracks with workflow.

- **Knowledge silos.** Enable open communication across all levels of the enterprise through Chatter, to eliminate many of the decision and communication issues caused by limited methods such as email. Alerts can be sent by a community of operators who handle exceptions, allowing for a collaborative effort in real-time, providing faster resolutions. Alerts can be accessed via mobile phone, or at home via the web. Visibility into exceptions is now more widespread, making finding the answer easier than before.

- **A home for resolutions.** Social networks in the enterprise create a permanent "home" for exceptions where users can communicate and collaborate around the answers. Exception management through social networks gives management clear insight for handling these exceptions. Viewing and monitoring interactions and necessary actions taken to resolve exceptions can lead to better implementation, revisions, or training on these systems, and increase productivity throughout the enterprise.

Improve decision making

- Increase the speed by which workers receive information through the use of Chatter.

- Deliver the right information to the right person at the right time through workflow.

- Provide shared, common access to the latest information at all times through an enterprise database.

- Automatically consolidate information from multiple sources in an enterprise database.

- Ensure employees are aware of pertinent information at all times through Chatter.

- Isolate the specific information each worker needs so they don't have to look for it and extract it themselves through task- and role-specific mobile apps.

Reduce errors

- Reduce re-keying of information by providing single data entry facilities for multiple systems.

- Provide a central shared database to ensure everyone is working from the same data at all times.

- Eliminate paperwork by providing online and mobile forms.

- Allow the sources of information to enter information themselves (e.g., can customers enter their own orders) through any device.

- Prevent things from falling through the cracks through automated notification of missed deadlines.

- Deal with problems more quickly by automating red-flag reporting through monitoring (e.g., automatic reporting prompts the appropriate user to take action, such as when a project is overdue or over-spent).

Provide better information faster

- Ensure accuracy of information by having clients take responsibility for entering and maintaining it.

- Improve timeliness of client information – they can update it themselves when their information changes.

- Provide quick access to data through a single, easily accessible repository and personalized views and reports, to significantly reduce search time.

Improve attention allocation

- Reduce the need for constant follow-up by using automated notifications and Chatter.

- Reduce the need to search for information – make the information come directly to the users when they need it.

- Reduce the amount of clutter the user needs to push through to get the exact information they need.

- Track assignments and issue automatic alerts to ensure all team members know exactly what they're responsible for.

Increase customer satisfaction

- Improve customer loyalty by making the client feel you care specifically about *their* unique needs (by creating highly customized solutions for each client).

- Respond faster to customer queries by making information easy to find.

- Provide customers with the ability to serve themselves.

- Keep the customer informed through automated notifications

- Decrease miscommunication by increasing visibility into processes that impact the customer.

- Identify problem trends early by automating data monitoring of customer-related activities.

Increase competitiveness

- Gain insight by unlocking and re-mixing information in new ways.

- Make it easier and less costly to try new ideas.

- Free up more time for innovation by automating common tasks.

- Make it easier to implement new services – and withdraw them easier – for lower "sunk" costs.

- Make building prototypes faster, cheaper, and easier.

- Facilitate disaggregation of services – make it easier to split up work that can then be outsourced and reintegrated.

- Promote innovation by empowering users to write their own solutions.

- Increase agility by dynamically assembling new applications and bringing them to market quickly in response to changing conditions.
- Reduce missed commitments by improving the visibility of commitments and automating the notification of missed deadlines.

Increase employee satisfaction

- Reduce stress through automation.

- Provide software that is better suited to each user's unique needs.

- Provide users with the ability to create their own solutions.

- Provide easier access to enterprise and web data.

- Improve the coordination of work among employees.

- Provide critical insight into the projects' status, sales goals and other objectives, helping to identify potential issues early on.

- Identify problem trends earlier by automatically triggering alerts when jobs fall off schedule, so corrective action can be taken to get quickly back on track.

Improve IT-business alignment

- Rapid prototyping provides improved communication and requirements sharing, leading to more customer-focused applications.

- Support self-service capabilities, especially for Millennials.

- Use situational application tools to deliver certain types of applications faster and cheaper and using less expensive skills.

Reduce cycle time
- Improve visibility of commitments so decisions aren't delayed due to missed commitments or poor coordination.

- Reduce miscommunication by keeping accurate and appropriate data, making it always available, and by making changes immediately visible.

- Reduce lag time by automatically notifying the next person in a workflow to start a process (e.g., once a warehouse employee marks all items in an order as received, it comes up in the Chatter feed of the delivery scheduling department, allowing them to start processing the order immediately, without human intervention).

- Bring together all the information required from inside and outside the enterprise; remixing it allows users to solve edge problems quickly.

- Save time by reducing unnecessary communication such asking others for status updates.

- Increase the use of systems by personalizing them to the exact needs of the users.

Reduce costs

- Make data collection more convenient by providing access through widgets and mobile devices.

- Eliminate incomplete paper forms by providing consistent data entry screens, with required and validated fields.

- Improve collaboration to facilitate the transfer, sharing, and simultaneous processing of information.

- Make clients responsible for entering and maintaining their own information.

- Build applications that allow partners, clients, and employees to serve themselves.

New types of applications with force.com

The economics of cloud computing lets innovative companies create products that either weren't possible before or are significantly less expensive than the competition (or just more profitable). This part of cloud computing is an arms race and there are short windows of opportunity since competitors can often put the economic advantages of cloud computing into their product formulations fairly quickly once they see that it works for you.[75] – Dion Hinchcliffe

Doing the same things everyone else is doing is going to yield less and less benefit as time goes on. Doing the same old things in an agile way will not provide nearly as much value as applying agility to accomplish brand new things.[76]

Businesspeople who see new opportunities and new, yet simple ways to deliver these opportunities can reap the rewards. With the incredible leaps forward in technology, no one should be afraid to question conventional wisdom and try different approaches.

The following describes new types of applications that can be built with force.com as you ride the wave of the new digital economy.

Make your applications proactive

Airlines proactively phone you with flight and gate announcements and changes, enable you to check in online, have your boarding pass sent to your mobile phone, allow you to use it for scanning at ticketing and security gates, and email you suggested future travel itineraries based on your history. What applications do you have that can be as proactive as this?

Build mobile apps

There are exciting new ways to leverage mobile technology, including:

---

[75] Dion Hinchcliffe, *Eight ways that cloud computing will change business*, 2009

[76] Michael Hugos and Derek Hulitzky, *Business in the Cloud: What Every Business Needs to Know About Cloud Computing*

- Real-time mobile communications and presence technologies (i.e., knowledge of where people in work groups are, including the ability to communicate with them instantly). Composite applications that enable the automatic update of disparate information and disparate data stores, based on a certain transaction by a mobile user. Location-based services, allowing presence and location to be layered in along with some sort of context within mobile applications. The ability to accelerate or improve business processes (e.g., the ability to automate order-to-cash or an invoicing cycle, sales fulfillment or ordering of inventory). The ability to fundamentally re-engineer existing business processes by using embedded phone features and technologies, such as utilizing camera and location features for accurate and timely safety incident reporting at a work site. Built-in functionality includes:

- Plug-and-play accessories

- Location identification/compass

- Image/barcode recognition

- Camera/video

- Accelerometer/gyroscope

- Speech-to-text and text-to-speech

- Near-field communication

Monetize your data and services

"Opening an API" means creating new business models that were not possible without an API. Connecting different software programs, APIs are gateways that allow businesses to transfer, track, and monetize valuable calls to their data, while connecting with partners and expanding distribution. Opening and launching APIs offers rapid entry to new markets via the cloud as well as fast ubiquity for monetizing your digital assets, data and content, and provides access to web services and mobile apps.

The big change in mindset is to recognize that data and services – a company's digital assets – must be released from the confines of a web site. Once they are free, and can be accessed from anywhere, the potential to grow the business can be realized.

Companies can realize significant benefits by providing access in the cloud to information and services they already sell, as well as packaging their data and expertise into new saleable products.

For example, manufacturing companies can expose their inventory and shipping processes as services so that their customers can get better visibility into ordering and fulfillment. The benefit to a small business of exposing certain of their operations is simple: if they make it easier to embed their processes into their customers' they can increase sales, customer satisfaction, and competitive advantage. In fact, companies that embed their suppliers' operations into their own will find it much more difficult to replace them – not because of technical difficulty, but because of their usefulness to the organization.[77]

Another example is where a company accumulates specialized knowledge as part of their business, and repackages this information as a completely different revenue-producing service. An insurance claims processor who accumulates data on product replacements from multiple vendors to support their claims business may discover that this information has value to other companies in the same or a related industry. By packaging this information and making it available as a service in the cloud for a fee, it can create a new revenue source that was not easily available before.

---

[77] Ronald Schmelzer, "Web Services are for Small Businesses, Too," Zapthink

Design new business models

force.com can facilitate new ways of handling businesses long in existence, and it also makes possible completely new types of businesses that simply weren't feasible prior to the advent of this technology.

The API explosion means it's feasible to create products that more precisely meet customers' expectations and desires. It may be to meet their use case in a small market niche, or to have access to data in a unique context, or to meet their preference to interact from a smart phone device. Ultimately companies will have the flexibility to design completely new business models. The ability to rapidly create and change supporting applications in the cloud make new businesses possible – such as offering time-shares of a jetliner, where multiple people can own the same jet and share it like a vacation home, but in much smaller time increments. Another example of would be renting out designer handbags for small time increments. This kind of app can also relate to the supply side of asset-intensive businesses like factories, warehouses, truck fleets, office buildings, data centers, networks, etc., where utilization rates can be raised by offering desired access in ever smaller increments of time.

Leverage the Streaming API

The force.com Streaming API takes us a step closer to the real-time organization. With the Streaming API, you can build solutions that react instantly to changes in data, threshold crossing, trend tipping points, etc. You can also build solutions that will synthesize and analyze multiple events in real-time, and send alerts or initiate processes.

Capture data on-the-go

Mobile reduces duplication and errors in sourcing data by enabling critical data to be captured at the time and place of its creation. Data is more timely, and information quality is improved.

Utilize mobility's location and time independence

Fundamental business processes that utilize mobility's location and time independence can be reengineered. Mobile provides opportunities to tailor offerings so that they're highly specific to a particular customer in a particular location. Such personalization significantly improves the overall experience the customer has with the business.

Leverage social networks

force.com provides a free set of tools and services that enables developers to harness the power of Facebook and force.com platforms to build business applications for Facebook. By making it easy for developers to build robust applications in areas like recruiting, productivity, and project collaboration that can be quickly integrated through the Facebook platform, Facebook users will be presented with new tools for activities such as sharing job opportunities or collaborating with co-workers or friends on events or projects.

Package knowledge

Embedding knowledge into an application helps eliminate the need to involve expensive resources when it is unnecessary. For example, a cable company needs to qualify leads based on how close a prospect is to an access point. Creating an application that instantly provides "distance scores" for each new lead (and associated potential construction costs) provides immediate information directly to salespeople without involving anyone from the engineering department.

Or take the example of a market research company where salespeople need to get input from many different departments to put together a single quote for a client. Every time the specifications change, the salesperson has to go back to each department. The amount of time wasted and the delays incurred can be enormous.

One of the major advantages of the force.com platforms is that each department can take responsibility for automating and maintaining its part of the bidding process. Because each department does this on the same platform, it's much easier to bring all the separate solutions together into a cohesive whole.

Also, once the knowledge required to estimate a job has been packaged, it may be possible to give clients (especially existing clients) the ability to estimate jobs on their own, and initiate an order process immediately – without any human involvement.

These kinds of savings are available in almost every organization.

Enhance Data Capture

Building force.com applications that are specific to the type of data being entered, how it is being entered, and by whom it is being entered can ensure that it does not have to be re-checked later in the process, or that it will cause unforeseen exceptions later on, or that it will have to be re-keyed into other systems.

force.com applications for data entry can have significant impact and usually can be done with minimal effort. Here are a few variations:

One source, multiple destinations

There is a single source of data for an application (e.g., a client), but the user needs to enter data into multiple systems. The solution is to build a front-end application that captures all the information in one place and feeds the data into all the systems that need it, thereby reducing errors and time.

Improved navigation

Data entry screens are often confusing. They may contain fields that aren't needed by the person doing the data entry, or are in the wrong sequence for easy entry. Frequently they force the user to move back and forth unnecessarily among multiple screens.

A typical indication of this type of problem is seen when information is written down on a piece of paper and keyed in later, which wastes time, and is an intermediate step that easily produces errors. A situational application can clean up screens to make it much more convenient for the user to enter data.

Data vetting

force.com applications can be built to vet data thoroughly, ensuring correctness from the start, which can eliminate significant problems down the line.

Glue systems together for individual users

Billions of dollars are lost every year because information systems don't work together. A vast amount of unnecessary time is spent in every office in every corner of the world just trying to act as the glue between systems.

This is particularly true when a single task that needs to be done requires information from more than one system. This means that a user has to take the time to compose the information they need to complete the task. Not only does it waste time, it is prone to error and can impair decision making.

force.com applications are well suited to these scenarios because no one knows the situation facing business users better than the users themselves. If they are able to build applications by pulling information from enterprise applications, departmental applications, and even desktop applications, their productivity can be increased significantly.

Make it easy to sell a combo

When a user feels hindered from taking a course of action that is desired by the company (perhaps because it's too difficult or extra work is required), chances are it will not get done.

A simple example occurs at the movie theatre, when they want to sell you a "combo" because it garners them a higher profit. But if the concessionaire needs to do extra work to fulfill a combo order, chances are they won't make offering it a high priority, and even if they do, it will slow down the fulfillment process.

Creating force.com applications to make it easier to streamline services by bundling and packaging them can go a long way to helping ensure that the practices you want to encourage are adopted.

Self-service everything

Self-service applications are a simple way to reduce costs and improve service. Perhaps the best example is FedEx allowing customers to track packages from their web sites, with no human intervention required. Leveraging and linking systems to automate processes for answering inquiries from customers dramatically reduced the cost of serving them, while increasing customer satisfaction and loyalty.

force.com applications can address these self-service areas:

Status checking. Allow clients to check the status of their orders, the progress of their projects, the statuses of insurance claims.

Knowledge access. Allow users to enter parameters and get answers they need. For example, enable users to find nearby physicians by specialty and distance.

Data entry and maintenance. Allow customers and partners to take responsibility for entering their own orders, support requests, and more.

Each one of these can be a separate mobile app specifically tailored to specific customer needs.

Rollup and consolidation

There are many instances where data needs to be collected from multiple sources and then consolidated into a single system. Most often, each source has slightly different ways of doing things, but the information required by the central system is the same.

force.com applications can be developed to take into account the unique needs of each source, and still automatically collect the common data that is required from all. An obvious example is in budgeting – each department can budget their own way, but still supply the numbers needed.

Once automated, additional functionality significantly improves efficiency is easy to add. For example, automated reminders can be implemented to ensure that necessary information is made available in a timely fashion.

Build Mashups

Mashups aren't invented during the IT department's annual offsite meetings. Instead, they spring from the minds of entrepreneurial virtuosos who are continually sifting through the services they discover on the Internet and imagining the emergent possibilities. – Andy Mulholland, Chris S. Thomas, and Paul Kurchina, *Mashup Corporations: The End of Business as Usual*

Mashups combine similar types of media and information from multiple sources into a single representation. A typical example is combining customer address data with Google Maps to show locations and print directions.

force.com applications that mash disparate data together in unique ways can be extremely powerful. Kelly Shaw from Serena provides a great example of a data mashup application in her blog.[78]

"Assume I run a fleet of ice cream trucks and I want to make the best use of the trucks. I could use a presentation or data mashup to help by pulling local event information from online community calendars,

---

[78] Kelly Shaw, "Business Mashups – mashup applications for and by the business," Oct. 22, 2007, http://businessmashup.blogspot.com/2007/10/how-close-are-we-to-overcoming-10.html

school activity calendars, business announcements and even law enforcement announcements. I could map these events on a Google Map along with information about the likely size and times of the events. Using this information I could develop a schedule to optimize the routes of my trucks.

"… [I could also] take the information from the mashup and use it automatically to schedule trucks, drivers and inventory to make sure the right trucks were at the right locations with the right inventory at the right time. … [The application] would know when trucks are due for maintenance and schedule the maintenance around heavy usage days based on the mashed-up information."

In this example, external data is mixed with enterprise data to produce actionable information that would not otherwise be feasible.

Giving users access to data that they can then mash into applications meaningful specifically to them opens up extremely powerful opportunities for increasing efficiency.

Bringing together just the right info from anywhere within the organization, combining it with info from other sources, and presenting it in a way that is optimized for both the individual and the specific task can increase productivity and produce whole new ways to deliver goods, services, and support to customers and trading partners.

Streamline touchpoints

An organization's touchpoints refer to its interactions with customers, suppliers, and employees. Each touchpoint represents a significant area of potential process or quality improvement, and competitive advantage. Most importantly, touchpoints represent areas where human interaction is often intense.

Touchpoints can be regarded as the periphery of an enterprise's central nervous system. As in human anatomy, it is the extremities that help to define the efficiency of our interaction with the world around us. Dexterity, mobility, and adaptability depend primarily on the nimbleness of our peripheral nervous system: fingers, toes, hands, feet, arms, and legs define how well we can react to many of the events around us. In this same way, an enterprise may have outstanding strategies, plans, and tactics, but they must be enabled through actions taken to satisfy customers, educate and leverage workers, and negotiate trade with suppliers.

To make these touchpoints more effective, it's critical to streamline any tiresome and repetitive tasks that otherwise consume employees' time and energy. Even a slight application of the right technology in these areas can have an extraordinary impact on a company's processes.

If it's easy, employees are far more likely to keep refining the way interactions are completed at the touchpoints of the organization, making them faster and including more value for customers. Enriching and streamlining individual transactions at the lowest level is something that will be difficult for competitors to replicate.

Spark Innovation

> *In a world where so many people now have access to education and cheap tools of innovation, innovation that happens from the bottom up tends to be chaotic but smart. Innovation that happens from the top down tends to be orderly but dumb.* – Curtis Carlson, CEO, SRI International, *Carlson's Law*

The sweet spot for innovation today is "moving down," closer to the people, not up, because all the people together are smarter than anyone alone, and all the people now have the tools to invent and collaborate.

And there is a need to invent and collaborate continually. As Peter Fingar has pointed out:

> *The whole notion of being able to set the pace of innovation in your industry becomes a radical thing that you have to be able to do, otherwise you immediately get commoditized.*

force.com applications offer the kind of self-service, continuous trial-and-error experimentation necessary to discover what works and what doesn't in a manner that is low-cost and fast.

Facilitate Innovation

Finding new and creative ways to solve business problems is key to remaining competitive. There have often been too many barriers to putting in place the software solutions needed to support innovation. Either IT doesn't have the bandwidth, or you don't have the knowledge or resources to build the solutions you need. Now with force.com applications, you can break out of the box and do it yourself. Who knows better than you what your business problems are? Why shouldn't you create the solution?

Keep an eye on things

force.com applications are very useful to people who need to keep an eye on volatile data such as currency exchange rates, machine availability, today's sales, or inventory levels. force.com applications are delivered as small, targeted mobile or widget apps that allow you to set up monitoring tools to watch data values while you do other work on the rest of your screen. Widgets create a consistent monitoring framework and allow applications to combine everything you're monitoring into one window, set alert thresholds when something changes outside of established parameters, or easily share tools even with others in different companies.

Create raving fans

force.com applications can be a useful mechanism for helping to create "raving fans."[79] People like to be remembered and valued, but in the day-to-day crush of things it may be difficult to take the time to send out a thank-you note, or a letter asking your customer how things are working out with the product they purchased, or the service received.

---

[79] Ken Blanchard and Sheldon Bowles, *Raving Fans: A Revolutionary Approach To Customer Service,* NY: Morrow, 1993

A situational application can be used to do all these things and more. For example, an association of pediatric occupational therapists built a situational application that automatically sent an email to its patients on their birthdays. The email contained a video of their therapists singing "Happy Birthday." It was simple to build – the system already knew each patient's birth date and who their therapist was. Once the video was made (a one-minute exercise), it was set to go. This is an example of how you create raving fans – and grow your business.

Other ways include:

- **Making it easier (and more pleasant) for customers to do business with you**. Provide them with systems that are tailored more specifically to their exact needs.

- **Knowing what your customers want by giving them an easy way to tell you**. A simple application to collect, categorize, and rank customer ideas could go a long way to help make this happen.

- **Knowing better who your customers are.** Collect and analyze information about them so you can better cater to their needs. To do this, build applications that automatically send out questions and follow-ups, and produce meaningful reports.

- **Making your clients feel that you really care**. The "happy birthday" video is just one example.

Don't let anything slip through the cracks

Continuity is all about making sure nothing falls through the cracks. Chatter is the perfect vehicle for sending instant notifications of events within a workflow to one or many users, and allowing users to monitor progress through the stages of workflow.

Leverage data in the cloud

When data is readily available in the cloud, it can be used in powerful new ways. For example, an industrial equipment vendor can know exactly where a piece of their equipment is and whether it's being used or in the shop for repairs. Customer service reps can get real-time information about clients' equipment on their smart phones. If data indicates possible problems, alerts can be sent to ensure action is taken before real damage is done.

This type of functionality helps vendors to be much more proactive and responsive, increasing customer satisfaction.

Leverage a revolutionary marketplace

When product information is available in the cloud as opposed to residing in each organization's own infrastructure, it becomes feasible to sell, exchange, or mesh together offerings and products from multiple providers together into the marketplace. The simplest example of this is the ability to create an ecommerce site that sells products from different vendors, such as Bonanza.com. The key to making this work is the existence of standard interfaces that allow developers to access services and data from diverse sources, regardless of what hardware or software they happen to be running on.

Build Business Networks

The global economy is reshaping companies' relationships. Gaining competitive advantage through networked business models, companies are tapping into talent across the globe to defend themselves against commoditization and disruptive innovation.

The cloud dramatically simplifies the ability for small and medium sized enterprises to build these *Business Networks* – defined as groups of companies that work together toward a specific objective for mutual benefit. New market opportunities are unlocked by combining the products and services of the business network participants in creative ways and leveraging each other's market access and infrastructure on a global basis.

Companies recognize that they must become more adept at managing external as well as internal operations, so there is an escalating demand for better inter-enterprise collaboration, coordination, and communication. However, entrenched client/server systems are ill-prepared for this shift.[80] Current IT infrastructures are:

- Optimized for internal processes, but weak on external-facing processes.
- Optimized for transactions but weak on collaboration support.
- Optimized for mature operations, but weak on support for emerging opportunities.

Cloud computing facilitates the development of highly collaborative, high-complexity challenges that require investing in relationship management. From the making of a movie to the development of a next-generation airliner, or the commercialization of a novel therapy, the focus is on leveraging a wide range of technologies and expertise to tackle a novel set of challenges, collaboratively creating not only new products or services but also whole new systems and categories that simply did not exist before.

The risks these projects entail, the capital they require, and the talent they must access cannot be encompassed by the efforts of any single enterprise. In effect, the need to operate as a collaborative business network is built into the very structure of the problems these companies must address. The cloud speeds the pace at which these business networks can be created and transformed.

This will lead to more symbiotic relationships between organizations, with collaborative services providing ad hoc, real-time IT services:

> Companies within a supply chain will be able to offer customers greater customization and choice because the supply chain can flex almost instantly, in response to customer demands.

---

[80] Philip Lay and Geoffrey Moore, "Business Network Transformation: IT's Next Great Opportunity to Shine," SAP Insider, June 2008

Consider the case of a car manufacturer. One of its customers may desire a green car with gold upholstery, a luxury stereo package, and alloy wheels. As is usually the case, one company might be responsible for providing the car chassis, while another company provides the stereo, a third the wheels, and another company does the assembly and shipping.

Traditionally, this level of customization would be impossible. Each component would need to be ordered weeks in advance, which is why companies would usually manufacture products according to standard configurations. However, in a cloud model, it is possible for every company in the supply chain to share data in real-time, enabling the car to be built-to-order by synchronizing the manufacture and distribution of the necessary parts.[81]

The cloud can facilitate the building of processes where multiple companies can collaborate, but there doesn't have to be any one person in charge.

Better align labor supply with client demand

Since the cloud makes physical location mostly meaningless, companies can more easily align labor supply with client demand. They can apply labor from other (and less expensive) geographies, and they can bring talented, part-time professionals back into the workforce.

Because the cloud is always on and always connected, professionals and their clients always share the same information in real time. This allows accountants, for example, to become proactive advisors – they are no longer simply looking at a QuickBooks file at the end of the month. For the average mid-sized accounting firm, the business impact of moving to the cloud is a significant increase in productivity. The computers take over

---

[81] *The Cloud and SOA: Creating an Architecture for Today and for the Future,* CAPGemini, 2008

the drudgery, accountants graduate from being bean counters to becoming business advisors, specialists can make the most of their expertise, and qualified professionals bringing up children or living in unemployment blackspots can rejoin the workforce.[82]

Aligning supply with demand is further enhanced by the fact that being in the cloud makes it far easier to contract work by the hour, or even by the minute. Companies can get as good or better results from workers in the cloud as they could from an employee in the cubicle next door if what's needed to do the job is easily accessible by using a browser. And when the business spikes or melts down, contracting in the cloud similarly bursts up and down.

Shifting more work to freelancers and outsiders and unbundling assets will lead to new pricing models that need to be tracked and adjusted frequently. It will not be possible to involve IT in every change that needs to be made to support this growing trend, making the new cloud-based custom development methodology essential to success.

Unbundle and re-aggregate Tasks

The cloud makes it much easier to for companies to segment work into discrete tasks for independent contractors and then re-aggregate the results of that work.

---

[82] Phil Wainewright, "Go Cloud, Young Man," ZDNet, August 5, 2009

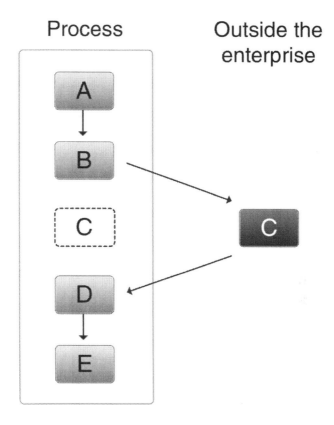

Figure 56: Any task in a business process may be a candidate for outsourcing. The cloud makes this easier to do by providing a standard way to build interfaces among disparate systems.

These applications allow companies to give substantial leeway to outsiders while still maintaining visibility and overall control over what is being done. This can substantially reduce costs and help get new products to market faster by eliminating the bottlenecks that come with inefficient communication mechanisms and processes. In addition, it becomes possible to mix different services – both in terms of the business service provided and the degree of management involvement required – from different service providers.

A good example of this is health care delivery, where elements of the process (e.g., reading x-rays) are handed off to external contractors who must have access to certain data, and return other data upon completion of their discrete task. Companies can more easily harvest the talents of people working outside corporate boundaries if they can rapidly create highly customized applications that cater to the specific needs of each relationship. This makes it more feasible to involve customers, suppliers, small specialist businesses, and independent contractors in the creation of products and services.

Appendix C: The Big Picture

The need to build back-office systems that are essential for accounting and other complex usages will of course always be with us. They are likely to remain in the realm of traditional IT (let's call it IT 1.0) for the foreseeable future.

The diagram below represents a summary of the ideas in this book. Taken as a whole, this summary represents an entirely new version of IT. Let's call it IT 2.0.

IT 2.0

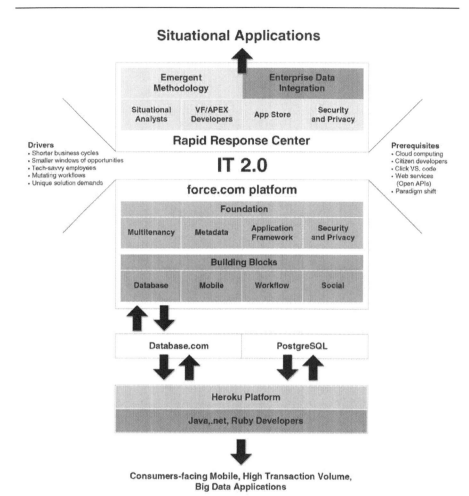

Figure 57: A vision of IT 2.0, featuring force.com and Heroku. IT 1.0 will soldier on for years, but this is where an organization succeeds or fails.

The IT 2.0 Wheel of Fortune

Here is the likely path to acceptance of IT 2.0:

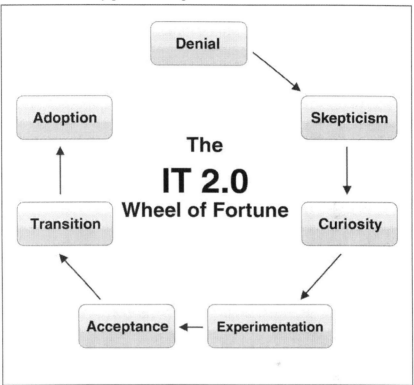

Figure 58: The wheel of IT 2.0 fortune. The faster you make it around the circle, the better your fortune.

Further Reading

Arthur, W. Brian. *The Nature of Technology: What It Is and How It Evolves*. NY: Free Press, 2009.

Bejan, Adrian and J. Peder Zane. *Design in Nature: How the Constructal Law Governs Evolution in Biology, Physics, Technology, and Social Organization*. NY: Doubleday, 2012.

Benioff, Marc. *Behind the Cloud: The Untold Story of How Salesforce.com Went from Idea to Billion-Dollar Company-and Revolutionized an Industry*. San Francisco: Jossey-Bass, 2009.

Bernard, John M. *Business at the Speed of Now: Fire Up Your People, Thrill Your Customers, and Crush Your Competitors*. Hoboken, NJ: Wiley, 2012.

Berridge, Eric and Michael Kirven. *IT.ER.ATE or Die, Agile Consulting for 21st Century Business Success*. Bloomington, IN: AuthorHouse, 2008.

Bonabeau, Eric, Guy Theraulaz, and Marco Dorigo. *Swarm Intelligence: From Natural to Artificial Systems*. NY: Oxford U., 1999.

Brynjolfsson, Erik and Andrew McAfee. *Race Against The Machine: How the Digital Revolution is Accelerating Innovation, Driving Productivity, and Irreversibly Transforming Employment and the Economy*. Lexington, MA: Digital Frontier Press, 2011.

Carr, Nicholas. *The Big Switch, Rewiring the World, From Edison to Google*. NY: W.W. Norton, 2008.

Carter, Sandy. *Get Bold: Using Social Media to Create a New Type of Social Business*. Boston: IBM Press, 2012.

Cowen, Tyler. *The Great Stagnation: How America Ate All The Low-Hanging Fruit of Modern History, Got Sick, and Will (Eventually) Feel Better*. NY: Dutton, 2011.

Dove, Rick. *Response Ability—The Language, Structure, and Culture of the Agile Enterprise*. NY: Wiley, 2001.

Enriquez, Juan. *As the Future Catches You: How Genomics & Other Forces are Changing Your Life, Work, Health & Wealth*. NY: Crown Business, 2001.

Fingar, Peter. *Dot.Cloud: The 21st Century Business Platform*. Tampa, FL: Meghan-Kiffer Press, 2009.

Fingar, Peter. *Extreme Competition: Innovation and the Great 21st Century Business Reformation.* Tampa, FL: Meghan-Kiffer Press, 2009.

Fogarty, Kevin. "How To Keep Rogue Cloud Software From Making IT Irrelevant," CIO.com, July 05, 2011. http://www.cio.com/article/685658/

Gladwell, Malcolm. *The Tipping Point: How Little Things Can Make a Big Difference.* Boston: Little, Brown, 2000.

Hagel, John. *Out of the Box.* Cambridge: Harvard Business School Publishing, 2002.

Hagel, John, and John Seely Brown. "IT Does Matter." *Viewpoint*, May 15, 2003. http://www.johnhagel.com/view20030515.shtml.

Hock, Dee. *Birth of the Chaordic Age.* San Francisco: Berrett-Koehler, 1999.

Hugos, Michael H. *Business Agility, Sustainable Prosperity in a Relentlessly Competitive World.* Hoboken, NJ: Wiley, 2009.

Hugos, Michael H. and Derek Hulitzky. *Business in the Cloud: What Every Business Needs to Know About Cloud Computing.* Hoboken, NJ: Wiley, 2010.

Hulme, George. "How to best fight the rise of rogue IT services? Compete," Cloud Commons, November 8, 2011.

Kelly, Eamonn and Peter Leyden. *What's Next? Exploring the New Terrain for Business.* West Sussex, England: Wiley, 2002.

Koulopoulos, Thomas. *Living in the Cloud.* Amazon Digital Services, 2010.

Linthicum, David S. *Cloud Computing and SOA Convergence in Your Enterprise: A Step-by-Step Guide.* Upper Saddle River: Addison-Wesley, 2010.

Maslow, Abraham H. *Maslow on Management.* Hoboken, NJ: Wiley, 1998.

Mulholland, Andy, Chris S. Thomas, Paul Kurchina, and Dan Woods. *Mashup Corporations, The End of Business as Usual.* NY: Evolved Technologist Press, 2006.

Mulholland, Andy, Jon Pyke, and Peter Fingar. *Enterprise Cloud Computing: A Strategy Guide for Business and Technology Leaders.* Kindle Edition. Tampa, FL: Meghan-Kiffer Press, 2010.

Pascale, Richard, Mark Milleman, and Linda Gioja. *Surfing the Edge of Chaos: The Laws of Nature and the New Laws of Business.* NY: Three Rivers Press, 2000.

Ramo, Joshua Cooper. *The Age of the Unthinkable, Why the New World Disorder Constantly Surprises Us and What We Can Do About It.* NY: Little, Brown, 2009.

Rifkin, Jeremy. *The Empathic Civilization: The Race to Global Consciousness in a World in Crisis.* NY: Tarcher, 2009.

Ring, Katy. "Salesforce as your strategic Cloud platform," businesscloud9.com, January 23, 2012. http://www.businesscloud9.com/ content/salesforce-your-strategic-cloud-platform/7609

Sapir, Jonathan. *Igniting the Phoenix: A New Vision for IT.* Bloomington, IN: Xlibris, 2003.

Sapir, Jonathan. *Power in the Cloud: Using Cloud Computing to Build Information Systems at the Edge of Chaos.* Tampa, FL: Meghan-Kiffer Press, 2008.

Schoemaker, Paul J. H. *Profiting from Uncertainty: Strategies for Succeeding No Matter What the Future Brings.* NY: The Free Press, 2002.

Smith, Howard and Peter Fingar. *Business Process Management: The Third Wave.* Tampa, FL: Meghan-Kiffer, 2003.

Stewart, Thomas. *Intellectual Capital: The New Wealth of Organizations.* NY: Currency/Doubleday, 1997.

Tapscott, Don. *Growing Up Digital: The Rise of the Net Generation.* NY: McGraw-Hill, 1998.

"The New Digital Economy: How it Will Transform Business," a research paper produced by Oxford Economics in collaboration with AT&T, Cisco, Citi, PwC & SAP, June 2011. http://www.pwc.com/gx/en/technology/publications/ transform-business-in-new-digital-economy.jhtml

Webber, Andrew. "How Business is a Lot Like Life," Fast Company, March 31, 2001. www.fastcompany.com/magazine/45/pascale.html?page=0,3.

Wheatley, Margaret J., and Myron Kellner-Rogers. "Bringing Life to Organizational Change," *Journal for Strategic Performance Measurement.* April/May 1998. http://margaretwheatley.com/articles/life.html.

Index

If you're reading this book on an electronic device, you already know that the concept of an index is meaningless, since its objective is to help the reader search for something in the body of the book. Because your eReader has search capability, there is no need for an index. You can search for whatever you want – and you aren't limited to the search terms the indexer chose to include.

Besides, an index assumes there are page numbers. Page numbers are based on the assumption that pages are of fixed length, with fixed margins, and a fixed font size. My Kindle, for example, has no idea what a page number is.

So, in the spirit of the ideas in this book, I decided not to provide an index. Of course, if you're reading the dead tree edition, you're out of luck. But look at it this way: it's a great example of how those still stuck in the physical world are being abandoned in the new digital economy!

About the Authors

Jonathan Sapir

Founder and CEO of SilverTree Systems

 Jonathan Sapir has over thirty years' experience helping clients leverage information technology to build their businesses. After starting out as a system engineer for IBM, Jonathan built a successful consulting firm in Chicago in the 1990s, then grew a software product development company which he sold in 2007. Returning to consulting, Jonathan started SilverTree Systems, Inc., to help companies migrate to the cloud.

Jonathan has written two other well-received books: *Igniting the Phoenix: A New Vision for IT* in 2003, which foretold many of the ideas that have become reality, especially in the areas of enterprise social software, cloud computing, and self-service application development; and *Power in the Cloud: Using Cloud Computing to Build Information Systems at the Edge of Chaos* in 2008, which looks at building information systems in the context of complex adaptive systems theory.

I'm an avid follower of Jonathan's thoughts and body of work. When starting down the current path of Web 2.0 three years ago, Jonathan's book and interviews captured exactly what is now transpiring in terms of business transformation. I have quoted Jonathan on many, many occasions; his insights into understanding emerging key business issues both from the IT perspective and the line-of-business have been truly visionary. – Rod Smith, IBM, VP Emerging Technologies

Jon is a wonderfully talented, exceptionally creative, and forward-thinking luminary who can add significant value to any organization and leap-frog their thinking. Jon

has proven time and again that he can think things through, not only at a practical level, but also at a level of fore-thought that few venture. – Ron Schmelzer, Zapthink

Steve Wood

Salesforce.com Vice President, Platform Business Development

Steve joined Salesforce.com in 2009 when his company Informavores was acquired by Salesforce.com. Informavores is now the basis for the force.com Visual Workflow tool.

Steve is responsible for working with platform partners in the areas of product completion, co-selling / co-marketing and OEM / acquisition.

Previously, Steve ran the Salesforce.com business process management vision and managed many of the force.com point-and-click tools (form builder, formulas, validation, etc.) as well as workflow rules, approval processes, and the new Visual Workflow. His job was to empower the business developer to automate business processes, while providing a scalable, extensible platform that is trusted by enterprise IT.

Before joining Salesforce.com, Steve created and built Informavores from the ground up. Informavores changed the way organizations such as Microsoft, PricewaterhouseCoopers, Hewlett-Packard, Dow Jones, the U.S. Department of Defense, the Internal Revenue Service, Aviva Norwich Union, and Symantec conceptualized process automation.

- *A world leader in visual thinking. –* Tony Buzan, inventor of Mind Mapping.

- *A truly innovative thinker – Steve has created an elegant solution to a very complex problem. –* Paul Smith, Global Head of Tax, PricewaterhouseCoopers

- *We have not seen any other products quite like those of Informavores... [they have] developed a technology that is easy to use, highly productive, clearly focused and is especially good at handling complex business rules: we are very very impressed... we have no hesitation in recommending the product and we urge any companies with relevant applications to seriously consider the Informavores products.* – Bloor Research

- *There is nothing new about young software companies making bold claims for their products, but in Informavores' case Wood's boasting is backed by some impressive endorsements.* – Information Age

Francois Koutchouk

President of Atlantic Decisions, Inc., and creator of EscapeNotes

 Francois was part of the very early team on Lotus Notes, pre-version 1 (sharing office space with Ray Ozzie, ex-CTO of Microsoft) until version 4, before assisting Steve Jobs at NeXT with their groupware endeavor.

With a complete understanding of the way Lotus Notes was built from day one, Koutchouk has written reference books and has consulted for large organizations, as well as architected a wide variety of applications on diverse platforms.

Francois now believes that Notes has become "all it can be" and cannot be taught new tricks: it's time for a transition to its closest related cousin, force.com.

Francois and his team's deep knowledge and maturity in Notes helps organizations to efficiently and safely migrate from Notes to force.com.

407

Peter Coffee

VP and Head of Platform Research at salesforce.com

Peter is best known for his longtime role as a commentator for Ziff Davis, where he was most recently Technology Editor for eWEEK, until joining salesforce.com in January 2007. He has over twenty years' experience in evaluating information technologies and practices as a developer, consultant, educator, and internationally published author and industry analyst.

Peter is the author of *Peter Coffee Teaches PCs*, published in 1998 by Que, and wrote Que's ZD Press tutorial *How to Program Java.*

Before joining eWEEK (then called *PC Week*) full-time in 1989, Peter held technical and management positions at Exxon and The Aerospace Corporation, dealing with chemical facility project control, Arctic project development, strategic defense analysis, end-user computing planning and support, and artificial intelligence applications research.

Andy Mulholland

Capgemini, Global Chief Technology Officer

Andy is a member of the Capgemini Group management board and advises on all aspects of technology-driven market changes, together with being a member of the Policy Board for the British Computer Society.

Andy is the author of many white papers, and the co-author of three books that chart the current changes in technology and its use by business. In 2006 he wrote *Mashup Corporations,* detailing how enterprises could make use of Web 2.0 to develop new go to market propositions. This was followed in May 2008 by *Mesh Collaboration,* focusing on the impact of Web 2.0 on the enterprise front office and its working techniques, and then in 2010, *Enterprise Cloud Computing: A Strategy Guide for Business and Technology Leaders*, co-authored with well-known academic Peter Fingar, and one of the leading authorities on business process, John Pyke. The book describes the wider business implications of cloud computing with the promise of on-demand business innovation. It looks at how businesses trade differently on the web using mash-ups, but also the challenges in managing more frequent change through social tools, and what happens when cloud comes into play in fully fledged operations.

Andy was voted one of the top twenty-five most influential CTOs in the world in 2009 by InfoWorld and is grateful to readers of *Computing Weekly* who voted the Capgemini CTO blog the best Blog for Business Managers and CIOs each year for the last three years.

Acknowledgments

Thanks are due to my excellent editor, Jill Bailin, who kept me on track and made the book readable; Scott Wilson, Michael Hugos, and Francois Koutchouk, who reviewed an early version of the book and provided excellent suggestions for how the book could be improved; Michael Hugos, Peter Fingar and Andy Mulholland, who are always willing to lend their deep expertise on this subject; Steve Wood, Francois Koutchouk, Andy Mulholland and Peter Coffee for taking the time to add their knowledgeable contributions to the text; Greg Olsen, whose Coghead ideas are deeply ingrained in this book; Dave Schafer for looking after our most challenging clients while I wrote this book; Ted Evangelakis, for successfully extending the reach of SilverTree Systems; Vince Sanchez, to whom I owe so much; Steve Sokol, for introducing me to the clients that made the ideas expressed in this book a reality; Eugene, Dmitry and Constantine and the rest of my team, who do such amazing work; Eric Wynn and Mark Hankins from Taco Bell, who saw the vision and were willing (and able) to give it a shot; Toma Carmanto for his excellent graphics; Marty Engel, for keeping me out of trouble; Brandon Buhai, for his always amusing conversations; and of course, my truly wonderful and always supportive wife Joyce and kids, Jorie, Jake and Jenna, who amazingly are willing to put up with me!

Over 750 years ago on the plains of Runnymede, King John was served papers containing a list of demands to be recognized and confirmed by his royal seal. The vestiges of royalty that survived are in large part due to King John's acquiescence to those demands and the principle of democratization. It was perfect irony that to survive, the monarchy had to open the door to its ultimate demise.

– Thomas M. Koulopoulos, *Web Services at the Desktop – A New World Order*